Contents

Contents

TACKLING THE ROOTS OF RACISM

Lessons for success

Reena Bhavnani, Heidi Safia Mirza and Veena Meetoo

First published in Great Britain in October 2005 by

The Policy Press
University of Bristol
Fourth Floor
Beacon House
Queen's Road
Bristol BS8 1QU
UK

Tel +44 (0)117 331 4054
Fax +44 (0)117 331 4093
e-mail tpp-info@bristol.ac.uk
www.policypress.org.uk

© Reena Bhavnani, Heidi Safia Mirza and Veena Meetoo 2005

Reprinted 2006

British Library Cataloguing in Publication Data
A catalogue record for this book is available from the British Library.

Library of Congress Cataloging-in-Publication Data
A catalog record for this book has been requested.

ISBN-10 1 86134 774 X paperback
ISBN-13 978 1 86134 774 9

Cover design by Qube Design Associates, Bristol
Front cover: photograph supplied by kind permission of Philip Game, pg@globaltravelwriters.com
Printed and bound in Great Britain by Hobbs the Printers Ltd, Southampton

Acknowledgements

We would like to thank Anne Harrop, Alison Jarvis, Emma Stone, Pat Kneen and Sue Bracewell at the JRF for their vision and enthusiastic support for this project. We also thank the many scholars and practitioners who attended the Racism Roundtable who contributed so openly and generously to our findings. Maria Hussain and Rhona Stephen at Middlesex University have to be thanked for their administration.

Our families have been understanding and supportive during the time it took to produce this book. Reena Bhavnani's particular thanks must go to her husband Ian Douglas and her children Anil and Anjuli for their patience and understanding; also thanks go to Reena's child care and household help, Maria Szabo, for allowing her to concentrate on the writing. Heidi Mirza would like to thank Stewart Phillips and Aliya her daughter for their long suffering and missed summer holiday. Veena Meetoo got married and gave birth during the production of this book. A special thanks to her husband Marcello Bertotti, her family, and new baby, Nadya, who carries forward in her new life our hopes and dreams for a peaceful, antiracist new world order.

Introduction

There is a growing worldwide consensus for human beings to live together in mutual respect of ethnic and racial difference. Governments have played their part through legislation and policy. But surprisingly, there has been very little evidence-based research on whether these policies have been successful. It is time to take stock.

In a climate of increasing bureaucracy in racial equality, we were commissioned by the Joseph Rowntree Foundation (JRF) to map the causes of racism and to review policy interventions aiming to combat it. In a far-sighted attempt to bring some coherence to the 'race' and policy debate the idea was to see what potentially successful elements of interventions could be usefully elucidated and in the process to suggest fresh approaches in tackling racism.

When we began the research for the book, we were sceptical: would we find anything new and illuminating given the mounds of paper already produced on social inclusion, diversity and racial equality? As we dug deeper, to our surprise, however, we discovered that there was little research literature that actually highlighted the *causes* of racism precisely. There has been little analysis and evaluation of the presence of institutional racism. And even less literature in the public domain that links these causes to policies aiming to promote equality and diversity.

There has been much rhetoric, but little widespread implementation of any real policy to combat racism over the last 30 years. This is particularly relevant because a growing 'rhetoric' on action, targets and implementation in the current context may actually increase the backlash against racialised minorities. Those implementing 'diversity' or 'race' equality policies feel besieged by being asked to demonstrate a certain type of accountability showing evidence of statistical outcomes, ticking boxes and bureaucratic assessments. These procedures have all become bywords in 'race' equality. There is little time for reflection, when having to meet 'racial equality targets' in terms of recruitment and demonstrating inclusion. It is therefore timely to ask the question: Are these recommended strategies actually the most appropriate approaches to tackling racism?

In the 20th century, there have been international UN interventions to tackle racism, European-wide directives and in Britain, specific legislation on 'race relations' and 'race' equality. Institutions and organisations have taken steps to conform to legislation, and both recipients of racism and their supporters have been involved. This book examines and categorises such policy interventions and their effectiveness by focusing on 'professional' social policy interventions. Professional policy interventions in 'race' equality are assumed to be a 'good thing' in tackling racism. In our approach, these assumptions are not automatically accepted, but instead we re-examine these interventions, and in the process encourage a fresh perspective.

We do not, however, detail the struggles or strategies of the recipients of racism and their supporters. Rather, the examination of grassroots interventions and antiracist protests requires another project. Here we focus mainly on the historical context of social policy interventions in Britain. While it is beyond the scope of this book to encompass the detail of interventions, historically, or by country or region, we do refer to international interventions, such as the Canadian government's approach to multiracialism in order to provide a comparative context to the British experience.

Any review of the causes of racism must recognise that it is multifaceted and complex in both its specificity and operation. All too often simplistic assumptions are made about what racism is and what it means. Yet understanding the nature of racism is crucial to developing effective interventions to challenge it. The scope of this book is to examine both the deeper causes of racism, and the reproduction of 'everyday racism' between individuals and groups, including the influence of politicians and the media. It explores too, the many different types of racisms. For example, there are different racisms against specific designated groups, such as, newer arrivals and asylum seekers, people of African Caribbean, South Asian and Chinese origin as well as Jewish and Irish people and Travellers.

Racisms are also not only different, but intersect with other discriminations and prejudices, of gender, class, age, disability and sexual orientation. Racisms can also be reviewed through the examination of their effects in different sites, such as schools, hospitals, prisons, youth clubs, theatres, sports centres or large workplaces. This enables us to see the specificity of racism as it is reproduced in different sites and situations, by local context. This context includes taking account of the multiple identities of perpetrators and recipients as well as the structures, processes and cultures of the institutions in question.

In putting this book together we held a one-day roundtable discussion to discuss the causes of racism and successful interventions to combat it. We invited 35 participants in the field of 'race' equality and racism to share their knowledge and help identify gaps in actions. This unique gathering of academics and practitioners informed the study. The interventions that emerged in our discussions left us feeling optimistic, but also a bit disconcerted at the scale of the issues. The energy and commitment of those involved in dealing with racism and delivering interventions was inspiring.

Projects ranged from top-down national initiatives such as the National Archive heritage project, 'Moving Here', which documents 200 years of Jewish, Caribbean and Asian immigration and their contribution to the diversity of Britain. There were 'middling' interventions which influence policy and legislation such as the Southall Black Sisters campaign for the reversal of the 'Primary Purpose Rule' which discriminates against migrant and refugee women suffering domestic violence by denying them access to welfare and support if their marriages to British citizens break up within a year of their arrival. Then there were localised projects such as the proactive conflict resolution project Aik Saath, which brought 'warring' white, Muslim and Sikh Asian young people together in a school setting to discuss their fears, beliefs and racist behaviour in carefully designed sessions. These broad-ranging approaches enabled us to explore how and if all these differing kinds of interventions addressed the causes of racism (see Appendix A (9) 'Aik Saath').

Organisation of the book

We begin in Chapter One by exploring the history and roots of racism. We consider the use of terminology, and clarify the origins and changing meanings of 'race' and racism. The meanings of 'ethnic minorities', equality, diversity and multicultural interventions are defined and analysed. Chapter Two establishes the parameters of the book, by defining interventions and assessing the meaning of 'successful' in professionalised interventions. Here we define equality interventions and difference or multicultural interventions. We suggest that professionalised interventions in these areas are not fixed but are reproduced time and time again, and are subject to changes in ideologies and national political objectives.

Chapters Three and Four unravel the ways in which 'everyday racism' manifests itself. Chapter Three focuses in particular on the notion of 'elite racism' as reproduced every day through the media and government. By investigating the vitriolic discourse on asylum seekers, multiculturalism and 'Britishness', we find power elites, who legitimate covert everyday racism. This illumination of elite racism suggests a different kind of intervention than that of 'ethnic' monitoring and recruiting 'race' relations officers. Chapter Four on situated racisms further explores the notion of everyday racism by examining how it is reproduced by ordinary people in local contexts. Local level successful interventions have understood, for example, the situational context of white young men's racist expressions and violence by initiating antiracist youth projects. However, these interventions require attention to the changing nature of working class or gendered identities, offering a different approach to one used in tackling the macro causes of elite racisms.

Chapter Five assesses the legislative framework of British 'race' relations, the introduction of immigration and nationality legislation and the relationships between the two. It charts the development of equal opportunity and diversity policies and reviews the literature on their effectiveness in tackling the causes of racism. It assesses the legislative framework which has introduced progressive antidiscrimination legislation such as the 2000 Race Relations (Amendment) Act in tandem with criminal restrictions and racialised anti-immigration and asylum legislation. Such mixed messages mean equality and antidiscrimination policies and practice have been limited by ad hoc and individualistic application. They are rarely evaluated to see if racism has declined. The new Single Equality Body proposed for 2006, based as it is on legislation, will be limited in its ability to recognise the complexity of people's multiple identities and collective racialised experiences.

Chapters Six and Seven explore research on the effectiveness of interventions based on 'equality'. Chapter Six discusses the conceptual issues inherent in ideas of equality of opportunity and their advantages and limitations in employment. Equality of opportunity, access to employment and training and equal or fair treatment in the workplace, particularly interventions on recruitment, promotion and racial harassment, are considered. Evidence suggests that there is very little evaluation as to whether policies such as positive action or specialist 'race' and diversity officers have been successful in tackling racism. Thus policies designed for enabling access are dealing with effects rather than causes. Organisational cultures, which reproduce racism are racialised, and continue to disadvantage minorities. Chapter Seven explores equality interventions based on equality of access to services. New government initiatives on social exclusion, social capital and neighbourhood renewal provide the framework for discussing interventions in various sites, including education, criminal justice, health and welfare and education. Dominant discourses singularly stress equality of access as stemming from the lack of social capital in ethnic communities which leads to social exclusion.

In contrast to equality interventions, Chapter Eight reviews research on the effectiveness of interventions based on 'difference', and the conceptual issues of multiculturalism. It examines the positive and negative effects of policies which recognise 'ethnic' difference in very different ways. This chapter discusses recent policy initiatives on community cohesion and intercultural understanding and analyses research on their effectiveness. The ways in which conceptual issues of multiculturalism are used to 'manage' 'race' and 'ethnic' minorities are explored. Many interventions based on recognising 'difference', whether faith schools, translation services, heritage projects, or projects on intercultural understanding have not been evaluated for their effectiveness in reducing racism and lowering intolerance. The hotly contested nature of multiculturalism in all its guises leaves many with deep ambivalences about the nature of these interventions.

Chapter Nine describes examples of successful interventions, and analyses what makes them successful. Not only should interventions address the causes of racisms and their everyday reproduction, but they should also address *the what, the why* and *the how.* Most professional policy interventions concentrate primarily on the 'what', and frequently ignore the 'why'. Successful interventions including youth programmes, and sports and arts initiatives are explored. Selective international antiracist and multicultural interventions in Europe, Canada, Australia and New Zealand are discussed to illustrate lessons for Britain. It is suggested that there is not one racism, but multiple racisms. Understandings racisms at macro (elite) and micro (local) levels help in planning interventions.

Finally, Chapter Ten summarises the key arguments and discusses the relationship of the root causes of racism to the everyday reproduction of racism. We conclude that racism changes depending on the macro and micro contexts. Understanding racism with reference to ideology, nation, identity construction, the role of whiteness and the nature of ethnicity, are essential to tackling racism. While many interventions are poorly conceived and implemented, we suggest a systematic strategy for thinking about future interventions in an integrated way, focusing on the three areas of education, communication and vigilance.

ONE

The roots of racism

The United Nations World Conference against Racism (www.un.org/ WCAR/) held in Durban in 2001 signifies the complexity of writing a book linking causes of racism with successful interventions. Despite admirable intentions to review progress in tackling racism, the Conference was beset with conflicts and controversies over Arab charges of Israeli racism against Palestinians, African demands for slavery reparations, and disputes over India's caste system, China's rule in Tibet and Europe's treatment of Romany and Gypsy communities. The roots of racism in slavery or the caste system as well as current manifestations through wars and conflicts over disputed territories all entered ideas about racism and its causes (Ajadi, 2002).

What the Durban Conference illustrated is that there is no one definition of racism, no one history of racism and no one cause of racism. Our purpose here is to explore the changing nature and specificity of racism. We are also concerned with mapping policy-based 'professional' interventions in racism against their effectiveness in tackling the root causes of racism in the changing British context.

We begin by examining the roots of racism, before discussing how these roots are reproduced every day. We conclude by exploring the terminology used in talking about 'race'. Following the clarification of these concepts, Chapter Two explores our understanding of interventions, the meaning of 'success', and the ways in which we categorise professional interventions.

The origins of 'race'

We rarely take time out these days to consider what terms such as 'race', from which 'racism' derives, mean. In fact, words such as 'race', 'race relations' and 'racial' have become so commonly used in everyday life in Britain that people assume that everyone means the same thing. It is important to disentangle underlying assumptions in order to understand these concepts (Back and Solomos, 2000). The words 'race' and 'racial' suggest that peoples of the world are grouped into distinct 'races', and that 'racial' conflicts, for example, result from contact between 'races' in and of themselves, rather than conflicts based on political or economic competition (Miles and Small, 1999). (See Appendix C, Glossary of terms, for definitions of the concepts used in this chapter.)

In its earliest conception 'race' did not have a scientific rationale. Through the 15th and 16th centuries religious writing alluded to variations between human beings but interpretations varied between those who explained colour differences due to the sun, compared to those who saw it as a curse of God (Husband, 1982).

However, with the growth of the slave trade in the 17th and 18th centuries, ideological constructions of superiority and inferiority between Africa and Europe began to emerge (McClintock, 1995). At the expense of high rates of adult and infant mortality, cruel and oppressive conditions of work, African slaves and Asian indentured labourers provided the profit for the infrastructure for Britain's industrial revolution. This profit has been documented as direct investment in the railways, coal and steel industries, ship building and the steam engine as well as the banking and insurance systems (Fryer, 1984, 1993).

The separation of the world's peoples into designated 'races' thus involved economic gain through the ascription of certain differential traits which were reinforced through literature, science and philosophy of the time. Today the reparations movement and the truth and reconciliation movements have been formed to publicly acknowledge the recognition of such a stain on the history of white people. Their aims are to heal the pain carried by generations of dispossessed and discriminated racialised peoples (Hutton, 2001; Mack, 2001; Ajadi, 2002; *Race and Class*, 2002; Adam and Moodley, 2003).

Scientific racism

With the ascendancy of science and the decline of religion, physical cause emerged as a predominant model in distinguishing 'races' in the 19th century. The meaning of 'race' changed from its literary sense, meaning a line of descent, or a group defined by historical continuity, to its scientific sense of 'race' as a biologically defined group (Husband, 1982). 'Race' was seen as a way of distinguishing people into biological categories, and these were used to explain differences between people in differing cultures, particularly the superiority of the Europeans.

'Race' was seen as unchanging, innate. This clarity was superseded with the publication of Darwin's *Origin of the species* in 1859 which argued that 'races' could be subject to change. Social Darwinism created a 'scientific' approach that 'races' had to be kept separate and 'pure', particularly the European white 'race', to prevent internal contamination. This framework was also applied to the 'feckless' and 'over fertile' working class in Britain (Husband, 1982).

Categorisation based on 'race' was not always based on colour. Ape-like caricatures of Irish people were produced, for example, in the Victorian period in Britain (Stepan, 1990). African people were likened to Jewish people, with a projecting mouth that had the 'African look' (Gilman, 1991). The eugenics movements of the 19th and 20th century sought to control the purity of the 'races'. Social Darwinism and the ideology of biological inferiority were introduced to eliminate any physical and mental dysfunction. The 'breeding' of those deemed undesirable such as disabled people and poor people was forcibly prohibited (Kohn, 1996).

Kohn writes about the 'Race Gallery' in Vienna's Natural History Museum, where, during a Hitler rally, a million people queued to see the 'parade of human skulls'. The human cranial hierarchy, arranged with Nordic at the top, insists that differences are real and measurable and can be divided into the typologies of Caucasoid, Mongoloid and Negroid. The Gallery, called the *Rassensaal*, remained open until the mid-1990s. However, 21st-century manifestations of 'race galleries' persist, with the Human Genome Diversity project mapping the DNA of indigenous people from around the world, and the American Census, that persists in 'race' classifications (Kohn, 1996).

Of course reputable scientists do not now believe that the human population is divided into distinct 'races' or species, such that those physical and genetic characteristics are related to social and psychological characteristics (Hannaford, 1996; Kohn, 1996; Montagu, 1997). But the words to denote those original meanings are with us today and are under constant revision and debate. The perpetuation of populist racist pseudoscience is evident in the intelligence testing of Eysenck (1971) and Jensen (1969). More recently Murray and Herrnstein (1996), with their controversial book *The bell curve*, show that the seeds of the earlier meanings of 'race' have not completely vanished (Kohn, 1996; Mirza, 1998). As such, commentators will frequently place quotation marks around the word 'race' since its original link with biology and genetics has been unquestionably challenged.

After the Second World War, the horrors of the genocide of Jewish people and Gypsies forced the academic community to challenge the so-called 'scientific' basis of racial difference. A variety of UNESCO statements between 1950 and 1967 appeared and papers on 'race' and difference came into being (Montagu, 1997). These were to argue that the biological basis of 'race' had no basis, and 'race' was a *social* construction. But the deep meanings of 'race', connected to the physical unchanging make-up of people, have still endured in different ways. The power of early scientific thought in this area, coupled with the legacy of colonialism and slavery, has left large footprints in our current societies.

Colonial power and discourse

The articulation of scientific discourse in the 19th century, coupled with a context of expanding colonialism, entrenched ideas of inferiority and superiority based on colour. By the mid-19th century, at the height of the Empire, Britain controlled over a quarter of the world. Ireland, Canada, New Zealand, Australia, the West Indies, Africa and India were conquered through violence, bribery and a divide-and-rule strategy. Edward Said's work on western colonial discourse explained the ways in which inferior beliefs of 'uncivilised', 'exotic' and 'backward' colonised peoples was not so much imposed as reproduced and reflected in the power of colonial discourse (Said, 1978). The creation of the 'white man' as 'civilising', 'enlightened' and 'rational' was both an idea and a lived reality for the coloniser. The discourses on difference between the East and the West created a social and material reality for the enactment of colonial subjugation. This was done though the creation of 'knowledge of the Orient'. Certain powerful understandings and codes, which regulated the colonised in their own lands, were laid down in language, literature, law, medicine and religion.

One such reality that was created concerned the intersection of gender and 'race'. The construction of white and Asian/African/Caribbean identities of women and men was linked to growing national identities in the 'West' and the 'East'. Gender and racial divisions were used to clarify these boundaries and to work as markers for European nations. They helped to define who was 'British' and who was a 'native' or a 'subject'. This definition of national identity was created and reinforced through sexual control and the idea of white women as mothers, who were important in reproducing the 'race' (Stoler, 1996).

These racial and sexual boundaries were regulated and became more distinct as the colonies became more politically stable, medically upgraded and economically secure. The centrality of gender in national discourse is still as strong. Fundamentalist notions of purity and redemption are deemed to belong to women so that they can be culturally transmitted to the next generation. Their bodies underpin the idea of the reproduction of the nation (Ware, 1997a; Yuval-Davis, 1997).

The new racisms

The culturalisation of racism

Authors now accept that racism changes according to political and social conditions. Over the last 20 years the new racism in dominant discourse has moved from a scientific biological basis towards a concept of cultural racism (Goldberg, 1993). In the 1960s and 1970s successful anticolonial struggles combined with the growing civil rights movements and the introduction of UN and other legislation covering human rights and equality, became part of the agendas of most countries (Omi and Winant, 1987). This was the era where integration was possible and efforts were made to encompass cultural difference, and it created the 'new racism' (Barker, 1981) and the 'culturalisation of racism' (Essed, 1991).

It was argued that the notion of cultural differences and a multicultural approach to social policy could still mask racism (Wimmer, 1997). In fact, such discourse could provide a breeding ground for both far right and everyday racism. Because the essence of multiculturalism lies in the idea that every culture is worth protection, so multiculturalism can be *re*-interpreted as a right of the indigenous to defend their homeland against 'mixture' (Solomos and Back, 1996; Wimmer, 1997). In fact it has even been argued that this 'new racism' also wants to be democratic and responsible, and therefore, begins by *denying* it is racist.

In the new racism, minorities are not biologically inferior, they are seen as culturally different. Cultural difference becomes a way of assigning blame for exclusion and poverty.

> They have a different culture, although in many respects there are deficiencies, such as single parent families, drug abuse, lacking achievement values, and dependence on welfare and affirmative action – 'pathologies' that need to be corrected of course. (van Dijk, 2000, p 34)

Discourses of 'race' and ethnicity are also contested by introducing antiracist strategies. Affected groups have also adopted the idea of 'race' in relation to ethnicity. They have tried to turn the concept around and use racial definitions such as 'black' for constructing positive self-identities and as a basis for political resistance, and to fight for participation (Wodak and Resigl, 1999).

Nation and 'race'

Global change has also changed interpretations of racism as technological change has accelerated the process of global communications. The technological revolution, the liberalisation of world trade and the financial markets has led to a growing interdependence of nations (Castles, 1996). Increasing global interdependence arguably threatens the nation state. It enables racism to be more overtly linked to ideas of sovereignty and nationhood. Those constructed as 'outsiders' (for example, recent late 20th-century immigrants) are constructed as outside of a mythical 'homogeneous national culture' (Parekh, 2000). These outsiders thus need to be 'integrated'. Culture, nation and identity are therefore deeply implicated with conceptions of racism.

Hall (1994) argues that a more explicit and visible debate on multiculturalism has resulted from a mass movement of people entering a huge number of nation states. The UK has seen not only immigration from its own ex-colonies, but more recently from Iran, Ethiopia, Bosnia and Kosovo, from people fleeing wars, political regimes and famine.

However, the notion of the nation being disrupted by such movements is mythical. National cultures were never unified in any case. Nations themselves are discursive devices representing difference as unity/identity (Anderson, 1983). Furthermore national identities are formed in relation to 'other' nation states. This has been particularly marked in relation to the creation of the 'East' and the 'West'.

The idea of nation is socially constructed and changes in relation to economic, social and political processes. This is an 'imagined community', imagined "because the members of even the smallest nations will never know most of their fellow members, meet them, or even hear them, yet in the minds of each lives the image of their communion" (Anderson, 1983, p 6). Nations are also constructed and reconstructed on the basis of gender and 'race', as we have outlined earlier in the discussion of colonial discourse. Gender differentiations can become essentialised with man as 'warrior', woman as 'nurturer'. So, although women are often evoked in nationalist discourse as in Britannia, for example, they are not autonomous but linked to the patriarchal structure of the family. This structure is seen as a microcosm of the nation. Families can guarantee the bloodline and so-called 'purity' of the nation (Yuval-Davis, 1997; Cockburn, 1998).

Ethnicity, culture and 'race'

The use of ethnicity and culture rather than 'race' now challenges the notion of biological differences as a cause of racism. Cultural differences become a legitimising force for racism. This 'new' racism (Barker, 1981) has implications for reconceptualising multiculturalism.

As argued earlier, the link between culture and 'race' is not totally new. Although colour has been integral to ideas of 'race' and hierarchy, particularly in relationships of slavery and colonialism, this has not always been the case, and ideas of religion or 'narrow' ideas of culture have also informed ideas about racism (Phoenix, 1998). In our current times, racism refers to the relationships between people based on colour, but this view also exists side by side with the idea of 'culture' to create 'ethnic' hierarchies, as well as 'race' ones.

This culturalisation of racism has led to both hidden and covert racism, such as an unstinting 'gaze' on all racialised peoples. This singular focus legitimates in a subtle way their *difference* from the 'norm'. It problematises all the cultures under the microscope. In this way white ethnicities, such as people of Irish and Jewish origin, have also been included (Back and Solomos, 2000). The culturalisation of racism has also re-formed to be overt about 'other' cultures such as 'jungle smells', being unhygienic and bringing disease (Ware, 1997b), as well as discourses that suggest that certain groups are only fit for a particular type of work. The Arts Council Diversity Plan, for example, tells a story of the father of a black director who went to buy tickets at a theatre, and was told the cleaner job had gone (Khan, 2002)!

Defining 'ethnicity'

This discussion then brings us to an understanding of the use of the terms 'ethnic' and 'ethnic minority', which have been discursively used as part of the culturalisation of racism. Ethnicity has been used frequently and interchangeably with 'race'. It was used to describe people who perceived a shared identity on the basis of culture, descent and territory, and it is essentially a process of group identification (Banks, 1996; Jenkins, 1998; Fenton, 2003). In the early 20th century it was used in the US by anthropologists and sociologists studying European immigrant groups and their relationship to American society.

The analysis of ethnicity in Britain normally begins with a study of the New Commonwealth immigrants of the 1950s (Solomos, 2003). This is an erroneous approach as we live in a society composed of a number of ethnic groups, one of which is the English (Alibhai Brown,

2000). In other words, everyone has an ethnicity. To use ethnicity to discuss the location of black people only is inaccurate. The term 'ethnic minorities' cannot be used solely in relation to those peoples from the ex-colonies in the Caribbean, the Indian sub-continent, East and West Africa, and Hong Kong. 'Ethnicity', it is argued, has to be separated from its discourse in relation to racism (Hall, 1992). It has to be predicated on difference and diversity:

> We are all ... ethnically located and our ethnic identities are crucial to the subjective sense of who we are. But this is also a recognition that this is not an ethnicity that is doomed to survive, as Englishness was, only by marginalising, dispossessing, displacing and forgetting other ethnicities. (Hall, 1992, p 258)

Despite the importance of ethnicity, an undue emphasis on it may suggest that differences are primarily due to a 'fixed' culture rather than to a dynamic changing relationship between such factors as 'culture', economy, 'race', class, disability and gender. As has been pointed out, for example in health research, explanations for and solutions to health problems are based on rigid and historical notions of culture and cultural difference, whereby cultures exist in socioeconomic and power vacuums (Ahmad and Jones, 1998; Nazroo, 1998).

In other words, we must constantly be alert to the ways in which we use the terms 'race' and 'ethnic minority' and not forget the origin of these terms and the ways in which assumptions are created about what they mean, particularly the relationship of 'ethnic' minority to 'culture'. To use ethnicity to discuss the location of black groups only, as in 'ethnic minority communities', is incorrect.

Ethnic groups (at least those designated as such) are not therefore the only groups separated by *culture*. Furthermore, homogeneity within the 'ethnic' group itself is also a faulty conception. We know that the heterogeneity of groups categorised as having one culture is absurd. Differences in culture may be separated by origin as well as 'routes'. The original educational or employment background of differing ex-Commonwealth immigrants and the white population, for example, may contain patterns between ethnicities, for example between Chinese origin, White Welsh origin and African Caribbean origin, but also overlaps between them, based on gender and class and type of employment or housing.

The connections between ethnicised groups and their connections with the dominant cultures will also influence the ways in which groups change. A variety of racialised groups interacts with and influences, as well as is influenced by, so-called mainstream society (Runnymede Trust, 2000). People are constantly forming new social mixes and creating new cultural forms and identities. For example, not all Muslims interpret their religion in the same way; similarly there are wide differences between Indians in the type of work they do and their involvement in mainstream institutions (Parekh, 2000). There are increasing separations between younger Bangladeshis and their family traditions. In addition, men and women within many of the different groups are represented differently (Mirza, 2003).

Differences within ethnic groups are also dynamic, interacting with the structures of society, influenced by and influencing each other. These differences may be rendered invisible in strategies to counter racism. Failure to recognise differences within ethnic groups and their changing nature subscribes to a 'narrow' and fixed definition of culture (Phoenix, 1988) and reinforces cultural racism.

The cultural differences *within* ethnic groups are also marked by overarching material differences. For example, there are differences between those who live in the poorer inner cities or those who live in affluent suburbs (Social Exclusion Unit, 1998). There is a growing polarisation between transnational migrant groups, some of whom are extremely wealthy while others are exceedingly poor (Vertovec, 1999). These material differences are part of a view of culture that is dynamic and integral to the shaping of people's beliefs, practices and identities. Within any cultural group, there are variations according to age, class, gender, disability and sexuality.

This foregoing discussion of the new racisms, based on a dynamic view of 'culture' and 'nation', now enables us to discuss the definition of racism.

Definitions of racism

'Race' is a social construct. Its changing manifestations reflect ideological attempts to legitimate domination in different social and historical contexts. Racism is therefore not about objective measurable physical and social characteristics, but about relationships of domination and subordination.

Fredman (2001) argues that racism operates along at least three axes. First, it is characterised by denigratory stereotyping, hatred and violence. Second, it sets in motion cycles of disadvantage. Third, it negates and even obliterates the culture, religion and language of the groups concerned (Fredman, 2001). Interventions to challenge racism thus need to be based on common definitions. They need to address all three characteristics within specific social contexts, for these axes of racism are related to each other.

Miles and Small have proposed a definition based on understanding racism as:

> … an ideology which constructs a social collectivity with reference to real or imagined biological and cultural characteristics, which are negatively evaluated. (Miles and Small, 1999, p 145)

This is useful, but these references to real or imagined characteristics of groups do not remain static. These negative evaluations are perpetuated by being reproduced every day.

Furthermore, there is also considerable historical variation in both the conception of 'races', and in the kinds of social expression we categorise as 'racist' (Goldberg, 1993). Racism is expressed in different ways in particular historical, regional and national contexts. In other words, there are different racisms (Gilroy, 1987). As Fredman argues:

> There is no single racism, but multiple racisms; colour racism must be examined together with cultural racism, which includes ethnicity, religion and language. (Fredman, 2001, p 2)

Furthermore, we must seek to understand how ideas of 'race' inform and are informed by other oppressions of age, class, gender, disability and sexuality.

This takes us back to understanding complexity. We recognise that the ideas about 'racisms' do not come from nowhere, but from the ways in which societal structures and ideologies are produced and maintained. Racism is implicated in social relations; it is not something *outside* of our social milieu. We need to include a perspective which takes account of how ideologies and structures in wider society support the ways in which beliefs about group differences are ingrained in our everyday lives. One way to examine how deeper roots of racism reappear in our societies is to examine not only the social milieu, but also the ways in which we think and talk about racism. These reproductions are critical in tackling the causes of racism.

Reproducing racism

The social and the cognitive (van Dijk, 2000) both reproduce everyday racism. The social component consists of everyday discriminatory practices at a micro level, and organisational, institutional and legal arrangements, for example, at the macro level. The cognitive component concerns people's beliefs, namely, knowledge, attitudes, values, ideologies and norms. Van Dijk argues that these *beliefs* are reproduced through discourse, and these beliefs are critical sources of the reproduction of racism:

> In the system of racism, thus stereotypes, prejudices and ideologies explain why and how people engage in discriminatory practices in the first place, for instance because they think that the others are inferior (less intelligent, less competent, less modern and so on), have fewer rights, or that 'we' have a priority for a job or a house.... Discourse, as a social practice is at the same time the main source for people's racist beliefs.... Indeed we learn racism (or antiracism) largely through text or talk. (van Dijk, 2000, p 36)

Essed's work (1991) on the experience of black women has analysed micro inequities which are perpetuated through everyday practices. She links the micro with the macro level of racism. In other words, the micro level of everyday behaviours and attitudes maintains the social structures of racism. It is these which become critical to the causes of racism and racist social practices, and it is these ideologies and discourses which need to be addressed in any interventions.

This particular conceptual understanding of the causes of racism may sit uneasily with the 'problem' of having to always produce 'evidence' of racism in order for it to be tackled. This evidence gathering usually means demonstrating current data ('ethnic' monitoring), often within one institution, together with/or the evidence of, the existence of *overt* beliefs and actions about 'race' (for example, I have a superior brain to 'them'). This can be too restricting – we need to understand how these ideas about group differences have been historically produced and sustained, and we have to understand how these ideas also achieve legitimacy in the context of other constructed group differences in Britain. Ideas become accepted and consensus gained due to prevailing economic and social conditions. We have to understand how they can be coded and overt, and that they are also subject to contestation. Most important, however, these ideas and beliefs are embedded in the ways in which we perceive the world; they are not an *added-on* prejudice.

We therefore need to recognise the concept of 'racialisation' to better understand racism. In other words, *all* group differences are racialised, since notions of inferiority and superiority define not only those who are perceived as inferior, but also define those perceived as superior. The concept includes the ways in which ideologies and structures construct certain groups in ways that presume they are naturally distinct. Although the origin of these constructions for groups is in science and biology, since the early 1980s there has been agreement that racism has increasingly been linked with 'culture' – meaning a way of life, with religion, dress and rituals. These 'fixed' scientific constructions have been replaced by 'fixed' cultural constructions.

Having now discussed the ways in which the roots of racism are reproduced theoretically, it will be useful to examine how the cognitive aspects of everyday racism are evident in the terminology we use.

Terminology: the way we talk about 'race'

As argued above, racialised knowledge in our society is constantly changing and open to contestation (Goldberg, 1993; Modood et al, 2002). What is 'common sense' or acceptable in one place or time can offend in another. For example, nowadays the use of the term 'coloured' is offensive to young 'black' people (of African heritage) and to those of 'mixed' heritage origin (which is also a contested term; see Ifekwunigwe, 2004). However, it was used as a term by older (postcolonial) 'West Indians' (a term now replaced by African Caribbeans) to positively self-identify themselves in the 1960s. In the US 'women of colour' is still used to collectively encompass the various shades of African American womanhood. In South Africa, however, the term 'coloured' invokes negative connotations of segregation under apartheid when Indian and indigenous 'mixed' people were referred to thus. Terms such as 'hybrid' were once seen as a racist concept. Hybridity now refers to the mixing of people of 'colour', and has now been reclaimed to denote the privileged, positive and creative space of difference such people occupy (Hall, 1992; Modood and Werbner, 1997).

In developing theories to look at the social construction of identity it is now generally accepted that there is no scientific or biological foundation for racial difference. Thus when people use the term 'Black' it is understood not to constitute a 'race'/racial category. Instead, it is

a politically contested homogeneous collective term which has co
to mean those who are visibly and politically racialised as 'other'. It
has been appropriated positively by some groups, such as 'black' African
and Caribbean women and politicised British non-white women
including some women of Asian origin to identify themselves (Brah,
1996; Mirza, 1997).

Ethnicity, on the other hand, includes self-defining religious and
cultural groups, who can be similarly racialised as culturally defined
groups. Because of differential power among and between *ethnic* groups,
inherent differences in worth may not necessarily apply in the same
way as with 'black' groups (Cornell and Hartmann, 1998; Runnymede
Trust, 2000).

These examples of different ways in which terms are evaluated in
different societies and contexts help us understand current terms in
use. The government has adopted as their 'official' term 'black' and
minority ethnic, shortened to BME, in many of their reports (Social
Exclusion Unit, 1998). This is not a term many 'ethnic minority'
communities tend to use to describe themselves. Indeed, there has
been much controversy about what it really signifies and to whom
(Modood et al, 2002). The term has evolved due to the political context
of racial definitions.

Recently those defined as ethnic minority people have contested
this collective term. In the absence of 'ethnic' being used for *all* groups,
they prefer the label 'minority ethnic'. The rationale is simple. While
those defined as 'ethnic' make up majority populations globally, they
find themselves defined as 'minority' migrant communities in Britain.
Thus the term 'minority ethnic' rather than 'ethnic minority' is now
used.

In this literature review we recognise the fluidity of racialised
terminology. As the 2001 Census categories show, there is no one
rationale in the current discourse which underpins our thinking about
'race'. Sometimes the Census uses visible colour; sometimes citizenship
and place of birth (for example, Pakistan). At other times it uses language,
religion, regional or country location to identify 'ethnic origins'. Thus
we use words such as 'ethnic minority', 'black', 'Asian', 'minority ethnic',
as interchangeable. In so doing we recognise the heightened and
sensitive (and often reductionist and essentialist) nature of using 'racial'
terms and categories but also acknowledge that there is no consistency
or one way to do it. We are guided by the context and what feels
appropriate for what we are discussing. Sometimes visible colour may
be appropriate, hence the collective use of 'black' people. Sometimes
ethnicity or religion may be more appropriate as when discussing the

nce 'South Asian' or 'Muslim' may be appropriate.
alised status may dominate, for example, 'Muslims'
rs', who are now increasingly racialised by their

...usion

Racism was rooted in the scientific discourse of Social Darwinism and the search for identifiable physical differences, based on a biological idea of 'race'. These physical differences were then linked to character traits and ideas of inferiority and superiority, and these constructions were legitimated by slavery and colonial domination. They helped to construct the identities of white women and men as well as those people of 'colour' subjugated in the British Empire. They helped define notions of 'East' and 'West'.

- Scientific racism has been partly replaced by the culturalisation of racism. Since the mid-20th century it has been publicly recognised that 'race' is a social construction and not a biological one. But differences between groups are now 'judged' on the basis of 'cultural differences'. This culturalisation of racism has led to both hidden and covert racism, such as an unstinting 'gaze' on racialised peoples, legitimating in a subtle way their *difference* from the 'norm' and therefore problematising them. Racism in our current context does not always refer to colour directly, but implies inferiority through the ways in which different cultural groups live.

- We are all part of 'ethnic' groups. To use 'ethnic' to refer to people of colour or new immigrants is incorrect. Similarly we all have 'culture'. Defining and understanding 'culture' requires an understanding of how 'cultures' intersect with broad structures and processes in society.

- Racism changes with context and historical periods. It has no one cause and no one solution. There are multiple racisms, which intersect with societal norms. The racisms concerned with culture, class, gender and nation are developed and reproduced differently, although there may be certain prevailing overall patterns.

- These differing understandings of racism suggest its multifaceted and complex nature. Racism cannot be viewed as one explanation or one theoretical framework. There are macro racisms and micro racisms, and these different racisms need to be examined in their specific contexts.

- Beliefs, attitudes and actions on racism are reproduced in social contexts, within the workplace, on the street, between neighbours, in the media and in government. Understanding the specific reproduction of racism is critical to tackling the causes of racism.

TWO

Defining successful interventions

Chapter One argued that the multiple, situated and changing nature of racism in different times and places means that it is impossible to find one solution, that is a 'holy grail of antiracism'. As such, this chapter begs the question, 'What is a successful intervention?'. Like the idea of multiple racisms, there are a variety of possible interventions, which may be based on understanding particular conditions. An intervention, for example, may be about the *way* in which an action is understood, spoken about, and/or taken further. It might also be about tackling racism or a more general 'institutional racism' through change management. An intervention might also be informed by different academic disciplines as well as the cultures of different countries and their particular laws. However, as we often found, what appears to be a successful intervention may not really get to the root causes of racism as the connection between cause and effect is not made.

Analysing professional interventions helps clarify what is 'successful'. Three questions emerge on the drivers of interventions, their evaluation and whether they tackle the causes of racism:

• What drives current interventions in racism?
• How is their 'success' evaluated?
• Are the interventions tackling the causes of racism or just dealing with the symptoms?

While the concept of an intervention is hard to pin down, the definition of an intervention as 'stepping in to affect the outcome of a situation' is one that is most appropriate for this book. But it does beg certain questions. What constitutes 'stepping in'? Who is doing the stepping in? Is it always important to intervene? What does 'successful' actually mean? In this chapter we explore these questions in order to provide the parameters for our argument.

Professionalised interventions

It is argued that 'intervention' in our current discussion on racism has a connotation of 'professionalism', the discourse of 'interventions' being 'owned' by professionals, that is, policy makers or practitioners (Harris, 2004). By using this discourse, professionals thus view their actions as proactive. They are seen as the doer while those who respond to the interventions are reactive.

We argue that ordinary black people, as well as those who have been racialised (such as the Irish and Jewish origin populations) have, of course, also *intervened*, that is, fought for space and the right to be heard. They have intervened every day with their struggle for the right to define the language of racism, for voicing their disaffection, for living a daily life despite hostility. They have, over the years, and for the most part, managed to negotiate 'settlements' with the country and neighbourhoods in which they live, although these are constantly being renegotiated (Runnymede Trust, 1999; Mirza and Reay, 2000a; Harris, 2004). As racism changes, these settlements or everyday interventions become part of the norm, and are thus overlooked as interventions, as they are often not thought of as influential in changing the ways racism is experienced and expressed.

While the focus of this book is on professionalised policy interventions, this does not mean that we are seeking to exclude the critical importance of these settlements, or even anticolonial and postcolonial protests and rebellions. We will continue to refer to these interventions throughout this book in order to indicate that change in racism is frequently triggered by people's struggles for change.

What is a professional policy intervention?

As ideas and definitions of 'race' change, so does the idea of a social policy intervention. Ideas about what works are not neutral or objective. They are affected by politics, ideology and resources, and what is possible in different times and places. For example, the current trend for evidence-based knowledge dominates our increasingly politicised policy-making processes (Fox, 2003). The focus now tends to be for short-term high-profile initiatives where empirical results can be visibly demonstrated. This emphasis on the demonstration of empirical effectiveness may arguably be increasingly important as public spending decreases, and there are cries for efficiency and effectiveness in the allocation of resources.

Such practitioner-based approaches which are informed by cumulative surface knowledge, rather than deeper understanding, often stress the '*how* but not the *why*' (Alderson et al, 2004). *How* can we encourage more 'ethnic minorities' to work for our company? Instead of *why* are members of racialised groups absent as influential leaders in our company? As we will show, what works, or is seen to work, does not necessarily tackle the root causes of racism.

Defining 'success'

Despite the fact that there is a wealth of literature on theories and explanations of racism, as well as how it is experienced in different parts of the world, interventions in racism and their impacts have received little scrutiny and research (Banton, 1997; Bulmer and Solomos, 1999). It is thus extremely difficult to assess if interventions to combat racism have worked or are deemed successful. This problem is partly related to a lack of clarity about what racism means. 'Race' equality, institutional racism and racism have often been used interchangeably. The notion of equality, however, as we argue, is linked to accessing opportunities, and is not necessarily concerned with tackling the root causes of inequality.

Tackling the 'why', the 'what' and the 'how': towards action-based approaches

If we assume that racism exists in our societies, then we need to 'step in' to ensure that it is reduced or eliminated altogether. To not intervene, we naturally assume, may make it worse. On the other hand, some studies indicate that both understanding the nature of what you are intervening in, and how you intervene, is critical, since some interventions, albeit with sincere motives, may actually end up making things worse.

For example, having a wonderfully worded policy which is *not* implemented can give the impression of 'doing lots of things for ethnic minorities', but in effect leads to a growing gap in perception between those committed to changing racism and those who are *not* identified as 'ethnic minority'. Charges of lip service may be made by those committed to change when nothing happens; whereas those who are not identified as 'ethnic minority' may become resentful, particularly where there is trenchant competition for scarce resources. The gap between those who are committed to change and those who perceive they are missing out may therefore increase, despite the sincerity of the motives behind the intervention in question.

Tackling the 'why', the 'what' and the 'how' in its specific context are important for successful outcomes. We will use these parameters to explore the success of professional interventions in later chapters.

Patterns of professional interventions

Categories of interventions

There have been two key types of professionalised interventions in relation to racism. These have included those which are concerned with promoting *equality* and those which are about the promotion of *difference*. In this book we look at initiatives to do with *equality of opportunity* which concern *employment* and *equality of opportunity* in *accessing services*. The interventions on 'difference' concern initiatives aimed at different ethnicised groups, especially multicultural policies. These latter policies have been introduced to both recognise and legitimate 'racial' difference. Community cohesion policies assume 'cultural' or 'racial' divides as being key to bringing groups together rather than gender or class.

It is helpful to begin by defining the key terms used in categorising professional interventions, particularly *equality of opportunity*, *diversity*, and *multicultural interventions.*

Equality of opportunity, or the policy of equal opportunities (EO), is an 'equality' intervention based on the notion of equal access. The European community uses social exclusion to signify the lack of EO. An equal opportunities approach aims "to equalise the starting point by removing barriers at the point of selection for employment, education or other benefit" (Fredman, 2002, p 6). Although these policies have been partially replaced by policies on 'diversity' within organisations, the EO approach still largely determines access to employment and training. British legislation on 'race' equality and discrimination has provided the main rationale for interventions. The legislation provides a basic framework on antidiscrimination, and it is backed up by Voluntary Codes of Practice on employment, which advises employers to implement EO policies. These policies are not mandatory, but voluntary. Underlying these policies are concepts of 'justice' and 'fairness'.

Diversity policies, which include policies on sex, 'race', religion, sexual orientation, disability and age, have been introduced for several reasons. A disappointment with the impact of EO policies and a failure to progress underrepresented groups (see Cockburn, 1991), together with a backlash against EO policies, has been argued as a key reason for their demise (Faludi, 1992). The changes in wider society, with recognition of the need for 'excluded' groups in an expanding service sector, have also led to a change of discourse about needing those 'other' than white middle-class men in the labour market. Demographic changes, with a projected ageing population in Britain and reduced fertility, have led to a push towards a *business* case for the employment of women and racialised groups, that is, the need to utilise all sections of the labour market for competitive and business reasons, because there is going to be a shortage of white men in the future labour market. Leaders are now under pressure to encourage 'diversity' in the workforce, and in service delivery (see DTI, 2004, pp 13-16).

Multicultural interventions include national policy interventions based on ethnic or racialised difference which have been implemented side by side with notions of equality of opportunity. These we have termed the 'difference' or 'multicultural' interventions (Runnymede Trust, 2000). More recently, these types of interventions include faith schools, separate funding streams for differing ethnicised groups, and translation and interpreting services. The separation of different racialised groups in social policy, particularly via monitoring categories, has also encouraged a stronger self-definition by the groups themselves. Recent policies on social and community cohesion have been introduced under the banner of 'multiculturalism'. These policies have emerged partly in response to the presence of asylum seekers, the disturbances in the northern towns, and the subsequent concern about conflicts between 'cultures'. They have particular resonance with the re-imagining of the British 'nation'.

Intervention strategies: the 'how'

These professional policy interventions have invoked a variety of strategies or approaches (Runnymede Trust, 2000; Bhavnani, 2001). They include:

- education and training courses
- legal sanctions or enforcement
- counselling and mentoring
- changing policies and procedures within institutions
- monitoring the evidence of discrimination
- setting specific goals and targets
- writing new policies
- cross-community contact.

Recent 'multicultural' initiatives also include working on the ground with differing groups. Specific services may be 'targeted' at certain groups, or groups based on religion, race, ethnicity may be brought together to resolve conflict. These initiatives frequently target 'racialised' groups and white working-class people.

The strategies have also been formulated for specific groups or individuals in particular places, such as, for example, children in schools, employees in a large corporation, or prison officers. A key legislative intervention has also, for example, highlighted activities aimed at specific racialised groups, termed 'positive' or 'affirmative' action, in the UK (Fredman, 2002) and US respectively (Sniderman and Carmines, 1997).

Thus interventions can be categorised by type, by strategy or by method (including who they are aimed at) or their legislative origins. It is not within the scope of this review, however, to list all these interventions or to classify them according to all these different kinds. Rather it is the intention of this review to thematise the interventions by type, and to suggest in the process certain historical and contemporaneous patterns.

Institutional racism

There has also been much talk recently about 'institutional racism', a term used extensively in Britain as a result of the Stephen Lawrence Inquiry (Macpherson, 1999). The Macpherson report defined institutional racism as:

> The collective failure of an organization to provide an appropriate and professional service to people because of their colour, culture, or ethnic origin. It can be seen or detected in processes, attitudes, behaviour which amount to discrimination through unwitting prejudice, ignorance, thoughtlessness and racist stereotyping which disadvantage minority ethnic people. (Macpherson, 1999, p 28)

The term, however, did not originate in 1999. Two North American writers and Black Power activists, Stokely Carmichael and Charles Hamilton (1967), first used the term 'institutional racism' about 35 years ago. They made the distinction between 'individual' and 'institutional' racism – the latter being more covert and associated with respectable societal institutions. Both stressed the historical nature of its origins and the way it was reproduced by *interconnected* relationships across all of society's institutions. They used the concept as a way of understanding the *consequences* of institutional racism rather than to analyse its operation. The term did not denote an ideology,

... rather ... a range of other processes. These include
decisions and policies which had been designed to
subordinate/control blacks; active and pervasive anti black
attitudes and attitudes which are said to *result* in racial
inequalities. (Troyna and Williams, 1986, p 50; emphasis
not in the original)

Institutional racism was often used interchangeably with racism, or
subsumed under it, giving it a breadth of meaning. In Britain, the
term was developed for application by Humphry and John (1971),
Dummett (1973), Allen (1973) and Fenton (1982) and used to suggest
strategies for black activists to overcome racial oppression.

But 'institutional racism' has now become a key rationale for
intervention by government (Macpherson, 1999). The term has been
adopted in policy formulation in different sectors or organisations.
There is, however, confusion and a lack of clarity about institutional
racism and it has been subject in its current usage to a number of
criticisms (Anthias, 1999; Solomos, 1999; Bourne, 2001). The definition
adopted by Macpherson above encompasses differing conceptions of
racism, but it does not cover all kinds of racisms. It incorporates the
ideas of racism based on colour; it also includes culture and ethnicity,
and takes account of racism being 'unwitting'. It includes ideas of
changing behaviour and attitudes. While it appears to be all-
encompassing, it *excludes* ideas of differing racisms based on gender,
class and nation (Mirza, 2003). Understanding racism with reference
to ideology, nation, identity construction, the role of whiteness and
the nature of ethnicity are essential to tackling racism (see Chapter
One).

The ways in which institutional racisms are interconnected has also
been ignored in interventions. The ways in which racism is embedded
in British society has not been confronted. Instead, organisations are
examined in isolation from each other and from societal norms, to
monitor procedures and processes, and specifically to monitor 'ethnicity'
to show evidence of either exclusion or discrimination.

The concept as used in organisational interventions has therefore
been interpreted in a rather narrow manner, disconnected from its
original use. One criticism that has emerged is that institutional racism
has become a way of examining bureaucratic procedures and
recruitment of ethnic minorities (Bhavnani, 2001; Cashmore, 2002).
The term, as defined by Macpherson, suggests that 'unwitting' processes,
attitudes and behaviours underpin discrimination and prejudice within

an organisation. But if there is a concentration on organisational procedures only, this can end up ignoring the ways racism is expressed.

Perhaps we ought to accept that the use of institutional racism to tackle all kinds of racisms may be limited. Furthermore, although the definition includes stereotyping, prejudice and ignorance, these are not used as vehicles to challenge racism in organisations. Institutional racism, as currently used, has been utilised more in order to re-examine policies, procedures and empirical data, for example, monitoring information. By emphasising organisational processes (that is, the 'how'), the 'why' can be ignored. Recruitment procedures may be re-examined to eliminate 'unnecessary criteria' for a particular job, for example, but black people may still not be recruited into the organisation. And if they are recruited, they may not experience equal treatment. The focus on numbers and examining bureaucratic procedures (much removed from the initial conception of institutional racism), and gathering data on who are 'excluded' for jobs or services, is taken as evidence of 'race' inequality. Tackling these procedures, then, it is assumed will also tackle the *causes* of racism.

Confusion in understanding institutional racism adds to our problems. For example, what does the term 'institutional racism' mean in relation to an everyday experience of being abused in the street, or by neighbours? Is it only way national policy can challenge racism? Do people have to wait for institutional racism to be tackled by organisations, in which case everyday racism will just disappear? Is the law, the media, politics and the political system in Britain institutionally racist?

This lack of clarity in unravelling racism, in all its facets, is closely connected to a lack of a clear definition of 'success' in relation to an intervention. What does 'successful' mean when you are tackling a problem which has not only been around for several hundred years, but keeps changing form and appears in different ways, in different societies, including being reproduced at all levels of society?

But the problem may not only be about the understanding of racism and the ways it is reproduced. Success is also hard to measure when effectiveness of interventions is not addressed. Unspoken assumptions are made, for example, because we do not question the ways in which action through legislation or Codes of Practice is encouraged. We assume this action will automatically be effective in addressing the causes of racism. This lack of analysis results in initiatives rarely being fully evaluated in terms of the decline of racism; rather *assumptions* are made that racism has declined if, for example, more minority ethnic people have been recruited into the police.

Calculating numbers recruited into an organisation, therefore, can be highly misleading, since the experience of being inside the police continues to demonstrate an internal culture suffused with racism (Runnymede Trust, 2000; Cashmore, 2002; Panorama, 2003). Of course, this strategy of appointing police officers who are racialised may be part of a longer-term approach in changing racialised attitudes, but this is often not written into policies or what people are aiming for in the long term. The change in representation is seen as a way of tackling 'racism' when it may or may not be a small part of wider strategy to tackle underlying attitudes, behaviours and cultures.

Conclusion

- We have focused on professional national and local policy interventions introduced (ostensibly) to tackle racism. These professional interventions are not fixed interventions that are reproduced time and time again. They are subject to changes in prevailing ideologies, and national political objectives.
- These interventions are grouped into two broad categories: *equality* interventions and difference or *multicultural* interventions. In reviewing the data on these types of interventions we have incorporated ideas of 'success', particularly measuring success to tackle the causes of racism. This review of research has included not only how these concepts of equality and multiculturalism are defined, but also if action has been taken, what impacts if any it has had, and whether behaviour or attitudes have changed.
- We must continue to unravel racism in our current context. How are the roots of racism reproduced every day? And how far do different people at different levels of power influence the operation of, and the challenging of, everyday racism?

THREE

Everyday elite racisms

When we think about racism from the late 1990s to the present, what images do we conjure up? We may think about 'racial' genocide in Serbia or Rwanda or the aftermath of September 11th and the ensuing attacks on many innocent Muslims. We may remember 'The Secret Policeman', the Panorama programme (2003) about the racist remarks made openly by ordinary police officers. We will recall the racist murder of Stephen Lawrence. Anti-Semitic attacks on Jewish cemeteries by right-wing groups may flash through our minds. We may recall the shock and horror of the election of Le Pen's Party and the election of representatives from the British National Party (BNP) in some of our cities. Our daily newspapers may remind us of the many racist attacks against asylum seekers, young black men and women (*The Guardian*, www.guardian. co.uk/race).

Other commentators will point to the fact that these examples of racism, although extremely wide ranging, ignore other manifestations which are more covert. It is argued that the idea of 'race' has been used as a displacement activity about social problems and moral panics. For example, vitriolic 'racist' anger about refugees and asylum seekers from outside Europe, or more recently against Eastern Europeans, whipped up in local areas by the media, is but the outcome of deeper problems of our changing Western postcolonial wealthy societies (Spencer, 1994; Harding, 2001).

We might think of the 'race' riots in Oldham, Burnley and Bradford. These towns partly represent 'post-industrial' Britain, with decaying housing estates and the loss of stable jobs and identities. Racialised fights between Pakistani and white English working-class young men exacerbated by racist state policing, are the result of the tensions that urban decline produces between groups (Kalra, 2003).

Others will point to the increasing gap between the rich and the poor in Western countries and ask why the substantial proportions of poor people are those of colour and/or immigrants (Mason, 2003). They may point us to appreciating that certain minority groups according to ethnic origin, class, gender, age and disability continue to be excluded from full citizenship and employment because of the experience of both overt *and* covert racism, fuelled by social 'problems'.

In conjuring up this range of images, it becomes clear that many complex factors in these examples are at work in producing or even causing these everyday experiences of racism. These factors are both general and specific for certain groups. They include the ways in which ethnic conflicts might flare up as a result of media racism, the ways in which black and Asian origin young men are criminalised by the police, the displaced envy and resentment of white working-class young men and women towards these 'others' in their midsts. Government policies on immigration exacerbate racism, and certain people are excluded from their rights as citizens, through access to employment benefits and so on.

These causes of everyday racism range from what has been termed 'elite discourse on racism' (by the media and government), unexposed and rarely discussed, to ways in which professional and managerial groups exclude others (a kind of middle-class racism; see Mac an Ghaill, 1999), to working-class expressions of racism such as overt attacks by the young working class (primarily men) of all ethnic origins against each other (see Cohen, 1997). These fights and attacks are sometimes based on skin colour, but also on territory, difference and exclusion. These actions of racism are frequently about ensuring the maintenance of power and status, imagined or real. These images also need further unpacking, since contained within them are both the symptoms and the causes of racism, which are sometimes extremely difficult to separate.

This chapter is therefore concerned with unpacking the contexts of everyday racism and their specificities. We are concerned with examining the everyday social practices which perpetuate racism. In order to do this we will focus on the *ideologies* as well as the *structures* of racism, the ways racism is expressed and acted on and the relationship of this expression to concrete acts. People from all walks of life incorporate these ideologies into everyday contact. They are reproduced on a regular basis and it helps us to see that a more successful intervention will result from one that targets the place of power where racism is reproduced. We thus focus our discussion on how everyday racism is reproduced by elites, via the media and government. These are critical but often overlooked *causes* of racism in our current world. We turn first to conceptualising 'everyday racism'.

Understanding everyday racism

Essed (1991) suggests that racism is created and recreated through routine practices by 'agents', that is, by human beings. For Essed, racism is an ideology, a structure and also a process, because "structures and ideologies do not exist outside the everyday practices through which they are created and confirmed" (Essed, 1991, p 44).

Routine and repetitive practices help to maintain existing social structures and relations. These social practices and ideas are incorporated into the way people live their everyday lives. They are reflective of and re-constitute the deeper roots, or causes of, racism. Essed locates the processes of everyday racism as the integration of racism into everyday practices. These practices activate underlying power relations, and these processes come to be seen as a continuum through which the integration of racism into everyday practices becomes part of the expected and the unquestionable. It becomes 'normal' to the dominant group to see 'others' as different and inferior, particularly in relation to the colour of their skin. These prejudices are frequently hidden and are not something *added* on to people's thinking and behaviour, but remain embedded in how we see the world (Williams, 1997). These racialised social practices visibly appear and disappear, according to specific triggers, either when impending change is being anticipated which requires individuals and groups to change, or when there are already changes in wider social relations.

In other words, racialisation and ideas of 'race' are embedded in our consciousness and are dynamically constituted in the ways in which people understand change. Actions of overt or covert racist behaviour are not based solely on ignorance, but are reflective of the interaction with the deeper roots of racism and the ways in which change is understood, or even promulgated. These social practices are rarely addressed in professional interventions, and rarely researched (Bhavnani, 2001). When these actions and behaviours are repeated, they become part of the perpetuation of racism. They become our everyday experience. As such, it becomes increasingly difficult to even *see* that these attitudes and behaviour are present, unless of course they are overt, such as the practices of the BNP. More importantly they remain unanalysed within their social and local context.

In order for causes of racism to be addressed, there is a need to expose the operation of the ways in which macro racism within wider societal structures interacts with everyday racism. More importantly there is a need to document the different everyday racisms, particularly ones which are perpetuated by those who have more power in our society.

How are these everyday racisms expressed? Who is responsible for expressing them most powerfully? We begin by examining elite racism and then go on in Chapter Four to discuss the expression of racisms by ordinary people, who have less power.

Everyday elite racism

How is racism legitimately perpetuated or reproduced? How do members of the public come to view racism as 'commonsensical' despite living in a society underpinned by values of liberal democracy and humanitarianism (Malik, 1996)? This chapter examines the concept of elite racism in order to better understand local situated racism as expressed by ordinary members of the public (Chapter Four). However, *both* these types of everyday racism are important to tackle in successful interventions.

It is generally agreed that people are differently involved in the reproduction of racism according to their gender, class and status. The more access to power human agents have, the greater the consequences for racist practices. Racisms expressed by the powerful players in our society will have a major influence on shaping the public discourse. Their views are widely disseminated and reported as if 'true' or authoritative. Those who have more power, such as politicians, senior executives and those in the media, are more accountable, since the powers of their actions have more widespread effects than those made by one neighbour to another. These social practices, named 'elite discourse' (see van Dijk, 1993a, 1993b, 1999), we have termed here *elite racism*.

Who are the 'elite'?

The composition of the 'elite' has changed remarkably in the last 20 years (Sampson, 2004). The influence of hereditary peers, trades unions leaders, diplomats and academics, together with many elected politicians, has receded. On the other hand, the power of corporation heads, treasury personnel, accountants who become chief executives, nominated peers, the Prime Minister, public relations experts, lawyers and media professionals has increased. In the process these 'newer' members of the elite have become less accountable and more secretive (Sampson, 2004). In other words while there has been a reduction in power for some members of the elite, newer members from a range of fields have become more powerful. Sampson (2004) argues that the elite have not become more democratic, but in fact *less* so.

On the other hand, 'race' equality and human rights legislation have now become acceptable as necessary in the world (Klug, 2000). These attitudes and behaviours by powerful people can, therefore, be challenged and limited by the actions of the public. Not all members of the public mimic the ways in which the elite expresses racist or antiracist attitudes and behaviours. The norms and values of human rights as well as antidiscrimination legislation have changed public sensitivities in societies which no longer tolerate the overt expression of racist attitudes and expressions (van Dijk, 1993a; Fredman, 2001).

The social context of racism needs to be established. Some of these 'racist' expressions need to be unravelled, since they are not immediately obvious. They can all too easily become *invisible*. This invisibility can be interpreted as 'normative'. It is assumed that asylum seekers 'do not want to work', as reported in the media, or that black young men are 'often involved in crime'. If these causes of the reproduction of racism are ignored, pre-existing attitudes to 'race' and racism can be strengthened.

The media and the reproduction of everyday racism

The media occupy a key site and perform a key role in public representation of racialised inequalities and the reproduction of 'race hate' (Law, 2002). Sampson (2004) has recently argued that no sector has increased its power more than the media in the last few decades, and are acting as the "new aristocracy" (2004, p 223). It is true to say that no elite, in particular the political elite and their discourses, could be as powerful as they are without the mediating and sometimes powerful reinforcement of the press, radio and television (van Dijk, 1993a). In this age of sophisticated technology and mass communication, the media play a powerful influence in not only reflecting social cognition, but also *informing* other elites, within and across borders and nation states.

Through various representations the media can construct notions of who 'we' are, who 'they' are (insiders and outsiders), and whether 'they' are associated not just with the label 'foreigner', but also 'criminal', 'deviant', 'illegal' and so on. For example, a major study in the 1970s showed how black youth had become criminalised in the media in the moral panic about 'mugging' (Hall et al, 1978). This moral panic paved the way for a new state authoritarianism which had popular appeal in a time of economic decline and political disagreements.

At the same time, since the media *bridges* cultural changes in society, the media can also affirm antiracism, and cultural diversity (Cottle, 2000). The media is influential in informing the public about ethnicity and 'race', since large sections of the white public have little or no alternative sources of information on these issues. As a recent Commission for Racial Equality (CRE) study on interracial friendships shows, many white people have little or highly superficial everyday contact with 'ethnic' minorities (van Dijk, 1993a; CRE, 2004a). Similarly, a Danish study showed that given that 85% of Danes have no contact with minorities, 83% of Danes confessed to having low to high racist attitudes (Hussain, 2000). Hussain argues that the media in Denmark exert a very important influence on the negative portrayal of minorities, particularly Muslims. Although popular attitudes were not reproduced exactly, the themes were extracted from news discourses, which people used to build their own attitudes. These discourses emanated from politicians, the police, cultural elites and academia. They also provided gate-keeping as to what was selected as news. The media hardly ever reported political and social activities designed to oppose racism and xenophobia.

In both the US and Britain, research shows gross underrepresentation and stereotypical characterisation in entertainment genres, negative and problem-oriented portrayal within factual and news forms, and a tendency to ignore structural inequalities and lived racism experienced by ethnic minorities in both (Cottle, 2000). A CRE study on stereotyping in the media (1998) found that white participants perceived that black and Asian communities were using up resources, housing, education, healthcare, which 'rightly' belonged to white people. Racialised groups felt that the media presented them in limited ways, as one-dimensional characters or as problems, being portrayed as criminals, drug pushers and so on. A survey of the top 10 programmes from each of the five main channels examined portrayal of ethnic minorities and concluded that there was an absence of ethnic minorities from TV drama serials and general leisure programmes, such as gardening, cookery and other lifestyle interests (Cumberbatch et al, 2001). Audiences from ethnic minority groups complained about tokenism, stereotyping and simplistic portrayal of their communities (Hargraves, 2002).

The ways in which Muslims are portrayed in the media have also been subject to some analysis by Poole (2000). Poole found that over a three-year period from 1993-96 (before 9/11), Muslims were identified as a threat to security due to their alleged involvement in 'deviant' activities. Muslims were also presented as a threat to British mainstream values, provoking concerns that *they* found it hard to integrate. There were also more divisive representations of inherent cultural differences between Muslims and non-Muslims in Britain which then resulted in problems in interpersonal relations.

Of course these views are not homogeneously expressed. For example, young white people felt it was divisive to have separate television programmes on different ethnicities, whereas some members of ethnicised groups said that they wanted to be more differentiated regarding their ethnicity.

The press and coverage of asylum seekers

We are now familiar with the kinds of language used particularly by the tabloid press about asylum seekers:

> Foreigners do not arrive by plane or train; they 'invade',
> 'swamp', 'flood', 'pour in' or 'take over' – they are soldiers
> of an enemy onslaught. (Harris, 2000)

The use of negative language and misinformation is very common in the pages of tabloid newspapers. "Bogus", "illegal asylum seeker", "a tide of humanity that sees Britain as a land of milk and honey", "conmen", "asylum crime", "bogus asylum seekers are draining millions from the NHS", "Britain the No 1 refugee magnet" are all expressions that have appeared in *The Star*, *The Sun*, *Daily Mail*, *Evening Standard* and *Daily Express* (Refugee Council, 2002).

The media's whipping up of panic about asylum seekers has fuelled commonsense racism. Academics at the Cardiff School of Journalism spent two years monitoring asylum coverage in newspapers and on television. They found that British media coverage of asylum seekers was overwhelmingly characterised by stereotyping, exaggeration and inaccurate language (Kundnani, 2003). The number of asylum seekers was distorted, imagery was used of the 'threatening young male' and a variety of stereotypical made up labels, such as asylum 'cheat' and 'bogus', were often used.

Such racialised reporting has gone hand in glove with increased attacks on asylum seekers and refugees. A government study which monitors social attitudes in Britain claimed that a marked increase in overt racism in Britain had been due to the negative media coverage of asylum seekers and immigration (Rothon and Heath, 2003). Similarly it has been reported there has been an increase of 75% in racist attacks on refugees as well as other minority ethnic groups in Scotland (*The Scotsman*, 9 March 2004). The British Social Attitudes Survey found that there was a high correlation between those holding racist attitudes and those who were hostile to immigration (Denney and Elliot, 2004).

A report by Liberty claimed that politicians and the media were to share responsibility for public hostility towards asylum seekers and that negative representation had led to direct attacks on them (www.liberty-human-rights.org.uk). Furthermore, the report, which was also supported by Amnesty International, the Bar Human Rights Committee and the Law Society as well as others, argued that the media and politicians' discourses led to a greater hostility towards all those from minority ethnic communities and heightened racial tensions (RAM, 2001).

The racist language used in the press against asylum seekers was explicitly exposed by a complaint by Simon Hughes MP to the CRE. The issue was debated in the press and media. Journalists and trade unionists such as Bill Morris accused the government and political parties of fuelling racism. The debate centred on newcomers' dependence on British people's money and jobs, and the issue of begging (Bhavnani, 2001). New regulations from the 1999 Asylum Act placed asylum seekers in a trap. They were told not to seek work *and* not to be dependent on the state. These debates became an important topic for populist party political point scoring in the 2005 General Election.

The Press Complaints Commission, who had received a number of complaints about the coverage associated with asylum seekers and refugees, was forced into publishing guidance on reporting in this area (www.pcc.org.uk/reports). The press, however, dragged its heels in apologising and in publishing counter-stereotyping stories.

Interventions such as the Refugees, Asylum seekers and the Media Project (PressWise Trust) provide a good example of the way in which interventions in exposing these discourses and their effects have taken place and created conflicts in the reports by journalists (see Appendix A (16) 'PressWise Trust').

Overt public racism: is it just a joke?

On the other hand, overt racist jokes and throwaway comments have also been condemned by the media. The broadsheet press can legitimate racism, but they also play a role in condemning overt racism, particularly when they can expose those in the public eye. Comedians have been condemned for their racist jokes, and overt racism spoken by senior politicians, public commentators, and the royalty has been similarly exposed. This condemnation is unsurprising given the analysis in Chapter One on the changing nature of the acceptability of societal racism from a more overt to a more covert kind.

The examples of overt remarks and jokes given below are not so much illustrative of what 'some people' say, but the ways in which some powerful people feel they can legitimately defend their remarks. They are also illustrative of how these remarks might be part of their 'everyday' thoughts and conversations. The remarks themselves are reproduced here, since they perpetuate notions of inferiority of black and other 'ethnicised' minorities compared to the comparative superiority of white British and Europeans. Unfortunately they reproduce everyday racism, and because the remarks are contested by powerful people who have made them, there is a danger that they may legitimate the expressions of such racism by others.

Examples of overt racism

Recent remarks allegedly made by the royalty were widely reported. One particular member of the royalty told a group of African American diners in an exclusive restaurant in New York "to go back to the colonies". She tried to redeem herself in a television interview by saying that she was not a racist. She explained that Africans were "adorable" and that she herself had pretended to be "half caste" to ease her travel in Africa (Branigan, 2004). Many people would feel that these comments were patronising.

The Conservative MP who told racist jokes about "Pakis being ten-a-penny", and the drowning of the cockle pickers as being linked to "Chinese take aways" was also exposed in the press. The MP herself did not see why she should apologise, arguing that she was the "victim of political correctness" (www.Manchesteronline. co.uk/news/s/82/ 82615). A member of her family condemned her sacking by the Conservative Party, claiming that the Leader was suppressing "free speech" and argued that our society "was now living with George Orwell's thought police" (www.Manchester online.co.uk/news/s/82/ 82615, p 1). The same member of her family also pointed out that telling jokes was an everyday "storytelling thing". He explained in a subsequent newspaper interview that the MP was not making a formal dinner speech, but speaking at a private dinner party relating the sorts of stories that "were doing the rounds" (www.Manchesteronline.co.uk/ news/s/82/82615). Here the 'joke' uses the term 'Paki' (recognised as a term of racist abuse), perpetuates the idea that one human life is less valued than another, and implies that there is a continuing "threat of *numbers* of Pakistanis, probably 'all alike'". Once more, while these remarks were condemned, they can also act as fuel for those who would willingly espouse everyday overt racism.

The football commentator (www.Manchesteronline.co.uk/news/ s/82/82615) who made off-the-cuff remarks about a black footballer as "an ugly lazy nigger" was similarly condemned. However, the comments were only exposed because a TV station unknowingly picked up the remarks on a microphone. The context of the remarks is important. They were made in everyday conversation to his co-commentator, when he presumed he was off air. Because they were picked up by a microphone in the Middle East that had not been turned off, they were reproduced in several media and he was forced to resign. It is unclear whether the remarks would have been exposed publicly by his co-commentator.

This commentator, unlike the MP cited above, did apologise. But his denial expressed bewilderment at not understanding what racism was, as his comments reveal: "Look all I can say is sorry. I genuinely did not mean to offend anybody. What else can I say? I am an idiot, but I am not a racist. A racist is someone who won't give a black man a chance. My actions over the years prove I have no problem with that" (*The Observer*, 25 April 2004). The connotations of stereotypical traits associated with certain black people together with the use of 'nigger' (once more a term of racist abuse, and widely reported in the comments made by Stephen Lawrence's alleged murderers), reproduces racism and its associated relations of domination and subordination.

A recent media presenter made comments about Arabs and the fact of their "not having contributed anything to civilisation":

> They are trying to terrorise us, disrupt our lives. Then they expect us to be careful of their sensibilities? We have thousands of asylum seekers from Iran, Iraq, Algeria, Egypt, Libya, Yemen, Saudi Arabia, and other Arab countries living happily in this country on social security.
> We are told by some of the more hysterical critics of the war on terror that it 'is destroying the Arab world'. So? Should we be worried about that? Shouldn't the destruction of the despotic barbarous and corrupt Arab states and their replacement by democratic governments be a war aim? After all the Arab countries are not exactly shining examples of civilisation are they? (*Express on Sunday*, 4 January 2004)

This text evokes a 'colonial' discourse about the 'uncivilised Arabs' and their terrorising ways. A proposed case against the presenter on inciting racial hatred was dropped in July 2004, and he has now accused the BBC of political correctness "gone mad" (Barber, 2004).

These examples illustrate how even overt racism by influential people exposed in the media and liberally condemned is justified and defended by influential people. This is a common tactic used by deniers of racism and has been called 'condemning the critic', which includes the tactics of "they have exaggerated what I said", "I have plenty of support" or "they are motivated by ..." or that "you are being politically correct" (International Council on Human Rights Policy, 2000). This kind of denial that you have done nothing serious or that you resort to blaming someone else to defend yourself can entrench racism.

'Inclusive Britishness?': 'elite discourse' and multiculturalism

Rhetoric on multiculturalism

There has been a long history of political discontent with 'Britishness' and a 'multicultural' society. (For further analysis of the policy context of multiculturalism see Chapter Eight.) In fact, the nationalist project in Britain in the late 1970s, 1980s and early 1990s was to redefine and contest 'Britishness' (Runnymede Trust, 2000).

In many public statements on Britishness (some refer to "Englishness" since devolution) black and 'minority ethnic' people have been seen as a problem in the past. For example, Margaret Thatcher, former Prime Minister, talked about the 'swamping' of Britain by 'different' cultures. Norman Tebbitt asked South Asian and Caribbean origin people to seriously consider who they supported in national cricket teams. He argued that the 'cricket test' could be applied to determine allegiance to England. By this he meant that you could not support both England *and* the West Indies – to be truly English you had to support England (Brah, 1992).

Contesting 'Britishness' has been more visible in response to social and global change, and these long-term changes have included the loss of the Empire and a challenge to ideas of what is considered the 'East' and the 'West'. More recently, growing integration with Europe and devolution, together with negative media coverage of refugees and asylum seekers, has brought forth a series of statements about our 'multi-cultural' society, and the meaning of 'Englishness' as well as 'Britishness'.

Large numbers of migrants many of whom are fleeing economic destitution and political repression have had an enormous impact on notions of nation and sovereignty. While devolution in the UK gave firmer identities to Scottish, Welsh and Irish people, 'Englishness' was left floating. The issue of purity, oneness, and an attempt to find a lost identity was echoed by John Major in his comments about 'villages with bicycles' and 'village greens' where cricket was played.

Current Britishness is steeped in a backward-looking, pathological nostalgia (Gilroy, 1999, 2004). Gilroy calls this a state of 'melancholia'. Britishness, he suggests, is in crisis and needs to unhook itself from its racist origins and embrace a sense of living together in a state of 'conviviality and multiculture' which diversity brings.

Contested, dismissed and inclusive?

More recently, however, debate about Britishness has intensified. There have been isolated attempts to include a positive idea of multiculturalism in some government speeches as well as those rejecting the notion of multiculturalism. Once again these arguments have to be disentangled. Some of the positive ideas about multiculturalism may not have evoked the benefits of pluralism and shared and diverse cultural values (Parekh, 2000; Runnymede Trust, 2000), but rather classless, timeless, intrinsic 'British' values, which have 'imagined' the nation of Britain. These values, honed in the days of the Empire, were about 'tolerance', 'fair play' and the 'love of the rule of law' (see Brown, 2004; and Gordon Brown and Mike O'Brien's speech reported in Alibhai Brown, 1999, pp 1-7). Robin Cook, on the other hand, has referred to 'chicken tikka masala' as a 'national dish', to attempt a more inclusive comment (Cook, 2001), presumably symbolic of a changing Britain.

Heated public debates have recently been played out in the press. These debates have concerned the importance of 'ending' multi-cultural policies (Goodheart, 2004) as well as celebrating them, by working towards plural societies based on a 'community of communities' (Runnymede Trust, 2000). The findings of the Commission on the Future of Multi Ethnic Britain (Runnymede Trust, 2000) were greeted with press hostility when they suggested that there was an historical and contemporary connection between racism and British identity (Runnymede Trust, 2000; McLaughlin and Neal, 2004).

In the light of harking back to the past, comments made by the Chair of CRE, Trevor Phillips, for the abandonment of multiculturalism, since it is said to suggest 'separateness' (*The Observer*, 4 April 2004), may appear understandable. Instead, Phillips argued the solution lay in reasserting an old-fashioned version of Britishness based on '"common values'.... The common currency of the English language, honouring the culture of these islands, like Shakespeare and Dickens" (*The Observer*, 4 April 2004).

But this vision of a past, with imagined common values, carries a weaker charge these days because these so-called 'common' values that Phillips refers to are intensely class-specific (Winder, 2004). What is more, modern Britain itself is full of variety:

> A cross section of Britain today would include the ticking of church clocks and the stack of shoes at the door of a mosque; the scarlet blaze of a letter box and the smell of corn grilling at the Notting Hill Carnival; the bleat of new born lambs and the rasp of muzak in shopping malls; sponge cakes in village halls and the flash of gold and turquoise in a passing sari; the fine mist of water sprinklers on suburban lawns and the blare of police sirens at night; the lilt of choirs heard across fields and the roar from the nearby dual carriageway. (Winder, 2004, p 462)

As Winder argues, people who construct thumbnail sketches of national identity, such as the one developed by Phillips, are usually lamenting the passing of their own youth, "the fraying of the iconography with which they grew up" (Winder, 2004, p 462).

Right-wing philosophers and commentators such as Roger Scruton and David Goodheart have also led the debate against multiculturalism (*The Observer*, 4 April 2004). Goodheart, editor of *Prospect Magazine*, argued that '"we prefer our own kind" and that diversity ('ethnic' difference?) made it difficult to adopt common values and to celebrate a common history. Those who were 'visibly different' were acting as a drain on the welfare state (Goodheart, 2004). Even though he admitted that 'welfare' was hardly redistributive, he argued that this *perception* was created and thus multicultural societies had to be questioned.

The tide has also turned legislatively against multiculturalism. In 2004 the Home Secretary responded to media cries of the 'swamping' of Britain with asylum seekers. He introduced nationality and immigration legislation and attempted to argue that new migrants have to conform to 'British' values. In response to the uprisings in the northern towns, the Home Secretary argued for the need for people to adapt to 'British' norms. This is an extract from the Home Secretary's speech, made after the 2001 urban disturbances:

> ... people should have the wherewithal such as the ability to speak English, to participate fully in society. This is not linguistic colonialism as my critics allege – it is about opportunity and exclusion. And just as we seek to defeat

racism, so we must protect the rights and duties of all citizens, and confront practices and beliefs that hold them back, particularly women. (Dodd, 2001)

The statement problematises racialised communities by pointing to social practices (such as forced marriages, or genital mutilation), which are already against the law, as pointed out by various commentators (Mirza, 2003). In fact, the most excluded 'ethnic' citizens are in fact second, third or even fourth generation settled communities who speak English very well. It may be true that some older members of minority groups have not learned to speak English fluently, but reasons for this range over a variety of factors. The statement implies that 'these' communities have not bothered to learn and integrate, and that the problem of not speaking English has been laid solely at their doorstep.

By speaking in these terms, David Blunkett, the then Home Secretary, implies that Britain is more 'progressive' and has not got social practices that hold women back, an idea that can easily be contested. Notions of superiority and inferiority are once again implied in this discourse on multiculturalism, suggesting a covert racism.

Analysing the rhetoric

These discourses on the 'multicultural' question (Hall, 2000) are important to examine since they contain within them ideas about 'race', racism and ethnicity and their links to 'nation'. There is an assumption that it is *ethnic* difference' which breaks up ideas of Britishness, rather than global change and mass migration. On arrival, new and established 'other' communities, are faced with growing privatisation and a decline of the welfare state in most advanced economies. Competition for scarce resources in the public sector is therefore stepped up. Tensions between poorer people can be exacerbated and become quickly racialised.

Strong arguments have already been made that Britain has always been multicultural (Gundara, 2001), and that 'immigrants' contribute more to the economy than they take out (Spencer, 1994; Harding, 2001), and that the common values of Shakespeare and Dickens evoke white middle-class men's 'cultures' rather than, for example, the antislavery movement, the influence of Salman Rushdie, Mary Seacole or Sylvia Pankhurst.

Discourses on multiculturalism are bound up with national identity. This is extremely complex. Interventions based on 'difference' are imbued with ideas of racialised groups as 'not belonging' to a place or country. Despite dominant discourse about tolerance and valuing 'other' cultures:

> The central issue facing central and local government is how to promote and reconcile ethnic diversity and simultaneously resurrect an older version of the British nation – which is seen as ethnically homogeneous, benign and tolerant. How in other words, to align the pursuit of (a narrowly conceived) multiculturalism with a recourse to tradition and an unchanged Britain. (Lewis, 2000, p 265)

National identity, which had come to stand for 'beyond ethnicity', has come to stand for the dominant majority, and all those defined as 'ethnic' come to stand for 'other' and 'minority' (Lewis, 2000). This construction of nation is important in understanding how racism is perpetuated. We need to return to our concept of ethnicity and insist on its use for *all* groups, not just those who have been racialised.

We also need to understand the ways in which all differences intersect with each other, such as class, gender, age and disability, rather than talk as if difference only means 'racialised difference'.

Multiculturalism: the more things change, the more they remain the same...

The London bombings by some British-born Muslim young men in July 2005 have ushered in a renewed contestation with multiculturalism. David Davis, Shadow Home Secretary, has argued that the cause has been our politically correct anti-racism which has resulted in, "allowing people of different cultures to settle without integrating [which] let the 'perverted values of suicide bombers' take root" (http://news.bbc.co.uk/1/hi/uk_politics/4740633.stm). Norman Tebbit of the Conservative party has also joined the debate by predicting an inevitable contest between competing cultures and the "impossibility" of multiculturalism. (http://news.bbc.co.uk/1/hi/uk_politics/4163484.stm). The backlash against multiculturalism has swept through the media with numerous articles and radio interviews aiming to understand this traumatic attack by highlighting 'Muslims' who have somehow 'failed to integrate'.

However, there are two reasons to question multiculturalism as the cause and explanation for the British terrorism. First, there is a need to continuously explore the changing nature of racism as it manifests itself in our British towns against the backdrop of an uncertain globalising world (see Chapter Two). The draw of fundamentalist religious ideology based on faith, truth and certainty coupled with sophisticated information exchange at a global level explain why some groups, such as these British-born young men, designated 'Muslim', find a sense of belonging within a wider community or 'umma'. Such a sense of purpose and belonging sits in stark contrast to the exclusion and racism experienced in the country in which they were born. Second, as Naomi Klein (2005) has argued the media has fuelled these young men's, "rage at perceived extreme racism that ... American and European lives are worth more than the lives of Arabs and Muslims, so much more that their deaths in Iraq are not even counted?".

But many of these questions and answers do not look for the complexity of causes. The media seek to polarise our understandings with the 'clashes of civilisations', the 'evil' Islamic fundamentalists, the West versus the rest, which place the two sides in opposition with each other, as if they are truly separate. In the wake of the London suicide bombing on 7 July 2005 there has been a massive increase in reported racist attacks. The Islamic Human Rights Commission received 320 complaints in one month and Scotland Yard reports hate crimes are up 600% over the last year (Klein, 2005). Whether these increases in attacks are connected to the terms of the debate or not, the idea of good versus bad (West versus Islam and immigration) has been reconstructed to make 'common sense' at a national level not without racist consequences.

The impact of 'elite' racism can emerge through the media via a drip-drip approach, and we must engage with the debate cautiously. Although the terms of the debate have already been determined by influential commentators, it is critical to question ideas about 'separate' cultures as if they did indeed exist (see Chapter Eight). The ways 'ethnic cultures' are defined and confined by politicians and media analysts into certain categories does not sit well with everyday life in Britain, where fusion and hybridity as well as differing foods and dress are plentiful, across and within all groups, black, white, women, men, old, young, working class, middles class and so on (see Chapters Three, Four and Eight). Everyday life indeed may be more complicated than our commentators suggest.

In fact, as Klein (2005) observes the real problem in our society is not too much multiculturalism, but too little. Multiculturalism as practised "in Britain (and France Germany and Canada) ... is a Faustian bargain, struck between vote-seeking politicians and self-appointed community leaders, one that keeps ethnic minorities tucked away in state-funded peripheral ghettos while the centres of public life remain largely unaffected by the seismic shifts in the national ethnic make up". She argues if a 'deep multiculturalism' was allowed to evolve and there was real equality of participation at the centre of power, we would have a more powerful humanism at the core of our government.

However, in our 'shallow multicultural' society, as we have it, religion has been used by the state to define people's identities, when religion may not be the most important identity for many people, whether Christian, Hindu, Sikh or Muslim, or even agnostic or humanist? Does the foregrounding of religion (that is, Muslims) as a 'separate' social policy category help to push the clock back on integration? The category 'Muslim' now appears as a 'norm' in the localised British context. Such a fixed and separate category did not exist in social policy previously, but has been created and legitimated by government policies with the willing compliance of so-called 'community leaders'. Perhaps we need to capture a different language and terminology to shake the foundations of the debates on multiculturalism. Some authors argue that the buzzword could be 'polycultural':

> Strictly speaking, multi- and poly- mean the same thing – many; the first is Latin, the second is Greek. But there is now a distinction: multicultural suggests an array of discrete cultures; polycultural suggests a mixture of ingredients too closely entwined to be distinct, a whole greater than the sum of the parts. In emphasising the connections rather than the barriers between 'cultures', it is plainly the more cohesive and optimistic ... term. (Winder, 2004, p 467)

Unless the terms of the debate are transformed, ideas about racialised 'Muslims' responsible for 'not integrating' remain on our radar. We need to keep a watchful eye on the ways in which debates led by politicians and the media quickly become the norm and end up fuelling racism, despite protests by these same commentators that they are not really attacking a 'racialised other'.

Normative 'whiteness': invisible elites?

While there has been much emphasis in the literature on postcolonial and 'black' identity (Owusu, 2000), studies looking at white identity are a relatively new development. Writing on the need to focus on whiteness has emerged from the US (for example, see hooks, 1989; Delgado and Stefancic, 1997; Fine et al, 1997; Frankenberg, 1997; Hill, 1997; Lipsitz, 1998). There have also been some studies in Britain

(Hewitt, 1986; Back, 1996; Cohen, 1997; Phoenix, 1997; Bonnett, 2000b; Puwar, 2000).

Most argue that whiteness as a category has to be distinguished from the term 'white' used in relation to white supremacy and right-wing political movements. This distinction allows people to understand how whiteness functions without having to label anyone a racist (Wander et al, 1999). Key points emerging from the unpacking of whiteness include:

- white is seen as the majority, and the norm, giving the concept status, which implies that it is tied to power;
- whiteness lacks racial/ethnic features, thus making it invisible;
- whiteness becomes naturalised so that it means nothing except a category which excludes any cultural traits. Such traits are applied only to minority groups;
- whiteness is confused with nationality, which is an expression of power in that it relegates members of black ethnic groups to a marginal role in national life;
- those who refuse to label themselves as white are expressing the fact that ethnicity can only be applied to non-whites. Thus white does not seem like a label (Nakayama and Krizek, 1999).

It has been argued that there is a pressing need to deconstruct whiteness in relation not just to racialisation but also to elite identity formation (Brah, 1992).

Solomos (1999) has written of our poor understanding of institutional racism and the paucity of work which shows how minorities experience their treatment in institutional settings. The focus on *whiteness* among elites at the top of the Civil Service also reveals a more covert racism, not amenable to be recorded as racial incidents. Puwar's study of the civil service (Puwar, 2000) questions the ways in which senior civil servants are represented as the pinnacle of rationalism and impartiality (the universal individual). In interviews with black civil servants, she argues that 'black bodies' are out of place in this environment and the (white) norm imagines leadership as based on whiteness connected with leadership qualities. People are shocked to find black people in these positions; they are assumed to be junior (infantilised) and constructed as being incompetent.

The importance of 'race', she argues, is dismissed in liberal discourse because it insists on the *sameness* of humanity. The abstract civil servant represents a thinking *mind*, universal, impartial, objective. This is because whiteness is not seen as racialised – it is defined as the norm. This *disavowal* (see the discussion of denial of racism below) is seen to be a key feature of how racism lives on in institutions.

Denial

In terms of establishing successful interventions to combat everyday racism there first needs to be a recognition that there is a problem. A recent global study on racism concluded that denial of racism is almost as ubiquitous as prejudice itself (International Council on Human Rights Policy, 2000). This denial itself represents a prime obstacle to progress, and can be more appropriately a *cause* of racism in our current context. Denial consists of denying the facts, as well as their interpretation. Policies or discourses that have had discriminatory effects are presented as if they are *justified* by existing conditions of economic and social inequality, and not ones about human rights. A social consensus develops which prevents acknowledgement of racism and euphemisms are used instead. For example, an emphasis on 'illegal' immigrants confirms a notion that immigrants are crime-prone. The 'drain on welfare' implies that immigrants are taking benefits, when this is not the case.

In some countries, such as the Netherlands, the term 'racism' is only applied to the expressions of right-wing extremists. As long as other manifestations of racism are denied, there is no need for official measures to combat them. There is no need, for example, to review regulations and processes and there is no need for moral campaigns to change the biased attitudes of white people. Racism is now rarely a self-description; it is mostly a label applied to groups or individuals by others. Petrova explains why,

> In western democratic societies most people who share racist opinions and act accordingly would deny that they are racists because racism is officially and culturally condemned while tolerance and racial equality and human rights are dominant ideological values. (Petrova, 2001, p 49)

Racism in the Metropolitan Police illustrates the operation of denial (Bhavnani, 2001). During the Stephen Lawrence Inquiry into the police handling of the racist murder of a young black man, denial was expressed in different ways. For some officers (across the hierarchy) there was an absence of any talk about 'race'. Senior officers' denials of racism resorted to positive self-presentation; a cry about sincerity; or a notion that racism existed in the inner cities, or among 'disadvantaged' black communities. As van Dijk suggests "white speakers engage in strategies of positive self-presentation in order to be able credibly to present the 'others' in a negative light" (1993b, p 193). The minority of police who did accept the existence of racism argued that it lay with a small number of bad individuals (the 'one bad apple' syndrome), or that it was about a misunderstanding of cultural differences. For those who discussed racism openly, denial consisted of a meritocratic, colour-blind approach which said that everyone was treated the same.

Conclusion

- Racist discourse is reproduced at the everyday level through multiple acts of exclusion and marginalisation (van Dijk, 1993b). Ideology and sets of attitudes that legitimate difference and dominance sustain these acts. While overt expressions of racism are inconsistent with norms of equality and the democratic humanitarianism of present-day society, we find the new power elites reproduce and legitimate covert everyday commonsense ideas of racism.
- However, the label 'racism' refuses to stick to the everyday manifestations of racist discourse. Thus the vitriolic media discourse on asylum seekers, multiculturalism and Britishness, or the reporting of localised working-class discontent, all of which are deeply imbued with racialised meaning, appear 'unraced', neutral, and unattached to their source of origin – that is, the politically powerful and influential. They are therefore 'legitimately' denied.
- These examples of illuminating whiteness and elite racism suggest an altogether different kind of intervention from monitoring ethnicity, changing recruitment procedures or appointing 'race' relations officers. The hidden nature of this racism requires constant and continuous *vigilance* and exposure, particularly since it is so powerful, as well as coded. We need more research and projects on whiteness, what is considered to be the norm, and elite racism. At the same time, we also need to be aware that overt everyday racism as expressed by elites has not completely vanished.

FOUR

Everyday situated racisms

The examples of media and elite discourse on racism, often based on denial, can affect the ways in which attitudes are expressed on an everyday basis by the public. Chapter Two explored the roots of the ideologies of colonialism, slavery and national identity. But the realm of social psychology and new anthropology may be equally valid in understanding how *everyday* racism is reproduced and maintained and reproduced as 'commonsense racism', expressed by ordinary members of the public.

We turn first to social psychology and theories of stereotyping. We then consider social anthropological work, particularly with white and black working-class men and women. These studies explain how attitudes and behaviours are reproduced on an everyday basis in locally situated contexts.

Learning to discriminate: stereotyping the 'other'

Explanations for the maintenance of racism through stereotypes are important for understanding the reproduction of everyday racism. *Stereotyping* refers to cognitive aspects of the reproduction of racism, while *prejudice* refers to affective manifestations. *Discrimination* refers to behavioural outcomes (Fiske, 1998). Understanding the process of stereotyping has implications for how to learn or unlearn racism.

The development of the 'authoritarian personality' dominated early thinking about prejudicial beliefs originating in childhood (Adorno et al, 1950). The idea of a 'fixed' personality has now given way to more subtle notions of covert and ambivalent expressions about the 'other'. It is argued that stereotypes emerge from what social psychologists call in-group/out-group dynamics. People like to feel they are part of a group. As villages, clans and other traditional groupings have become broken down, our identities have attached themselves to more ambiguous groupings, such as 'race' and class. We want to feel good about the way we are, so we denigrate those outside. Although we are differentiated, those outside are viewed as an undifferentiated mass (Paul, 1998).

Stereotyping as habituated responses

Recent social psychology discusses the almost 'automatic' way in which stereotyping takes place, because of the 'default' explanation (Fiske, 1998). People are so used to knowing and experiencing white men in key positions that those who have been racialised, as well as non-racialised women or disabled people, are all seen as the 'other'. They become stereotyped as such because they are 'marked'.

Experiments found that people made *immediate*, almost reflexive, associations with social groupings. They associated black and white people with different social traits at a subliminal level. Since these connections are made often enough, they become part of the unconscious. Our culture is suffused with these images. We are surrounded by notions of equality and tolerance, but the reality of these concepts is lacking in our society. Thus our conscious minds check or limit our responses. But sometimes our non-verbal behaviour gives us away through eye contact, hand gestures, how far away we stand and so on (Fiske, 1998).

It is argued that stereotypes are activated as the 'other' in our minds because this activation is efficient for cognitive processing. A greater amount of effort is needed to cognitively *counter* the automatic stereotype these activations require (Fiske, 1998).

On the other hand, all these theories locate prejudice and racism in individuated processes rather than societal structures and institutions (Leach, 2002). Furthermore, by suggesting that categorisation and stereotyping are almost natural, prejudice itself becomes almost 'natural' and inevitable. This limits notions of subjectivity and intentionality, and thus limits social responsibility.

These social cognitive theories on stereotyping have been contested by discursive theories. Rather than measuring prejudice on various scales and instruments, the discursive approach looks at everyday encounters and conversation on racism to understand how and where it emerges in particular contexts and institutional structures. This approach to discourses has found that the language of contemporary racism is ambivalent, flexible and contradictory. It brings us back to understanding the concept of everyday racism. We explore this situated context below. But first, the puzzling nature of the ambivalent expressions of racism might be better understood by turning to psychoanalysis and the role of the unconscious.

The influence of psychoanalysis

Cognitive associations in stereotyping may also be linked to subliminal associations, a concept derived from psychoanalysis. In psychoanalysis, unconscious unmet desires are powerful. These desires produce ambivalence about white, black or other identities.

In his seminal book *Black skins, white masks*, Franz Fanon (1986), a black political activist and doctor of psychiatry wrote in the 1950s that the black man experienced himself 'through not being white'. In a state of mind he calls 'negritude' (a negative but powerful combination of the psyche and the social), the 'black man' desires to be that which he is not. He is not seen as a man by others, but as a 'black man'. The colonial subjugation is assumed to be complete, when the 'black man' submits to unconscious self-hate. He is characterised as sexual, emotional and primitive. On the other hand, the white man is constructed as a rational, thinking human being. But each 'side' may desire the other's characteristics.

The unconscious follows its own system of thought and is structured like a language. The ambivalence in identity formation is based on splitting different parts of ourselves into masculine, feminine, good or bad (Rattansi, 1994). We can only form our identities through representations of those who may be like ourselves, via language, images, film and art. These identities position us as to who we are, but this *who we are* is always looking for the 'ideal', the perfect fit (Hall, 1997). It is never final, never complete.

Role of the unconscious in racist discourse

Rational arguments therefore may be too simple a way of challenging racism, since these opinions and views are part of the unconscious, and if they have not been expressed, are not amenable to rational discourse. The role of the unconscious in racist discourse is powerful. Cohen (1997b) has argued that it is an important tool to use in education. He considers the racism of white working-class young men to be intrinsically tied up with identity and their body image. New identities have to be constructed with them as partners and learners by educators, so that contradictions around racism can be resolved. He argues that censoring racism as the only or key strategy will bring forth resistance, particularly in the context of school disciplinary cultures.

Understanding and challenging racism through the unconscious requires a longer-term educational approach. Attitudinal change becomes a complex issue not amenable to the giving of facts and persuasion by statistics. This complexity also suggests that short-term training courses based on a rational approach will be limited, or at worse, merely repress racism.

Situating local racisms

Ethnographic work has helped focus on the 'why' and 'how' racism is reproduced in particular local contexts, taking to a deeper level our understanding of stereotyping and discrimination. Clearly, any attempt at educating about racism, without first addressing wider issues of identity and belonging in neighbourhoods, is not relevant as a strategy for tackling racism. Amin (2002) suggests that broad frameworks and national interventions, as well as understanding the conditions of protest and rebellion, are important interventions in tackling racism. However, he argues that we can only intervene successfully in racism if we understand the everyday enactment which centrally confirms identity and attitude formation. This means taking into account both ideas of stereotyping and prejudice, as well as the local context in which these attitudes and behaviours are expressed.

Class

The complexity of everyday life with regard to white and black (male) 'youth' ethnicities is evidenced in work by a variety of authors (Alexander, 1996; Back and Nayak, 1999; Alibhai Brown, 2000). Local contexts of social mobility, gangs, exclusions from schools, name calling, friendship loyalties, strong black street cultures and territorialism, as well as poverty, all influence the experience of popular racism, which varies across local contexts. These have to be understood so that the most appropriate interventions can take place.

Hollands (1990) examines the types of racism adopted by white working-class groups in urban institutionalised sites. He suggests a typology of different racisms across and *within* class, gender and age. He uses three class codes adopted from Cohen's work on antiracist youth work in schools (1986). In examining different forms of white racism expressed among young trainees, he suggests that there is firstly the 'aristocratic breeding code' where black and white are believed to be each 'bred' into particular codes and differ physically, emotionally and intellectually. Secondly there is the 'bourgeois/democratic scientific code'. This supplements the breeding code with a biologically based justification centring on sexuality and the body. Finally there is the 'working-class code', emphasising the inheritance of labour power and skills and control over private and public territory (Hollands, 1990; Mac an Ghaill, 1999).

Research shows that working-class white racism is not homogenous (Cohen, 1997a) and that it varies in strength according to place and time as well as in relation to gender and age. Cohen's research showed that there were differences in attitudes towards racism among the young white men on a Youth Training Scheme. Those on schemes with better job prospects and with fewer young black trainees were more likely to have a laissez-faire attitude to 'race' than other young men on the scheme because their relative privilege had been maintained. When these privileges were challenged there were cries that this was 'unfair' and that there was a need to resort to 'appropriate' rules of behaviour. Where the prospects were less good for trainees, 'race' was a highly charged issue and white trainees resented being on schemes dominated by black young people. In their eyes, this confirmed that such schemes were rubbish. Such racisms may also be contradictory. The same young white people might support the racist immigration policies of the National Front, but may also take an active part in concerts on Rocking Against Racism.

Back (2001), for example, has noted the strong 'shared' masculinised culture of white and Asian origin young men after the disturbances in the northern towns: "common aggressiveness, common gang codes and a similar body language" (Amin, 2002, p 6). Not all aspects of the conflict are seen to be about 'ethnic difference', "while others were about the common frustrations of youth alienation, unpromising socio-economic prospects for all, and masculine demonstrations of turf and territory" (Amin, 2002, p 8).

Hewitt's study of young people in a predominantly white part of Greenwich explores the 'routes of racism' (1996). He shows that young men and women do not straightforwardly accept and take on the non-racist or racist language or views of their parents. For young men, in particular, their peer group is far more influential. It is through young male peer groups acting together that an individual may take the route from expressing racist abuse through engaging in vandalism and graffiti, and ultimately to attacking a young black man walking on his own through 'their' territory.

The argument that racism is not a single monolithic phenomenon of social power is particularly evidenced in work on 'place' by Back and Nayak (1999). The suburb in Birmingham on which they focus is an almost totally white estate, highly deprived, overlooking fields, yet next to a prosperous borough. The embracing of racism by young white men represents, for them, a deep sense of crisis of working-class culture, where communal ties have been broken and 'white' corner shop owners have disappeared. The men and their fathers were no longer defined by their manufacturing jobs, which were associated with belonging, pride and masculinity. These jobs have now been replaced by a service economy, rampant consumerism and growing home ownership. The presence of Asian-owned corner shops are seen to be symbolic of white working-class marginalisation and dislocation, and so the young men use graffiti to inscribe 'white spaces', marking 'their' territory.

> Young men are faced with a dilemma: Who are they in a situation where their identity is not defined by their relationship to work? Race provides a means to resolve these contradictions and express belonging, entitlements and identity: It's the Pakis, the Niggers that have taken our jobs – this is our country. (Back and Nayak, 1999, p 278)

The young men who resorted to racist violence were distinguished from others who had no connection with racism. They were influenced by peer groups and family who did not challenge their racism.

While working-class racism has traditionally laid emphasis on territory and labour power as a means by which working-class identity could be maintained, some commentators believe that middle-class racism is more an exercise of choice (Wieivorka, 1995). This choice results in segregation from minority ethnic communities. Although Wieivorka's research focuses on France, the author maintains that his conclusions hold for Western Europe as a whole. Such racism has been given virtually no attention when drawing up public policy or designing training.

The middle classes are defined by participation in consumption, mobility and opportunities for going up in the world rather than dangers of going down. They have attempted to mark themselves off not so much from poor manual workers as from the immigrant population, which they see as a threat to their ethnicity and religion. The middle classes have deserted certain areas and moved to homogenous suburbs. They have resorted to private education and taken their children out of schools with high immigrant numbers. This creates ethnic segregation, which is itself imbued with racism. It has contributed indirectly to the rise of populism, which has found its chief expression in France in the Front National, where racism is part of their platform. By operating on a logic based on segregation and keeping the racialised population at bay, the middle classes mark their distance from people who signify both social decline and a different racial identity. This builds the racialised group into a threat and a scapegoat.

Gender

The relationship of gender to racism and locality has also been explored by Ware (1997b). She discusses the rise of the BNP in 1993. After the 1993 General Election, attacks against Bengalis rose. The perpetrators appeared to be white men in their twenties and thirties. However, Ware points out that white working-class women expressed their racism, referring to threats to the kinship among their families; to religious incompatibility; to Bangladeshis being 'unhygienic' and 'bringing disease'. Bangladeshis in council houses were perceived to be jumping the housing queue because of their large families or by making themselves homeless by migrating. The white women appealed for families to be kept together, in one place. These views supposedly represent a 'feminine' point of view as they involve domestic space, smells, spitting, disease and all the things that are seen as a threat to the home. Ware argues that women like these help present racism as a heartfelt appeal for justice, in opposition to the 'macho racist thugs'. At the same time, the women's racism is contradictory. For example, the housing given to Bangladeshis was seen as undesirable by whites. The discourse among these women also evoked the 'old' racism of white supremacy, which is both highly racialised and highly sexualised (Ahmed, 2004). For example, the women expressed fears about their safety and of being "mugged by blacks".

The context and the people who express racism connects to the role of the unconscious, described above. Cohen's study demonstrates how white working-class men use gendered and patriarchal characteristics to represent differing ethnic groups. They viewed young men of African Caribbean origin as 'macho', 'hard' or 'heavy' and Sikh Asians as 'wimps'.

> In effect certain elements are selected from African Caribbean 'culture' and privileged because they are associated with the street code of manual working class masculinity; in contrast certain elements are selected from the Asian cultural heritage because they can be made to signify petty bourgeois and effeminate traits. (Cohen, 1997a, p 168)

It is these everyday relationships of 'race', class and gender inequality that need more thoughtful interventions. From this analysis of localised embedded white working-class racism, and the role of the unconscious, it is clear that we have to stop thinking about racism as something 'we have to do to black people' or something that is separate from society. We also have to stop thinking about 'race' and ethnicity as the most important determinant of people's identities in all contexts. Poverty, disadvantage and social exclusion need to be addressed. Class and gender operating in very specific situations, with the aid of unconscious and conscious stereotyping, are not the sole axes in understanding situated racisms. We also need to consider disability, age and sexuality.

Multiple racisms

Recent studies which have examined multiple identities we all hold, suggest that issues of the opposing contrasts of black/white, majority/minority are limited. In fact, what is clear is that neither the majority nor the minority is homogeneous or unified. It is fragmented. There are differences within the so-called minority ethnic groups as well as between and across all social groups. A recent study by Chahal (2004) found that differences between the experiences of women and men in accessing service provision were greater than those between 'ethnicised' groups. He suggests the limitations put on women by families because of their cultural 'rules' often restricted the independence of disabled women. Similarly religious and cultural identities, which were important for some young people in care, were often overlooked by mainstream services.

When attempting to unpack the issues around multiple racisms and its parallel perspective, multiple identities, the situation is complex. In fact a fundamental dilemma for people who are tackling racism is that there are very few 'pure' oppressors or 'pure' victims. Those who are at the receiving end of racism often consciously and unconsciously engage in oppression of others, who deviate from the norm. Just as there is a simultaneous experience of gender, masculinity, class and racism, there is a simultaneous experience of disablism and racism for black disabled people, or homophobia, religion and culture for lesbian Muslim women, for example.

The official discourse on equalities cements singular identities. For example, when seeking legal remedies in the system you have to be *either* a woman or black (you cannot be both) (Crenshaw, 1998). However, a recent study on multiple identity and ethnic minority women found that they did not describe themselves in terms of the imposed identities of being a woman or black or young or old (Mirza and Sheridan, 2003). Instead the women saw themselves as holistic individuals, as wives, mothers and carers, and expressed their experiences in terms of poverty, family and cultural knowledge (food and religion). When talking about access to health services, they talked in terms of neglect, misinformation and discrimination. They did not find the services of the equality bodies useful for accessing justice or helping them with their daily health needs. Ultimately cultural assumptions and preconceived attitudes about the women obscured their rights to be seen as individuals and limited their rights to access services and thus gain health equality.

Disability and age

Official concepts of multiple identities may therefore not be *so* useful since they do not apply in the same way every day in terms of lived realities. It may be more useful to conceptualise them as multiple racisms. The difficulty with multiple identities is that they depend on context and situation and who is involved in the social interaction (Shakespeare, 1998). They need very appropriately targeted interventions to gauge situational context. Multiple identities need to be linked to multiple racisms. For example, the social model of disability has been challenged by many authors as suggesting we conceive of disability as applying to white men with spinal injuries in wheelchairs (Morris, 1998). Furthermore, all disabilities are lumped together ranging from cystic fibrosis, deafness, visual impairment, mental illness and so on.

Similarly, racialised children with disabilities in residential schools will need a very specific intervention, which may alternate between recognising ethnicity, disability, both or neither, as appropriate. Day centres where age, ethnicity and disability come to the fore are also a case in point. Setting up an Asian day centre for all 'Asians', that is, Hindus, Sikhs and Muslims, where they have to share facilities and pretend to be the same, can cause conflicts. We need to acknowledge that there are huge differences which may not be resolved. There may be issues of class, disability, ethnicity and age. The singularity of emphasis on 'race' or ethnicity in all situations might make the intervention totally inappropriate and will have dangerous consequences of 'fixing' identities.

A recent study on the views of young black disabled people on independent living showed a huge complexity in their views and experiences (Bignall and Butt, 2000). Many had experienced racism in their schools, but it was difficult to explain teachers' low expectations of them as solely due to racism. Their experiences were a mixture of how much education they had had, their impairment, and the assumptions others made about their 'cultures'. Some of these young people voiced the view that their experiences differed from white disabled people; others did not. Deaf Asian origin children expressed difficulties in feeling a sense of belonging because of not being able to communicate in their 'home' spoken languages, since their first language was either English and/or British sign language. Some did not feel they could practice their religion because of issues of access to places of worship.

In another study (Hussain et al, 2002), Asian origin young people felt independence was something they wanted in life, but that it was not only related to leaving home, but about having more control over their lives. These Western assumptions about independence are important to know about in interventions with young disabled Asian origin people. On the other hand, although many young people and their families wanted to hold on to their religious and cultural identities, they also felt they were treated better in Britain than in South Asia. Young women in particular felt that their families had low expectations of them and tended to be overprotective.

The demise of separate equality bodies in favour of more inclusive human rights and a single equality body (DTI, 2004) signals the importance of understanding the dynamics of multiple identities together with multiple racisms. Research needs to show how multiple identities are both expressed and experienced if interventions to tackle multiple discrimination are to be successful.

Conclusion

• Unpacking the causes and manifestations of everyday racism is complex. Acknowledgement is the first step in challenging racism (Petrova, 2001). What is clear from these two chapters on elite and situated racisms is that for an intervention to be successful, it needs to be aimed at the specificity and the location of the cause of the discrimination. This may be the pervasive power of the media and judiciary, the poverty and neglect of the disenfranchised and emasculated white, black or Asian working class, the crisis of national identity among the British, or the strategies of a popularist government which scapegoats asylum seekers. It may be about responding to the way disabled black children express their experience of unequal treatment, or the ways in which white women use domesticity discourse to inferiorise Bangladeshi women.

- An accurate understanding of the causes of racism 'in situ' includes attitudes expressed by members locally, and an understanding that examines *all* identities. Strategies for change must address both how you self-categorise or are categorised, for example, white and black, asylum seeker, or not, woman or man, disabled or able-bodied. The solution is not to put the sole onus on the black and minority groups to do the changing. The problem is not theirs, but they will need to be involved. With such wide-ranging causes there is no 'one stop solution' to endemic everyday racism.

FIVE

Racism and the law

This chapter begins by charting the ways in which legislation on 'race' equality has been introduced, followed by a brief analysis of its related policy effectiveness. Professional interventions have been primarily defined by 'race' relations legislation and this chapter is devoted to exploring its background. The social context in which antidiscriminatory laws have been passed constitutes a critical way in which racism is both reproduced and challenged.

When it comes to 'race' relations, Britain is both liberal and conservative. On the one hand, it prides itself on providing sanctuary and safety for refugees and those fleeing persecution. National campaigns against deportation protect families in churches and local British communities act in ways that may be uniquely liberal and radical, Christian and 'British' (Church and Race: www.ctbi.org.uk; National Coalition of Anti Deportation Campaigns: www.ncadc.org.uk).

On the other hand, the conservative tendency is also evident. For example, progressive antidiscrimination legislation is passed at the same time as racist immigration legislation. Policy and media coverage on asylum seekers and refugees adds to the trenchant conservatism. *The Dover Express* (1998) aimed at local people in Kent, where asylum seekers first arrive, published an editorial calling asylum seekers 'human sewage' and claimed that they were running brothels. The far right BNP and National Front supporters have capitalised on this discontent and leafleted, marched and carried baseball bats, threatening asylum seekers in the process (www.canterbury.u-net/Dover).

Race legislation as a framework for interventions

One of the first British national policy interventions to tackle racism in the 1960s was through legislation. A series of studies in the 1960s and 1970s established the extent of discrimination faced by black people, particularly in getting jobs. Reports documenting the state of 'race' relations, Select Committees on Race Relations and Immigration, and other independent sources established time and again the persistence of racial discrimination (Solomos, 2003). In the labour market, studies found that a substantial proportion of employers rejected black applicants before an interview in favour of white applicants, and furthermore, the discrimination was based on colour, not experience or qualifications (Daniel, 1968; McIntosh and Smith, 1974; see Brown, 1992 for an overview). This evidence of blatant racial discrimination experienced by black people in employment and in housing, as well as their overt criminalisation (Hall et al, 1978), led to the passing of the 1965, 1968 and 1976 Race Relations Acts (see Appendix B, Table 4).

But these Acts themselves arose not only out of a response to pressure for change, or a simple recognition that discrimination had to be tackled. The 1965 Race Relations Act was a response to party political competitive responses to the Notting Hill and Nottingham riots and attacks in 1958, and huge cries for immigration control by Enoch Powell and the Conservative Party, with support from large sections of the British population. The Notting Hill riots themselves, a response to a racialised fight, led to several days of disturbances and provocation by white British-born residents against West Indians, chanting "Down with niggers" and "Deport all niggers" (Miles, 1982). As Miles has pointed out, the White Paper to strengthen the 1962 Immigration Act produced in 1965 by a Labour government was targeted to restrict 'black' immigrants who were identified as 'aliens' (see Centre for Contemporary Cultural Studies 1982), rather than Irish, Canadian, Australian or New Zealanders who were not.

Moreover, the White Paper included a political initiative called 'integration'. Integration became officially associated in social policy with doing things *for* 'coloured' people, who did not really belong, and must be helped to adjust (Miles and Phizacklea, 1984). Integration, and subsequent race relations legislation, was defined in relation to limiting black immigration and containing the 'problem'. As Roy Jenkins, Labour MP and strong advocate for multiculturalism said in 1966: "without integration, limitation is inexcusable; without limitation integration is impossible" (see Runnymede Trust, 2000, p 318).

The link between immigration and 'race'

In British social policy responses to racism, one common pattern has been the link between the limiting of 'black' immigration to resulting good 'race' relations. Since 1990 we have witnessed the passing of at least five laws on restricting immigration and controlling citizenship and nationality. On the other hand, we have also seen the 2000 Race Relations (Amendment) Act (see Appendix B, Table 4) and the Macpherson Inquiry (1999) to tackle 'race' inequality. This pattern of juxtaposing talk about tackling racism with limiting immigration is not new. It has its origins in postwar reactions to the 'presence' in *Britain*, rather than *abroad*, of ex-colonial 'black' subjects.

The connections in policy have been based on two issues of concern to governments. First, there has been a negative response by the white majority in Britain to the arrival of ex-colonial black migrants. These negative responses have been reinforced by government discourses on immigration. Second, ex-colonised groups, because of 'racial' discrimination, have felt excluded from full participation in British society (Schuster and Solomos, 2003). The need to manage and control the potential for conflict between these two 'opposite' experiences has driven this association since the 1960s.

The causes of these possible and actual conflicts have rarely been addressed. The need for labour is fully acknowledged by government, but the provision of infrastructure, such as housing and so on, to ensure good 'race' relations' is not forthcoming (see Solomos and Back, 1995). There has recently been a growing decline of public resources for the public sector, in *male* manufacturing employment, and a concomitant emphasis on self-help and the privatisation of services. There is evidence that these socioeconomic changes have had a relatively greater impact on working-class people, who are more likely to rely on public, rather than private, provision of housing, education and health.

Immigration and nationality legislation

Although the 1976 Race Relations Act was a breakthrough in creating 'positive action' as a strategy to tackle racism, immigration policy, together with the 1981 Nationality Act, continued to entrench the idea of excluding 'coloured' immigrants. More particularly, the Nationality Act of 1981 included a definition of British as having a father or grandfather born in Britain. The notion of nation with 'race' became explicitly legitimated in British policy, and inextricably linked with immigration.

A series of restrictions on immigration continued to be passed. The 1988 Immigration Act made residents in Britain prove that they could maintain their relatives without recourse to public funds, implying that black people were a burden on the welfare state. The 1993 Asylum and Immigration Appeals Act made it more difficult for visitors to enter Britain. It was domestic evidence of the increasing harmonisation of stricter controls, both on immigration and asylum in Europe. Visitors were not given any right of appeal against refusal of entry.

The 1999 Immigration and Asylum Act encompassed carriers' liability for illegal passengers, and introduced visa sanctions before entry. Many refugees were thus prevented from fleeing even the countries internationally recognised for their abysmal human rights record. Those who did arrive were subject to poverty, exclusion and separation from a supportive community. Vouchers were introduced for food. The dispersal policy forced asylum seekers to be spread out over the country, where they were isolated and more vulnerable to hostility. Commentators even pointed out they would become marked as 'different' and 'dependent' and warned about dumping asylum seekers in sink estates, making these asylum seekers feel unsafe (Audit Commission, 2000b; Bloch, 2000).

The attacks on refugees and asylum seekers continued to be reported in Liverpool and Glasgow, and we saw the first murder of an asylum seeker (Schuster and Solomos, 2003). The 2000 Race Relations (Amendment) Act seems ineffective in this context, particularly since it was not extended to cover the racist role of public authorities in relation to immigration, asylum and refuge (see Appendix B, Table 3 for a summary of asylum and immigration legislation post-1945).

November 2002 saw the passing of the Nationality, Immigration and Asylum Act, preceded by a government White Paper entitled *Secure borders, safe havens: Integration with diversity in modern Britain* (Home Office, 2002). The discussion on citizenship and nationality in the White Paper refers directly to the disturbances in the northern towns in September 2001, and as such can be argued to be a partial social policy intervention in response to those riots and disturbances (for a discussion on the 'disturbances' and community cohesion see Chapter Eight).

There is discussion in the White Paper on the sense of failure arising from the disturbances, which highlighted the need to renew the social fabric of our communities, and re-build a sense of common citizenship. Most of the reports after the disturbances, including the central coordinating one by Ted Cantle (Home Office, 2001) pointed to the lack of action by the police on the repeated racial violence and harassment of Asian origin communities. In fact, 'concern' about new migrants, together with a decline of public services and a recurring story of lack of police action on racial harassment, was pointed out in various reports (see Chapter Eight).

These issues were mostly ignored in the White Paper. The White Paper proposed instead a *migrants-only* oath of allegiance and suggested the introduction of English tests that migrants would have to pass. It has been suggested that the then Home Secretary Blunkett's comments were about 'blaming the victim' (CARF, 2002).

While diversity (meaning 'race'?) as a term is included in the White

Paper, to signal 'integration', these terms are not analysed or considered in any depth. In fact, difference and diversity are presented primarily as a 'problem'. Difference is presented as something that needs to become like 'the way we do things'; 'they' should seek to embrace 'our' values and 'our' sense of belonging and identity (Schuster and Solomos, 2003). The inclusion of only racialised young men in the White Paper serves to further entrench them as a problem, while ignoring their experience of racism.

Here the government has deftly implicated racialised settled communities as, once more, needing to adapt to British norms. The causes of racism embedded in socioeconomic conditions have not been addressed in this legislation, and in fact, arguably, the White Paper reproduces the idea of racialised minorities as problematic.

The continuity of government policy on immigration, nationality and bettering 'race' relations then can be conceived of as a *cause* of racism in postwar Britain. Unless there are explicit attempts to disassociate these issues, racism will be perpetuated. Furthermore, issues of immigration cannot be understood and shared across Europe, unless these issues are disassociated. Black and white residents as well as new migrants in Britain can only really begin to engage in debates on Britishness, citizenship and Europe once these issues begin to be firmly disassociated.

Using legislation to promote equality

The 1976 Race Relations legislation did extend terms of the previous Acts to cover employment and services, which had been excluded in the 1968 Act. Sections 35 and 38 on 'positive action' were inserted. The section on positive action allowed organisations to take action to redress the underrepresentation of racialised groups in employment and training. Two voluntary Codes of Practice concerned with employment were published by the Commissions concerned with 'sex' and 'race' in 1984 and 1985. These Codes have been instrumental in the launch of equal opportunities policies (EOPs) and *monitoring* of the workforce by 'race' and gender in the 1980s and onwards. Monitoring has been highly influential in professional interventions and is discussed further below.

Equality and employment

Equal opportunities policies, since they were voluntary, were adopted by organisations for a number of reasons. Local authorities became the first to set up 'race' units (particularly after the Scarman Report, 1981, on the Brixton disorders), and to introduce policies on the employment of non-white people. Other reasons for the introduction of these policies included responding to the campaigning for change from various community groups; the impact of the 1980 and 1981 rebellions and uprisings in various cities; as a response to 'race' or gender disputes within organisations; to prevent tribunal cases arising; in efforts to promote a progressive public image; and for political appeal, and internal campaigning by activists (Jenkins and Solomos, 1989; Bhavnani and Cheung-Judge, 1990). These latter reasons can, of course, be accurately regarded as initial interventions to tackle racism with professional interventions taking place in response to these triggers.

However, where EOPs were introduced, the majority of the policies led to changes in tackling organisational bias in the recruitment and selection of employees, men and women, black and white, through the development of 'fairer' procedures. Some changes to employee relations practices were also put in place. These included extended leave, observance of religious holidays, job share, movement between full- and part-time work and workplace nurseries (Cockburn, 1991; Coyle, 1995; Davidson and Burke, 2000).

Diversity

These policies have now suffered a demise and been replaced by policies on 'diversity', including overall policies on sex, 'race', religion, sexual orientation, disability and age. Some authors have argued that there has been a disappointment with the impact of EOPs and a failure to progress underrepresented groups up the hierarchy (see Cockburn, 1991; Wilson, 1995). Others have argued that there has been a backlash against EOPs (Faludi, 1992; Cassell, 2000).

The changes in wider society, with recognition of the need for black and 'ethnic minority' groups in an expanding service sector in a global economy, have led to a change of discourse about the business need for under-utilised labour (see Race for Opportunity: www.bitc.org.uk; CRE, 1995; Metcalf and Forth, 2000). Demographic changes, with a projected ageing population in Britain and reduced fertility, has led to a push towards a business case for the employment of minorities. The need to utilise all sections of the labour market for competitive and business reasons has been the key appeal to corporations (Punch and Pearce, 2001). The employment of these groups, it is argued, will bring added benefits since they will increase access to certain customer groups.

Race relations legislation, then, has been absolutely critical in the British response to racism. It has provided the framework of action for policy, initially as an approach that discussed equal treatment, and later equal opportunity, primarily in the area of employment.

New 'race' equality legislation

The passing of the 2000 Race Relations (Amendment) Act, which requires public sector bodies to actively promote 'race' equality, has been hailed as a key change in the ways in which British social policy on 'race' equality has been transformed. Instead of a framework based on negativity, there is an emphasis on the 'positive'. The Act lays down the conditions not only for possible indirect or direct discrimination, but actively examining for potential (and unintended?) discrimination. It advocates steps to tackle potential exclusion. It also asks public sector bodies to promote good relations between groups. The legislation, for the first time, discusses the active searching for difference, based on 'culture', in order that services can be delivered for equity of access.

As a result of campaigning by many groups, including the CRE, the government was forced into amending the Act to include indirect discrimination (CRE, 2000). In fact, we should remember that recommendations from the Stephen Lawrence Inquiry were really responsible for the passing of the 2000 Race Relations (Amendment) Act. This inquiry itself and its impact in Britain, particularly the use of the term 'institutional racism', would not have come about if it had not been for the dogged and intense campaigning of Stephen's parents and friends over a period of years (see, for example, Bhavnani, 2001). This prolonged intervention over a period of years contains several lessons for policy makers and practitioners.

In Northern Ireland, a separate Race Relations Order was passed in 1997, as well as the 1998 Fair Employment and Treatment (Northern Ireland) Order. The connection with discrimination on the basis of religion was applied, and complaints are heard by a separate Fair Employment Tribunal (see Appendix B, Table 5).

Although the antidiscrimination measures relate to goods and services, as well as employment, most of British case law in this area has been concerned with employment (European Monitoring Centre for Racism and Xenophobia, 2001). There are also provisions in criminal law to protect against racial harassment. These include the 1986 Public Order Act, 1997 Protection from Harassment Act and the 1998 Crime and Disorder Act. The police investigate under these latter laws, and decisions to prosecute are made by the Crown Prosecution Service.

Human rights legislation

We have also seen further legislation to affect local government and the public sector, including the 1998 Human Rights Act, which came into force in October 2000, driven by the European Union. For the first time individuals will have the right to enforce the European Convention of Human Rights in UK courts. The right to be free of discrimination and the right to liberty and security, freedom of conscience, thought and religion, and the right to a fair trial are some of the rights included in the Convention. Spencer (2000) has written about the implications of the Human Rights Act in relation to 'race' or racism. She argues that the right to family life may enable families to challenge their separation by immigration controls or deportation. Freedom from degrading treatment may provide an additional ground on which to challenge discriminatory treatment or harassment. In each case the Act protects people from religious and racial discrimination in the enjoyment of their rights (see Appendix B, Table 6).

Multiple identity and equality legislation

Official equalities constructions are seen to divide people up by 'race', ethnicity, gender, age, disability, religion and sexuality. Therefore people are treated within the system as *either* black or a woman, rather than as one person with complex intersecting identities shaped by class, patriarchy and racism. The legal discourse on equalities arguably cuts across our natural multiple identities as experienced in daily life. However, in reality we experience our gendered racial and other identities in a continuous flow of one through the other (Brah, 1996; Mirza, 1997; Mirza and Sheridan, 2003).

This 'intersectionality' is not problematised in the official equalities debate. Intersectionality is overlooked within the systematic rationale of the legal discourse that artificially separates out our combined racial and gendered and other identities (Crenshaw, 1998; UN, 2000). Multiple identities are a lived reality and it is important that people are seen as 'holistic individuals'. They should not be 'objectified' in terms of preconceived political and social categories (Mirza and Sheridan, 2003).

A new inclusive equalities agenda that aims to bring together recent progressive European and British antidiscrimination and equality legislation, under the umbrella of a restructured single equality body, is an attempt to rationalise the debate (Hepple et al, 2000; DTI, 2002a; O'Cinneide, 2002). In 2006 one overarching Commission will integrate the separate work of the Commission for Racial Equality (CRE), the Disability Rights Commission (DRC) and the Equal Opportunities Commission (EOC). The White Paper *Fairness for all: A new Commission for Equality and Human Rights* (DTI, 2004) heralds the creation of a new Commission on Equality and Human Rights. This signals a sea-change in thinking away from discrete notions of identity toward more complex articulations of difference and diversity.

Equalities legislation in the UK has been far-reaching and progressive. The 2000 Race Relations (Amendment) Act, the 1998 Human Rights Act, the 2000 EU Race Directive and Employment Directive have all widened antidiscrimination, equal treatment and positive provision. Comprehensive principles and standards are established for equal treatment and unfair discrimination. These standards apply to employment, training, pay, and the provision of goods and services across the six grounds of sex, race, disability, sexual orientation, religion and age. Protection can now cover direct and indirect discrimination based on sex, 'race', colour, language, religion, political or other opinions, national or social origin, association with a national minority, property, birth, racial or ethnic origin, religion or belief, disability, age and sexual orientation (DTI, 2002b; Fredman, 2002).

But equality legislation is not harmonised. For example, there is as yet no legislation on gender comparable to the comprehensive 2000 Race Relations (Amendment) Act. However, employers with more than 150 employees are required to comply with the 1997 EOC Codes of Practice on Equal Pay and the 2002 Sex Discrimination Act.

From September 2002, the 1995 Disability Discrimination Act, as amended by the 2001 Special Educational Needs and Disability Act, makes it unlawful for providers of education and related services to discriminate against disabled people. There would have to be substantial good reason for an employer not to make reasonable adjustments to accommodate the disabled person. This applies to all recruitment matters including recruitment, training, promotion and dismissal (see Appendix B, Table 7).

It is of seminal importance that similar recognition for equal treatment, direct and indirect discrimination, and positive action along the lines of the 2000 Race Relations (Amendment) Act and the 1975 Sex Discrimination Act, has been achieved for people of different sexual orientations, religious beliefs, and age groups (Fredman, 2002). In 2006, legislation on employment to outlaw discrimination on the grounds of age, sexual orientation, religion and belief comes into effect (DTI, 2002b). This provision will have significant implications for expanding the practice of equality.

While the new equality and human rights agenda appears progressive, many black activist groups fear the submergence of 'race' issues into an inaccessible, liberal human rights agenda (1990 Trust: www.blink.org.uk/). Black activist groups such as Southall Black Sisters and 1990 Trust are concerned that racialisation of the issues they experience (that is, exclusion from school or unfair imprisonment of Asian women) will be seen as individual human rights issues and not as a collective 'racialised ' experience (Joseph Rowntree Racism Roundtable, 2004). This marginalisation of minority group rights has implications for the acknowledgement of racial discrimination as an embedded practice in racialised societies (McCrudden, 2001; Petrova, 2001).

Limitations of race and equality policies and practice

Legislation primarily deals with the *regulation* of the effects of racism. The law does deal with the concept of 'indirect' discrimination, which has the potential to be used to support those designated as belonging to certain 'ethnic' groups (such as Sikhs and Jews). However, all cases are individualised and discrimination is not regarded in law as systemic.

Admittedly, the concept of equal opportunity took equal treatment further by arguing that equal treatment could not be achieved if groups started at different starting points. An EO approach aimed "to equalise the starting point by removing barriers at the point of selection for employment, education or other benefit" (Fredman, 2002, p 6). However, although access to opportunity can be created, this does not mean that those who are on the receiving end can take advantage of these opportunities. Other barriers, for example, of child care, material deprivation, economic barriers to getting qualifications, or the effect of the stereotyping of groups, are highly restricting for people (Mirza, 2003). Societal discrimination extends beyond the bounds of individual prejudice, and should not be limited to compensating 'victims'; rather to restructuring institutions (Fredman, 2002).

Antidiscrimination interventions: how effective are they?

By the early 1990s, almost two decades since the key pieces of antidiscrimination legislation were passed, incorporation of their spirit into organisational practice was regarded as both tentative and marginal (Cockburn, 1991; Braham et al, 1992; Bhavnani, 1994). Employers developed policies, but implementation was poor. Organisations introduced these policies in piecemeal terms and there were great discrepancies in the embracement of these policies by organisations.

The 2000 Race Relations (Amendment) Act does have a requirement for public authorities to publish Race Equality Schemes, which consist of evaluating the effectiveness of policies. This legislation and the concomitant equality impact assessments are partly based on the Northern Ireland Fair Employment Order. However, in examining issues about carrying out Race Impact Assessments, it is clear the Schemes concern the ability of organisations to count/calculate those groups who may be excluded from a certain policy, or to argue that certain services are not accessible to particular groups, based on evidence gathered. For the first time, the idea of the difference of ethnicised groups is regulated and legitimised in law. In fact despite the progressive nature of this legislation, related policy implementation has so far been poor.

Although organisations can be given the benefit of the doubt about this statutory responsibility, one glance at the ways in which this might be done shows a complicated policy analysis exercise, which is intensely managerial and bureaucratically designed (Kandola and Fullerton, 1994; Collier, 1998; Sihera, 2002). A series of questions and boxes to tick reveal this exercise to be mostly mechanistic and very time-consuming. For example, a recent report in the *Financial Times* (5 May 2004) referred to the fact that guidance for employers from the CRE based on the 2000 Race Relations (Amendment) Act runs to over 93 pages!

In fact there is little empirical evidence that 'race' equality policies have changed the social and discursive practices of racism. In the search for empirical evidence on effectiveness, there is plenty of work that describe policies and action plans, but none which show what effect there has been in terms of the decline in racism. The few studies that exist, which evaluate how organisations are responding to legislation, suggest minimal progress and remain inconclusive and, more importantly, not critically analysed.

There has been visible evidence of the recruitment of racialised groups into organisations particularly in government and the public sector. But we do not know if racism has declined. In fact, evidence might show otherwise, not least the poor implementation of policy. For example, a recent Audit Commission report (2003) found low awareness and understanding of 'race' equality in the public sector. An independent evaluation of training for Metropolitan Police officers (Tamkin et al, 2003) found that many senior police officers think that the emphasis on 'race' is 'overdone'. These officers felt hostile to learning about 'race', were defensive about it, and felt it did not make any difference to their work. Local residents, particularly in racialised areas, found no evidence that Stop and Search procedures had changed. They continued to feel that their areas were stereotyped as being problematic.

More recently, the report from the Office of the Deputy Prime Minister (2003) examining the effects of the 2000 Race Relations (Amendment) Act, found that even now, almost 30 years after the 1976 Race Relations Act, in the public sector, Councils remained unsure as to how to integrate equality and diversity into service delivery, and demonstrated a lack of practical competence in addressing 'race' equality. Councils continued to equate 'race' with social problems and 'race' itself was imbued with ideas of fear and uncertainty. Many felt that targeting specific groups for service delivery might exacerbate tensions in their areas. There was an absence of clear sanctions for poor performance and non-compliance by staff and managers. Unsurprisingly, progress depended on personal and individual commitment. Councils were 'consulting' black and racialised users by providing information for them in various formats, but were not constructively engaging with them.

Another report examining the actions of public authorities after the Stephen Lawrence Inquiry found that policies were unlikely to translate into action, primarily because of a lack of monitoring, which only existed in recruitment initiatives (Mills, 2002). There was a failure to review policies and only a minority had adopted the concept of 'institutional racism'. Most had adopted the definition of racial harassment, but these complaints by the victims were dealt with through disciplinary measures, which address symptoms, rather than being tackled by addressing the underlying causes.

Conclusion

• Professional interventions on 'race' equality, based on legislation, are imbued with contradictions inherent in their development. For example, policies to reduce racism, notably the antidiscrimination legislation and the more recent 2000 Race Relations (Amendment)

Act, have often developed in tandem with other policies, notably on immigration, asylum, nationality and criminal justice, where racism has been implicated and entrenched (see Miles and Phizacklea, 1984; Bhavnani and Bhavnani, 1985; Solomos and Back, 1995).

- The limitations of the legislation with its individualist stance and the voluntaristic ethos of the ensuing Codes of Practice have also limited the ways in which policies have been introduced and their effectiveness.

- Equal opportunities policies introduced as a key intervention by organisations are rarely evaluated to establish if racism has increased or declined. They have also been introduced in ad hoc ways, and have primarily been concerned with encouraging access to employment and training. Policies on diversity have been introduced to put forward business reasons for promoting equality. There is limited empirical data that these policies have led to a decline in racism.

- An overarching Commission on Equality and Human Rights will deal with 'race', sex, age, sexuality and disability. Concern has been expressed that people's multiple identities will continue to be treated in an individualised manner, preventing an analysis and action based on collective experience.

SIX

Equality at work

In this chapter we discuss the patterns of achieving equality of opportunity given changing employment patterns and policies. We consider equality of access to employment and training, and to equal or fair treatment in the workplace, particularly interventions on recruitment, promotion and racial harassment.

Work on promoting equality in employment and training began in the public sector, in local government. The Greater London Council took a lead in the early 1980s. Most gains were made in local government and the Civil Service. 'Municipal antiracism' (Gilroy, 1990) was introduced. This was a particular brand of local authority antiracism, some of it concerned with actively campaigning against racism and targeting funding for underrepresented groups. Within organisations, however, it was criticised for narrow conceptions of 'race' and organisational change. Tackling racism, via 'racism awareness' training, was criticised for making white people 'feel guilty'. There was also a backlash on 'race' initiatives under Thatcherism in the 1990s (Cohen, 1999).

Concern also began to be expressed about poor implementation of EO policies in the 1990s. The CRE launched the 'Leadership Challenge' that encouraged leaders of organisations to prioritise 'race' equality. After the Stephen Lawrence Inquiry (Macpherson, 1999), and a huge flurry of activity, the Home Secretary set targets for senior management positions for 'black and ethnic' minorities in the Police, Fire and Probation Services. This arguably marked a shift in the delivery of workplace equalities. A top-down model of organisational change replaced a bottom-up model, which had been based on black and white employee-led antiracist initiatives.

The private sector was slower to embrace equality of opportunity in relation to 'race'. The 'Race for Opportunity' campaign was launched in 1995. Large employers in the private and public sector were persuaded to take action on 'race' equality. This campaign continues to persuade employers to demonstrate progress, primarily in recruitment and promotion (Race for Opportunity Update, 2003). It has encouraged the setting up of networks of minority staff, encouraged applications from minority groups and also supported inclusion efforts in the wider community, particularly schools (see Appendix A (7) 'Race for Opportunity').

Recruitment initiatives

Public authorities in the inner cities have showed demonstrable gains in the recruitment of black and minority ethnic people (Wilson and Iles, 1999; Goldstein, 2002; Creegan et al, 2003). Certain authorities in London, such as Lambeth Council, Hackney, Greenwich and Haringey, for example, have high proportions of black and minority ethnic residents and they have recruited high proportions of black staff. This is also true for the regions, particularly in Birmingham, Leicester, Manchester and Liverpool. Within the public sector, there have also been gains in recruitment in the civil service, the police force and in the employment of teachers. Within the private sector, banks and retail organisations were some of the first private sector organisations to institute changes in employment, and these showed changes in the composition of the workforce, by racial and ethnic origin (Business in the Community: www.bitc.org.uk/index.html; Metcalf and Forth, 2000). There may be differences in the ethnic origin of the groups that have been recruited, with Indian origin women and men, for example, more likely to be recruited into the private sector, and African Caribbean origin people more likely to be in the public sector, but these patterns are subject to change.

These gains in recruitment could be partly attributed to demographic, sectoral and labour market change. The impetus for change has clearly been changing urban demographics, which has seen a growing concentration of black and minority ethnic populations in particular areas since the 1990s. Since the Stephen Lawrence Inquiry, there is a political and moral case that services in such areas should represent their local constituents, and so there have been particular drives to actively recruit from more representative populations.

Demographic trends of smaller families among white communities, coupled with an ageing population, have increased the pressure to employ 'under-utilised labour', both in settled migrant communities and new migrant groups (Owen, 2003). The public sector has had to open up to partnerships with the private sector as a result of privatisation, and more women and black and minority ethnic groups have entered it. The growth of a service-based economy, especially in the areas of health, education and public sector social services, has led to an increase in jobs for women and black and minority ethnic groups, mostly in part-time and low-status work, but also in a limited capacity in managerial and professional occupations (Strategy Unit, 2003).

A change in numbers recruited has also not necessarily led to these workers being less negatively valued. Black workers, although increasingly employed in the public sector, and committed to serving black service users, have expressed the need to be recognised for their contribution. A recent study showed that they were being placed in marginalised positions in their organisations and not given extra responsibility or credit for their work. The situation was compounded by the fact that they were on the receiving end of taunts that they were *naturals* to work with service users (Goldstein, 2002).

Research on the Race Equality Standard in 1998 (Iganski et al, 2001) showed that most of these policies were in boroughs where there were significant numbers of ethnic minority populations. Linking the *spatial* presence of black and minority ethnic groups to the presence of racism explains why equality of opportunity has not had major effects on the labour market integration of black and minority ethnic people across the board. Equal opportunity is only effective in areas of significant minority ethnic populations, or is found in sectors where they are overrepresented as clients, such as criminal justice.

Employment and refugees

Government interventions to address the inclusion of new migrants into the labour market have created and sharpened divisions between those who reside in Britain and those who have newly arrived. These divisions, rather than encourage equality of opportunity, contribute to racism.

Inclusion initiatives for new arrivals such as refugees have been instituted by local and national agencies working together to facilitate integration into the labour market (Home Office, 2000). But the policy of managed migration (for example, the Highly Skilled Migrants Programme and the Seasonal Agricultural Workers' Scheme) sits rather uneasily with more repressive measures which do not allow asylum seekers to work in Britain until their legal right to be in Britain has been determined (Bloch, 2004).

These potential migrants or refugees with a right to remain in Britain might be waiting as long as between one and five years for their decision (Bloch, 2004). Lack of integration into the labour market will hasten deskilling, and entrench segregation between what people see as the 'deserving' and 'undeserving' poor. Regional dispersal, ensuring asylum seekers are more isolated, the introduction of a system of support under the National Asylum Support System (NASS) which is *separate* from mainstream welfare provision, and the increased use of detention, with separate schools, can only exacerbate racism in Britain.

Positive action recruitment interventions

Most of the interventions aimed at changing the recruitment patterns of racial segregation in the employment market have been through *positive action* schemes to change the representation at a particular type of job or for a particular level. These positive action initiatives have encompassed targeted marketing and advertising policies (see Race for Opportunity Update, 2003), such as word-of-mouth in the community, advertisements in the black press or using other formal and informal networks. They also include graduate schemes such as the Windsor Fellowship that places black and minority ethnic young people in work placements. These interventions have made a difference in heightening awareness, and creating an atmosphere of welcoming inclusion. There is internal organisational evidence of increases in applications to particular organisations, and recruitment to fast-track (for example, graduate) schemes (for example, in HSBC bank and British Telecom). There is evidence that legal requirements are a key strategy to force employers to change. A recent review of organisations' responses to the 2000 Race Relations (Amendment) Act showed that 80-90% had now written equality policies aimed at employment (Schneider Ross, 2002).

But implementation is patchy in different sectors. In the National Health Service it was found that only a small percentage of authorities had introduced positive action measures, and those that had implemented them ranged in the area between 10-12% (Iganski et al, 2001). Some organisations in this survey did not see it as important enough; others adopted a colour-blind approach. Some confused it with *positive discrimination*. Some of the nurse education centres in this study had collected monitoring data, but they did not use the data to strategise about recruitment methods. Iganski et al state that very few of these recruiters had ideas on how to target 'ethnic minority' students. Most interventions were poorly resourced and not based on 'action' strategies. 'Race' equality was marginalised and remained the responsibility of one person who was not centrally responsible for recruitment.

Persistence of racialised exclusion

Despite positive trends in recruitment, patterns of racialised social exclusion persist. Compared to their white counterparts, young people of African Caribbean, African and Asian origin suffer higher rates of unemployment as well as underemployment, whatever their qualifications (Berthoud, 1999; Heath and Yu, 2001; Mason, 2003; Strategy Unit, 2003). The government has insisted that getting people into employment is integral to tackling social exclusion.

The New Deal Programme for 18- to 24-year-olds and for 25+ was set up to design training programmes for those who can, to get work. Although it has achieved some success in getting long-term unemployed people into work, it failed to achieve equal results for different ethnic groups. The reason, it is argued, is that these gaps in policy initiatives mirror 'disadvantage' in the labour market. Without tackling the fundamental cause of differential ethnic employment, based on endemic racial discrimination, disadvantage and the racial segregation of the labour market, it may not be possible to tackle the effects of unemployment (Wilson, 2003; TUC, 2004).

Mainstreaming equal opportunities

Equal opportunity in the workplace is about removing exclusionary barriers to participation and access for all. One such barrier relates to the practice of 'institutional racism' (see the discussion of 'institutional racism' in Chapter Two). The Stephen Lawrence Inquiry (Macpherson, 1999), which highlighted institutional racism, focused on direct and indirect discriminatory practice within the police in particular, and public sector organisations in general.

Mainstreaming equality through meeting statutory requirements and enforcing the law has thus been seen as a central strategy to combating racism in the workplace. Mainstreaming as an ideal is about promoting equality through changing cultural practice in the workplace. It aims to do so by "building issues of equality into policies and practice, across a broad front, taking account of all the equality strands" (DTI, 2002a, p 10). Mainstreaming in this sense means engendering reflexive organisational change through the "process of assessing the implications for different individuals of any planned action including legislation, policies and programmes, in all areas and at all levels" (Runnymede Trust, 2000, p 286). From management, to staff interviews and appraisals, to day-to-day delivery of services with clients, equality and diversity are everyone's responsibility. However, as the evidence shows, this is often not the case across many public and private sector organisations.

Mainstreaming may be a good idea, but in day-to-day practice there are many obstacles. For example, perceptions on equality interventions vary between groups based on 'race' and gender (Creegan et al, 2003). As Creegan et al show, white men regard equality interventions as a big brother approach, and do not take monitoring seriously, black minorities continue to feel racism is a problem that has not been tackled. These black staff would like better grievance reporting and support mechanisms at work, whereas white staff would like more opportunities for career development and cross-cultural mixing.

Many of these ethnicised employees are employed in 'equality' jobs, where they are pressing for change, despite top level resistance or apathy. White women, as recipients of equality policies, are more critical of the failure of equality policies than their male counterparts. It is possible that as rhetoric about equality increases, coupled with poor implementation these divisions may increase.

Have equal opportunities been widely implemented?

The patchy implementation of positive action measures is also borne out in studies on the implementation of EO policies generally. Research by the Institute of Public Policy Research in 2002 revealed that out of 500 UK directors, very few had *implemented* change. Less than four out of 10 organisations monitored ethnicity. Only 10% had a policy to change the profile of their company. They had signed up to EO, but these policies were narrowly defined and poorly evaluated (Blink, 2002).

In Scotland, a recent study found that 61% of private sector employers said that their policy consisted of no more than a written statement, despite 99% having a policy. The majority of respondents replied 'No' when asked if they would implement a racial equality programme if it reaped commercial benefits. A total of 50% of respondents felt that the policy was either divisive, not cost-efficient or unnecessary. Employers introduced policies to avoid industrial tribunals. But the survey did find that those employers who had taken action agreed it had been very beneficial (CRE, 2000).

The lack of widespread implementation of the law has a variety of causes. Equality strategies on 'race' in the 1990s have been introduced in the public sector under the new managerialism, and the entry of the market into public service reform. This has occasioned devolved budgets, internal trading units and control to line managers (Creegan et al, 2001). Although the New Labour government has attempted re-regulation with antidiscrimination policies after the Stephen Lawrence Inquiry, the policies have been introduced in an atmosphere where implementation is getting harder. Cost-cutting, sub-contracting, organisational change and meeting 'targets' has led to middle managers feeling besieged (Wilson and Iles, 1999). They have been given a freedom to manage, but EO provides restrictions on their 'free rights' to manage. The possibilities of resistance to equality become stronger, particularly in the light of a lack of resources for education or training on racial bias and stereotyping.

On the other hand, where policies have been implemented, there have been positive benefits. Together with demographic changes and cost-cutting, recruitment policies have been streamlined. Formalised selection processes with more objective mechanisms have been introduced in order to make them less subject to personal favouritism. They have made a difference in welcoming potential minority employees. For example, it has been argued that introducing more 'objective' cognitive ability tests and personality inventories may be more valid predictors of job performance than unstructured interviews, even though we do not know enough of their ability to display a potential adverse impact (Iles and Auluck, 1991; Wilson and Iles, 1999). These mechanisms may or may not be related to the introduction of EO policies.

Have equal opportunities reduced racism?

We would further argue that despite some gains in recruitment, the pressure for mainstreaming and the drive to tackle social exclusion, discrimination has not gone away but has become more covert than overt (Jewson and Mason, 1994). Research shows that recruiters who are white men are still more likely to recruit in their own image (Prewett-Livingston et al, 1996). Access to good educational qualifications, together with recruiter perceptions of 'recruitees'' competence, may continue to be critical barriers for some black and ethnic minority groups.

These perceptions may also apply to promotion and training for minorities inside the organisation. Where positive action has been introduced, such as targeting groups for a training course, increased confidence in personal development was found among the attendees. However, organisational cultures remained untouched (Bhavnani and Coyle, 2000). Minority women wanted to leave the NHS, felt marginalised and unable to impact on the culture of exclusion that often ignored their needs, such as getting time off or financial support to help them upgrade their qualifications (Bhavnani and Coyle, 2000).

Similarly, research examining the experience of positive action training in the housing sector found that of the 1,000 trainees over 15 years, 80% obtained jobs they were trained for in housing management. Trainees felt confident about personal and career development. But the report argued that racial stereotyping and direct racism in the organisational cultures in which they worked had not changed and that the recruits felt isolated. They felt that they had experienced a glass ceiling with regard to promotion (Julienne, 2001).

In other words, attitudes towards the 'other' based on histories and roots of racism may not have gone away. A recent overview indicated that there was a widespread tendency in organisations for line managers to evaluate the performance of minority ethnic employees as lower than white staff (Tackey et al, 2001). Tackey et al concluded that managers evaluated performance levels more negatively for certain groups, which was seen to be an important explanation for the discrepancy in ratings. Moreover, good performance was attributed by managers to good luck or extraordinary effort rather than the skills/ ability and knowledge of an individual from an ethnic minority background.

A recent study for the Department for Education and Skills has borne this out (Powney et al, 2003). Ethnic minority teachers were most likely to go for promotion but least likely to get it. They were often qualified, but rarely found in positions that reflected their ability and skill. The teachers themselves felt that they were subjectively assessed for promotion by governors and head teachers. These 'assessors' were perceived as holding implicitly racist opinions (Powney et al, 2003). Similarly there is a growing body of evidence in the 1980s and 1990s that black people in the NHS experience discrimination in promotion and training prospects (Alexander, 1999; Coker, 2001). The relatively poorer representation of black people at higher levels in the health service reflected representation of black managers in local government (Andrew, 1996), and the civil service (Wilson and Iles, 1999). Cockburn's research (1991) in the public and private sector showed black employees tended to be concentrated in clerical jobs rather than those with higher pay and more career potential. Later work summarising the relatively poorer position of black and ethnic minority women managers by Davidson (1997) did not give any grounds for optimism.

Much of the evidence available suggests that organisational cultures continue to marginalise and inferiorise minority ethnic groups. These experiences are reported by minorities themselves, and the studies suggest that changing procedures alone may not make a difference to reducing racism. In the 1990s, discourse about 'equality of opportunity' shifted from recruitment. Policies were devised on career progression and promotion of minorities. There is now a greater use of 'competence' frameworks and systematic appraisals. The emphasis on 'competencies' does not necessarily mean a 'pure' objectivity has been created. A greater emphasis on self-motivation and self-development in careers may mask societal and organisational obstacles to access equal opportunity.

The business case for diversity

The pervasive discourse on equality and social inclusion discussed above is now based on the notion of 'respecting diversity in order to achieve equality.' Diversity is about good public relations, and 'inclusivity' is argued to be good for business. It is more about getting the right people for the job on merit and the business benefits of a more diverse workforce (Cabinet Office, 2001).

The switch to diversity policies may be of limited value. Business climates may and do change. Employing members of the same 'ethnicised' group may have both advantages and disadvantages. Organisations might now be able to access previously 'ignored' customers, but racially matching workers to customers does automatically assume they will be able to identify with one another, when in fact staff or customers may resist the idea (Fredman, 2002). Employing members of an ethnic group of colour and not Yorkshire/ Derbyshire/London white members, for example, does not imply that racist attitudes are being addressed in the organisation.

Diversity policies, which are couched in business sense terms, have to be underpinned by a set of more fundamental rights-based principles (Fredman, 2002). Changes in the attitudes of the public on ethical and social responsibility have persuaded companies that a 'rights'- based approach may also be good for business. Policies that have been primarily given momentum as a result of socioeconomic conditions can easily change with changing conditions.

A positive workplace ethos is a crucial variant to embed equality. The national survey on teachers' careers showed that black and minority ethnic teachers desire a 'nice' place to work. They want enthusiastic empathetic colleagues and head teachers who value them. This is no different from anyone else. More specifically, these staff want to be recognised for their general contribution, and not solely 'as token black representatives' (Powney et al, 2003).

Diversity does not mean employing more black and minority ethnic groups just to provide role models. It also means meeting the needs of individual employees and taking account of the individual's personal attributes, cultures and home/work parameters. We need to tackle the attitudes and behaviours, covert and subtle, of dominant, often white majorities, *and* their relationship with the 'other'.

In organisations a good intervention should ask 'How can we keep track of attitudes to difference and diversity?'. Change in behaviour away from discriminatory practices represents a change in attitudes away from prejudices. There is a need to go 'back to basics' and to work with people to make changes at the micro level.

One intervention that has confronted the issue of 'racism' in the workplace more explicitly has been actions regarding racial harassment. It is to this we now turn.

Racial harassment in the workplace

Professionalised action to prevent racial harassment or to monitor its occurrence did not begin until the late 1980s when strategies and procedures were introduced in local government, Civil Service and other organisations. The 1990s saw an impetus in discourses on racial harassment as the concept came to be legally constitutive of industrial tribunal decisions under the 1976 Race Relations Act. In fact the 1976 Race Relations Act does not use the term 'racial harassment'. Tribunals have become willing to see this form of labour market exclusion as 'less favourable treatment on racial grounds'. It therefore now constitutes unlawful racial discrimination.

The 1994 Criminal Justice and Public Order Act legislated that all forms of harassment at the workplace were considered criminal offences. The 1998 Crime and Disorder Act created new racially aggravated offences such as racial harassment, assault, or grievous bodily harm, which carry significantly higher penalties (www.racialharassment.org.uk; Shields and Wheatley, 2000). These interventions were partly due to the success of antiracist community monitoring and campaign groups such as Southall, Newham and Community Security Trust.

In 1999 the Stephen Lawrence Inquiry, which recommended monitoring of racially motivated incidents, added to the legal and social context of action on racial harassment. Since the Inquiry these strategies were given added impetus with the recommendation of multiagency working for action outside the workplace. Interventions consist primarily of encouraging the reporting of incidents, communications across agencies, sanctions and banning of behaviour, supporting victims and working with perpetrators. The last one is extremely rare, but some early work on it is beginning (see Chapter Nine on successful interventions).

Interventions in setting up confidential reporting situations have not proved very successful. The national survey on teachers' careers showed that reporting such personal and sensitive experiences was difficult. Open discussion of sexuality in places of work remains problematic. There are so few informal mechanisms for intimate disclosure without fear of reprisals (Powney et al, 2003). The official grievance procedure remains internal to the organisation; remedies rarely end in dismissal. Those on the receiving end understandably fear victimisation.

Surveys of racial harassment in the workplace exist, but evaluation of effective intervention strategies are sadly lacking (Lemos, 2000). Research shows racial harassment from staff, patients and relatives has been growing in the health service, with 40% of nurses reporting it as something they had experienced (Shields and Wheatley, 2000). NUPE's survey showed that many black and ethnic minority nurses were subjected to racial harassment by other staff and patients as did the survey in West Yorkshire (Lee-Cunin, 1989). All these surveys showed that the issue was escalated because black staff were disciplined for retaliating.

In a national survey of staff in higher education institutions, 27.7% of black and minority ethnic women reported racial harassment compared to 16.1% of minority ethnic men. The women were also more likely to express scepticism of their university's EO policies. Furthermore, these women were considerably unlikely to publicly report racial harassment. Gendered forms of racial harassment in overtly male institutions pose a significant issue for higher education (Carter et al, 1999).

Recently, growing concern has been expressed about the increase in the incidence of racial violence and harassment in the British context (Virdee, 1995; Khan, 2002). Despite legislation, racial attacks still appear to be on the increase in public spaces such as on transport, the street and in the workplace.

Ethnic monitoring

The 2000 Race Relations (Amendment) Act requires that organisations positively promote 'racial' equality. Benchmarking and impact assessments have become integral to race equality in public sector organisations. Ethnic monitoring has thus been given a new lease of life.

'Ethnic' monitoring is not new, however. As a foundational exercise to take action on 'race' equality, it has been around since the 1980s. Yet many organisations have failed to take monitoring on board (see the earlier discussion on the implementation of EO policies). Furthermore, this lack of action may have increased a lack of trust in monitoring as a strategic intervention for producing evidence of 'discrimination'.

The Audit Commission report (2003) found that black and minority ethnic staff felt 'ethnic monitoring' was a tick-box exercise and were suspicious of it. This is singularly depressing when the very people who policies are designed to help do not accept it.

Furthermore the conceptual basis of monitoring is flawed. As we have argued elsewhere (Bhavnani, 2001), the concept of ethnic monitoring does not allow for comparisons across class and 'race' or across 'race' and gender. It only highlights 'ethnicity'. This is a problem given our earlier discussion of the differences across and between ethnic groups in Britain (see Chapter One on definitions of ethnicity). It does not allow for an understanding of comparative outcomes, such that class and gender and 'race' are considered together.

In fact, 'ethnic' monitoring in isolation keeps the gaze on ethnicised peoples, and is not compared with the taken-for-granted 'positive action' that characterises white middle-class men's networks and alliances. Monitoring appears to be used as 'record keeping', rather than as a foundation for action. It further 'closes' ethnicised identities and assumes that this is always the most important category for analysing one's own experience. Ethnic monitoring is arguably about disciplining and regulating racialised identities.

Some would argue that ethnic monitoring fits into a larger 'performance' management approach to encourage accountability. But as part of a technicist managerial discourse, ethnic monitoring does not allow time for reflection or for the consideration of political choices. It stresses measuring outcomes, but fails to aid thinking about the means.

We now know that racism has become more subtle and harder to measure explicitly. A more subtle covert racism has implications for explicit measurement. We cannot use crude categories of, for example,

African origin, to design interventions. The category is too broad, encompassing a whole continent, assuming similar educational experiences or similar experiences of harassment, whether women or men, young or old. Groups are also constantly changing and we do not yet keep data on multiple identities, and multiple racisms, for this kind of data collection to be effective. It is also difficult to use ethnic monitoring to tackle the wider issues of subtle disregard, lack of value and marginalisation experienced by these groups.

Most importantly, we should not automatically ethnically monitor, without understanding why we are doing it. What is the issue we are trying to tackle? Should we count those who are designated 'ethnic'? Why? Who else should we count for comparison? And why are we keeping these figures?

Black staff networks and mentoring

One of the more successful interventions does not concern employers' initiatives but the organisation of workplace 'black' staff groups. In several sectors, including the Civil Service and in specific local authorities, as well as in banks, in education, in the police and in social services, black and minority ethnic groups have got together to form networks or associations to push for internal change, and to provide a support system for those who feel marginalised and disregarded by the organisation. A good example of this is the National Union of Teachers' Black Teachers Network that has a very well attended annual conference. The Black Police Officers Association regularly exposes and comments on racialised policing matters, and has provided visible support for police officers who have complained about police discrimination (www.blackpolice.org). In further education, the Commission for Black Staff in Further Education set up a study and action plan into institutional racism in education and produced guides for retention, recruitment and staff development. Networks of black staff in the Civil Service have also been prominent in pushing for change. Their union, the Public and Commercial Services Union (PCS), has seminars and training programmes for their black staff group.

In the UK, the mentoring of black young people by older, white and black adults began as a community sourced initiative (Appiah, 2001). Lessons from the US indicated that mentoring was successful within organisations in building confidence, encouraging a more proactive desire for improvement and job development and was important under the right conditions for tackling internalised racism. Mentoring as an intervention has rarely been evaluated for its long-term effects, but the literature of short-term effects shows that those black people who have been mentored, do increase their promotion rates and become more optimistic about their jobs and careers (Bhavnani et al, 2003). In the US, where a white mentor took on a black member of staff and the conditions were right, mentors reported gains in the understanding of 'race' and diversity through mentoring relationships. This aspect of positive action where there is mutual benefit may be an effective intervention in tackling racism, since both sides participate in change.

While mentoring can build confidence, it can also build powerful social networks which many black and minority ethnic people are not tapped into. As a mechanism for change it understands the importance of the persistence of 'who you know' in getting a good job (Mirza, 1992). While networking is problematic as it reproduces inequality through exclusivity, it is also pragmatic in appreciating the mechanisms for disadvantage and can open up new worlds of opportunity for young people. In the same way, black staff networks can also close down opportunities for mixing with influential white staff.

Mentoring can be seen to be fundamentally flawed as a philosophy in other ways too. It is based on the concept of 'role models,' which is deeply implicated in a cultural deficit model of black negative self-esteem and low self-image as an explanation for black underachievement and underemployment (Mirza, 1995). While many young people may lack the social and professional skills of self-presentation and have narrow horizons, this may be because of the lack of educational opportunities and social experience and cultural capital, all of which are limited if you are poor, disadvantaged and lack resources and support (Wilson, 2003).

Conclusion

- Professional equality interventions in employment have included policy development, monitoring of ethnicity, the appointment of specialist officers on 'race' or 'diversity', positive action training and changing procedures and systems with regard to recruitment and promotion.
- There is little evidence indicating that these interventions have been systematically evaluated. The limited academic and policy-based research shows that written policies are adopted by the majority of organisations when they have the force of the law. On the other hand, *implementation* of equality policies is patchy and ad

hoc. Those who have responsibility for implementation at middle management level in the public sector may feel besieged by continuous change, growing responsibilities, together with a greater emphasis on targets. This extra pressure on work may increase tensions since fewer resources are available.

- Changes in recruitment procedures have arguably made a difference to the employment of ethnicised minorities in both the private and public sectors. However, a case can also be made for other factors which have encouraged the recruitment of minorities. These include labour market and sectoral change, public sector reform, and demographic changes. Research on the New Deal (to tackle the social inclusion of ethnic minority young people) shows little impact on the disadvantage experienced by minorities in the labour market.

- Negative evaluations of racialised minorities continue to be found in various studies, but these perceptions and experiences are not generally shared *across* or *within* all groups. White men, for example, do not perceive minorities as being discriminated against, or being marginalised. White women empathise more with pushing for change.

- Promotion procedures are also arguably becoming more objective in assessing those with management potential. However, research continues to show slower progress of minorities in organisations and a greater tendency for minorities to receive lower evaluations of competence than their white peers. Organisational cultures continue to disadvantage minorities.

- The 'new language' of racial equality and inclusion in the context of the liberal democratic discourse on equality and antidiscrimination is now being constructed around achieving *diversity*. It has employed the dominant (arguably masculinised) agenda of objectives and targets, enforcement and evaluation, recruitment and audit. Diversity initiatives are also not evaluated and the business case for diversity based on economic conditions may not be so persuasive once the economic climate changes.

- Racial harassment policies in the workplace are rarely evaluated. It is difficult to argue that any of these initiatives have reduced racism. Equality interventions in employment have had limited success in the area of recruitment. The policies have been designed mainly for enabling 'access' to opportunity. They are dealing with the effects rather than the causes of racism.

- Black staff networks and mentoring can provide important support for isolated black employees. They are empowering and help build connections that are vital to overcoming racialised barriers at work.

SEVEN

Accessing services

Following on from our exploration of legislation and equality interventions in employment, this chapter summarises research on 'fair and equal access to services'. Two aspects of service interventions are relevant here. The first is concerned with ensuring that minority ethnic groups as a whole are not excluded from accessing services. The second type of intervention is based on cultural differences, such as language or religious observances. This second type of service intervention explicitly recognises 'difference', and it is this type of 'difference' intervention that will be considered in Chapter Eight on multicultural interventions.

Equal access to services, as with employment, has been primarily concerned with written policies and monitoring. Government social policies on Best Value and Modernising Government have also included consultation with groups that are 'hard to reach'. Many public authorities interpreted these groups as including minorities, as well as those with disabilities, older people and poor people. Consultation has now become part of the 2000 Race Relations (Amendment) Act.

There has been virtually no research which indicates whether these strategies on access to services have been implemented. We consider any research on these interventions under the various sites of housing, criminal justice, education, health and social welfare, and arts and leisure. We ask whether interventions in racism in these essential sites tackle the endemic problem of exclusion and inequality that seem to persist in service delivery.

We conclude by exploring a new concept in social policy, *social capital*, since social capital has been invoked in relation to the black voluntary sector. Its use has been to encourage 'access' and inclusion interventions for services that are now no longer solely provided by the local authority.

Racism, housing and neighbourhood renewal

Housing is indelibly linked with poverty and income. Housing access issues include housing tenure differences, regeneration programmes and minority relationships with majority/settled tenants, including the prevalence of racial harassment.

Investigations by the CRE in the 1980s into discrimination in local authority housing found widespread evidence of discrimination. In 1993 the CRE identified similar problems with housing associations. In 2001 The Housing Corporation published research confirming that Registered Social Landlords had a poor track record in tackling 'race' equality. The Runnymede report (Runnymede, 2000) highlighted differences between racialised groups in access to housing tenure. Nearly 50% of African Caribbean and Bangladeshi origin families live in social housing. Other groups of African, Asian and Pakistani origin may own their own houses, but as a whole all minority groups disproportionately live in overcrowded conditions and are disproportionately represented among poor people.

Intervention strategies have included monitoring housing allocation, as well as training for managers, but no evidence of effectiveness is available. Even though councils may argue that they can find no evidence of discrimination in allocations, particularly the ones that have monitoring systems in place, other research indicates that discrimination still persists (Power, 1999; Presentation Housing, 2000). In fact Power's research shows that some local authorities have actually entrenched segregation of communities – her research in Bradford showed social housing to be segregated on ethnic lines. The segregation was a result of policies that assumed that certain areas were suitable for Asian communities, while others were not. Thus Asian families were left on waiting lists, while properties remained vacant. Estate agents engaged in the practice of 'blockbusting', that is, selling a home to an Asian family and then informing white neighbours that their house price would fall. These policies created segregation, an outcome desired by neither community. In interviews and discussions with residents, it became clear that residents were unhappy with what had been created. Most did not want, for example, segregated schools for their children (Runnymede Bulletin, 2002).

Even when no evidence of unfairness of allocations is found by group origin, other action research shows that segregation takes place not between estates, but on the same estates (Bhavnani and Foot 2000). The most recent research from the Audit Commission (2003) found that black groups feel that discrimination exists in housing allocation, and they preferred more interaction across groups. Black-led housing associations, together with voluntary groups, have provided important interventions in patching up the effects of racism and lobbying for change (see Presentation Housing, 2000).

The Housing Green Paper (ODPM, 2000) did not even mention racism, and recent research argues that policy and practice responses in neighbourhoods and housing services ignore black and minority communities (Presentation Housing, 2000). A 'colour-blind' approach has also characterised the government's approach to regeneration. Research has revealed the exclusion and disadvantage of racialised groups, and regeneration has been linked to *geographical* areas, not to black and minority ethnic groups per se (Brownill and Darke, 1998). Regeneration research shows that the impact of such policies on black communities was not a priority for agencies set up for regeneration. Black groups lost out in resource allocation, and resources were not (re-)distributed or targeted even in the most recent National Strategy for Neighbourhood Renewal aimed at black communities (Presentation Housing, 2000).

The exclusion of Gypsies and Travellers from accessing housing has become part of our everyday experience, although recently, integrated strategies have been introduced. These aim to reduce tensions in areas where Romany Gypsies and Irish Travellers are present, but government interventions to tackle issues for these communities has arguably worsened the situation. No additional resources have been allocated for these communities. Their access to accommodation and services is almost impossible to mainstream where the social policy discourse is one of enforcement and eviction, rather than support. This can only escalate local hostility and negative media coverage. Abuse and violence are sometimes the result, and are not challenged (Crawley, 2004).

A zero tolerance approach to racial harassment has been advocated by government, who recommend that this approach be integrated into tenancy agreements (Social Exclusion Unit, 2002). The government has also recommended neighbourhood warden schemes, and the existence of these schemes has led to an increased rate of reporting of racial harassment. Findings from the British Crime Survey also found that reporting of incidents had gone up, indicating better recording practices by the police (Clancy et al, 2001). These strategies of sanctions or zero tolerance are clearly effective in encouraging greater reporting by victims, but they are not designed to address the causes of racism.

Evidence indicates, however, that racial harassment projects tackling the impact of racism on minorities can be successful. Providing a singular focus in support for victims of racial harassment provides a critical space for the client's experience to be validated. Caseworkers provide practical help and emotional support, raising confidence levels of victims. It is suggested they have become indispensable in challenging racist oppression (Chahal, 2003). Mainstream agencies, on the other hand, are viewed as offering little of this holistic approach.

A recent investigation by Lemos (2000) interviewed 250 agencies tackling racial harassment in 67 local authority areas. Interviews took place in areas where the majority of black and minority ethnic people lived. In one year (1999-2000) 42,000 incidents were reported. These incidents varied from borough to borough. Despite the doubling of recorded incidents, a high degree of under-reporting for some groups, particularly refugees, was also reported (Chahal, 1999). Interviewees frequently raised the question of resources. They also discussed the slow progress of taking action against perpetrators. Support strategies for victims and action against perpetrators were included as part of this study. Safety devices such as alarms, counselling and phone helplines were established in about one third of these agencies. But because of a division between housing managers about rehousing victims, a very low level of rehousing and transfers was the result.

Legal sanctions against perpetrators were rare. When the law was invoked, possession orders and injunctions were used to deter perpetrators. Working with perpetrators was also rare. Where this type of intervention had been introduced, it concerned probation officers working with racist offenders (see Chapter Nine).

Education

School interventions in racism have included those targeted at school exclusions, raising attainment of differing groups, teaching about racism in citizenship education, awareness raising for teachers, and changes in school management and leadership, including recruiting more black governors (Majors, 2001). Strategies in higher education and further education focus on monitoring, access and outcomes for staff and students (CBSE, 2003; Law et al, 2004).

The educational underachievement of young black and minority ethnic pupils is a long-running debate, since the Rampton (1981) and Swann (1985) reports highlighted the issues. In the 1980s, interventions included the introduction of multicultural education. This was designed to increase the self-esteem of racialised minorities through portrayal and the celebration of various religious festivals. Multicultural education also included English as a second language, mother tongue teaching, and a focus on involving parents.

Twenty years later, 'Aiming High' addresses the same issue but suggests a variety of differing interventions (DfES, 2003). It identifies 'hard' structural issues, such as leadership, school ethos, ethnic monitoring, and the importance of sharing best practice. But solutions and projects recommend 'soft' behavioral and social issues. For example, Excellence in Cities projects include programmes to raise self-esteem, breakfast clubs, summer schools, parental skills, role models and a pastoral curriculum. It could be argued that the government policy of focusing on black children and their parents, rather than on racialised structures such as setting and streaming and league tables, entrenches the idea that challenging racism lies within black communities. As a result, tackling racism in white rural areas, where there are few black children, is often overlooked (Richardson, 2004).

Funding interventions in underachievement centre on 'raising achievement'. The EMAG (Ethnic Minority Achievement Grant) has replaced Section 11 funding for minority children (Tikly et al, 2002). The success of such programmes as Excellence in Cities and EMAG is difficult to gauge. Base line data is lacking and evaluations are not longitudinally designed. Local authorities also set targets for black and minority achievement. There is often no rationale as to how or why these targets have been set. Some are set to increase the gap between black and white, and some are unrealistically set to make white children underachieve (Gillborn and Mirza, 2000).

The Quality Standards and Codes of Practice in delivering racial equality, and the requirements of the 2000 Race Relations (Amendment) Act have requirements to demonstrate positive action on tackling racial inequality. This means that schools are now sensitive to the penalties of not addressing the issues. While many black teachers cynically report that they have been identified as the ones to produce the school's action plan and equality strategy, the requirements have also provided positive impetus for many other schools to now discuss issues openly in consultation with governors and parents (Fekete, 2004a).

Teaching about 'cultures' of racism

Although funding extra teachers and resources to raise attainment at secondary level is a major intervention, interventions in the early years is also advocated. These interventions concern the training of teachers and practitioners in challenging racist attitudes. The work by the National Early Years Network is a case in point (Lane, 1999). The Working Group Against Racism in Children's Resources (WGARCR) has also worked on exposing and challenging racism in books and images for young children. The long-term effects of these interventions are not yet known.

Some efforts to tackle racism through education do show a direct relationship between analysis of the problem and the intervention. Many teachers teach about racism in personal and social education, in citizenship classes, and incorporate black history into their teaching. It does appear as if these sessions are taught in a special class or module, and they may not always be integrated into the mainstream curriculum. While there is much good practice in schools using theatre, geography, poetry, sport and literature and human rights to openly challenge racism in schools (Richardson, 2004), we do not know if these sessions are effective in tackling racism, since they are not evaluated.

Citizenship education has been hailed as a priority in Europe. In 1997 the Council of Europe launched an education for democracy and citizenship programme, which was seen as essential in tackling racism and xenophobia (Osler and Starkey, 2002). Antiracism has also been integrated into funding grants for transnational projects. However, the Crick Report, which recommended citizenship education in Britain, has been criticised for having a colonial flavour (Osler, 1999). In its discussion of national identity in a pluralist context, the report states that due regard should be given to the homelands of minority communities and to the main countries of British emigration. This, as Osler points out, precludes the idea that people have a variety of hybrid or multiple identities, which vary across contexts. Nor does the report make any mention of racism. Citizenship education needs to be more than civic responsibilities – it should also be about creating a more cohesive democratic society (Osler and Starkey, 2002).

Teacher training for diversity and inclusion does not incorporate racism but instead looks at the achievement levels of ethnic minority groups (Osler and Morrison, 2000). Teachers may feel ill equipped to handle those who they may view as 'difficult' pupils, and may also not have dealt with their own racism (Runnymede Trust, 2003). Several studies may be pertinent here. Initial teacher training courses have optional diversity or multicultural training, consisting of a few hours with a guest speaker. Only 30% of newly qualified teachers felt equipped to deal with diverse students (Multiverse, 2004). A recent study showed that 70% of trainees have overtly racist attitudes (Jones, 1999). There is some limited evidence from a teacher training module that challenging the racism of student teachers, without personalising the interaction, can produce a decline in racist attitudes, and, what is more, encourage students to take up the issue in their teaching careers (Gaine, 2001).

This lack of teacher understanding can have damaging effects. Gillborn and Youdell (2000) demonstrate the effects of unchallenged racism among teachers in the education system. In a modern version of the self-fulfilling prophecy, called the 'New IQism', teachers who hold stereotyped views of African Caribbean origin pupils make decisions to set and stream these young people into lower ability streams. As a matter of school policy, these pupils are entered into lower foundational levels of GCSE examinations. This level means that they are unable to attain a higher grade than a C.

The Teacher Training Agency has commissioned a comprehensive web resource for teachers to access information on race and diversity (www.multiverse.ac.uk/). Independent organisations staffed by committed activists such as Trentham Books produce books and journals for teachers and the Runnymede Trust has produced guidance on race and diversity in their booklet *Complementing teachers* (Runnymede Trust, 2003).

Exclusions

Research shows that the rate of exclusions from school for black Caribbean pupils is three times higher than for white pupils (Centre for Educational Research, 2003; CRE, 2004b). In fact, Britain has the highest rate of school exclusions in Europe (*Times Educational Supplement*, 19 January 2001). Department for Education and Skills policy on exclusions includes managing the situation rather than having a nil exclusions policy (Blair, 2001).

Intervention strategies have focused on setting targets to reduce exclusions. Some research shows that targets on school exclusions set by schools and local authorities in the 1990s did not address 'race' specifically, and so were not effective, as pointed out by the Social Exclusion Unit (2000). The recommendations from the Social Exclusion Unit, however, do not focus on this multiplicity of factors. Instead, they suggest working with black pupils and their parents, behaviour improvement programmes and mentoring schemes (Lewis, 2000; Centre for Educational Research, 2003).

However, wider research on how groups are constructed may help us explore different reasons for disproportionate exclusions. Research shows, for example, that stereotypes of 'African Caribbean' origin boys and girls persist. Their masculinity or femininity is interpreted by (mainly) white teachers as 'sexualised' and 'aggressive' (Gillborn and Youdell, 2000). The pupils 'stand out' and innocent actions are often interpreted as hostile (Sewell, 1997). Teachers also hold poorer expectations of black students (Barn, 2001). Bangladeshi and Pakistani youth are viewed as volatile, sexist and anti-authority (Alexander, 2000).

Pupil Referral Units are disproportionately filled with young black and Asian pupils and often refugee children, invoking patterns of educationally sub-normal labelling, or the 'sin bins' of the 1970s (Coard, 1971).

Some evaluations from 1996-2000 do show decreases in permanent exclusions (Centre for Educational Research, 2003; CRE, 2004b). The reasons for this decrease are not clear-cut, however. For example, decreases could occur because of a change in local school policy brought about as a consequence of parental, press and government concern. There may be a change in attitudes between teachers and pupils and parents. On the other hand, the decrease may be related to the fact that children of African Caribbean origin are more likely to be on fixed-term exclusions or unofficially excluded, so that they do not appear in the statistics and are, instead, kept in special centres within schools (Bhavnani and Foot, 2000). The reasons for the decline have not been systematically evaluated, and this lack of understanding encourages repeating interventions that do not address the 'why' of school exclusions.

Since 2001 rates of permanent exclusions have begun to rise again, disproportionately affecting young black pupils (CRE, 2004b). This increase is being evaluated in an effort to explain the pervasive racial differences that characterise school exclusions. Research aims to investigate the historical and policy variations in regions and schools (Centre for Educational Research, 2003).

School leadership

Teachers identify school leadership and ethos as key issues in addressing racism (Powney et al, 2003). A good antiracist schooling environment is made up through a multiplicity of factors, which include strong EO policies, the involvement of pupils, staff and parents, good pastoral support, the communication of high expectations, and clear procedures for recording and acting on racist incidents (Blair et al, 1998, 2004). Such practice is not widespread. The Stephen Lawrence Inquiry recommended the recording of racist incidents in schools. While bullying has been addressed, racial reporting has not been widely taken up. The ability to report experiences in confidence is an essential prerequisite to feeling safe, and an atmosphere of well-being aids reporting.

Black community-led interventions

There has always been a strong black (and minority) educational movement. Parents have campaigned for racial justice, have set up their own schools (supplementary or Saturday schools), and continually try to raise awareness of the issues (Mirza and Reay, 2000b). A strong desire for education characterises the ethos inculcated by the energetic women who frequently run these schools. These are places of black empowerment and knowledge. The ethos is one of child–centred pedagogy and a shared inclusive curriculum, not often visible in 'mainstream' schools. Community schools such as these include those for Greek, Turkish, Muslim, Jewish, Spanish, Somali and African Caribbean communities (Kempadoo and Abdelrazak, 1999). These schools are underfunded, and in our current context, they risk being absorbed into the government's education and community engagement initiatives. This may occur because these schools are often used as after-school or homework clubs as well as places for excluded pupils.

Health and welfare

Access to health services for ethnicised groups have been influenced either by 'fixed' definitions of culture, a colour-blind approach or an approach to disadvantage which constructs the groups as 'deficient' in some way (Ahmad, 1996). A recent review of the experiences of minorities in service delivery found that groups were subject to either mono-cultural or 'colour-blind' approaches or stereotypical assumptions about how they lived (Chahal, 1999).

Cultural assumptions are sometimes made to determine what people need (Mason, 2000). Health data are informed by acknowledged and unacknowledged 'racial' presumptions, but these are presumed to be objective (Ahmad, 1996). For example, there are studies documenting specific illnesses which disproportionately affect certain groups. However, this information is incorporated into 'fixed' ideas about 'culture' and is not linked with class, gender and/or poverty.

Conclusive assumptions are made about ethnic differences found in epidemiological data. These assumptions are interpreted either as genetic or cultural risks. Socioeconomic factors do not appear to be considered, and strategies to tackle 'equal' access are therefore made on the basis of cultural difference (Nazroo, 2003). 'Cultural awareness' programmes are devised in such a way that they concentrate purely on 'difference'. The issues become reified by discussing what people wear, what food they eat, how often they pray and so on. It is assumed that all members of the group act in the same way. These 'cultural practices' of diet and eating habits, rather than poverty or lack of access to health care, are then linked to poor health (Mirza and Sheridan, 2003).

Experience of health services may also be conditioned by both cultural *and* 'racial' constructions. The Sainsbury Centre for Mental Health report (2002), *Breaking the circles of fear*, documented the over-representation of black (African Caribbean origin) people suffering from schizophrenia. This over-representation is also evident among those detained under the 1983 Mental Health Act. In London black people are over-represented by 40%. Suggested explanations for this include perceptions by staff that black men are more 'threatening', more 'dangerous' and more difficult to treat in mental health. A review of best practice in mental health for black communities found that both service users and carers felt unvalued, misunderstood and patronised (Rai-Atkins, 2002).

On the other hand, there are also indications that a colour-blind approach may dominate, and this may apply in areas where few ethnicised minorities live. An Independent Inquiry into the death of David Bennett (DH, 2003), a mental health patient, found he was subject to racist abuse and racial attacks by patients in a Norwich clinic. He died while struggling under restraint. However, the Inquiry found that his colour or experience of racism had never been overtly discussed. A doctor from the clinic did not think being the only black man on the ward could affect his mood or his aggressive behaviour. Racial abuse experienced by David Bennett had been ignored by staff. However, perhaps 'unwitting attitudes' related both to colour and a desire to 'cover up' may have been in evidence. The Inquiry found that staff had been unwilling to disclose the circumstances of David's death to his family. The police had also prevented the Health Trust telling David's family until the next morning. This single Inquiry may have wider implications. For example, Rai-Atkins (2002) found that the advocacy services of black and minority ethnic mental health users were undeveloped and their needs often overlooked.

Some interventions in the health and welfare sector services encourage inclusion by targeting those considered disadvantaged. This fits into government strategies to stem social exclusion. 'Race' has been considered as an afterthought in measures to tackle exclusion (Bhavnani, 2001). For example, the Sure Start programme which aims to engage mothers in healthcare and education for themselves and their children was 'colour-blind' when first introduced, but included 'race' later by producing separate guidance on involving minority ethnic children and families. The resulting guidance gives examples of projects which encourage access to learning. Initiatives aimed at Travellers are included, whereby parents are shown the benefits of pre-school activities and games.

Other Sure Start strategies include projects where bilingual workers work with some groups to build confidence in women. There is one example of a project in Nottingham, termed 'antiracism', which aims to build and empower Caribbean communities to protect children from violence. In Camden a variety of minority ethnic and refugee communities are targeted for antenatal care, for example, supporting young parents from Bangladeshi families. There are also initiatives which encourage capacity building for women to enable them to participate in the labour market. These projects may be important for tackling exclusion, but these interventions are targeted at racialised groups and do not appear to include tackling the racism of other parents, children, or even Sure Start workers. It is debatable as to whether these projects can be designated antiracist. Strategies on 'inclusion' in this sector ignore the dominant majority and their related attitudes and behaviour.

Racism in the criminal justice system

Discrimination in the criminal justice system was particularly highlighted in the 1980s. The Scarman Report (1981) documented the overrepresentation of black people in prisons. Ethnic monitoring, 'race' awareness training and the appointment of 'race' relations officers were all adopted as key interventions for the criminal justice services. Even though the 1976 Race Relations Act was not extended to criminal justice by successive governments, in 1991 the Criminal Justice Act had a clause inserted agreeing for annual information about possible discrimination to be made public (Faulkner, 2004).

Monitoring and training appear to be the key interventions in relation to the presence of racism in the police force and in the wider criminal justice system.

Police

'Race' and diversity training has been a central strategy for challenging racism since the 1999 Macpherson Inquiry exposed the deep-rooted racist culture in the police service. However, these schemes have not been evaluated systematically and where they have, are shown to be ineffective (see Bhavnani, 2001; Tackey et al, 2001). A recent report for the Metropolitan Police Authority showed that many senior police officers thought the emphasis on 'race' in the organisation was overdone. The response to training was hostile and made officers defensive. Police officers themselves did not feel it led to any changes in behaviour. They felt easier with cross-cultural traditions and differences (Metropolitan Police Authority, 2003). No evidence was found that either monitoring or training interventions benefited the community, since they experienced no difference to Stop and Search procedures. Stop and Search continues to disproportionately affect racialised groups, particularly African Caribbean young men (Ghaffur, 2004). The Metropolitan Police Authority research with focus groups of minorities showed they felt stereotyped, particularly if they were in an ethnicised area. Police officers, on the other hand, wanted to drop the term 'institutional racism' which was used by the Macpherson report to describe the way they operated (Metropolitan Police Authority, 2003).

Prisons and custody

Within the Crown Prosecution Service recent evidence found that prosecutors did not monitor racial aggravation incidents even when the evidence was overwhelming (Gus John Partnership, 2003). Non-custodial approaches show that sentencing is different for black and white defendants, and racial discrimination is involved in the ways young African Caribbean origin males are treated. This is because they are more likely to be referred to Crown Court, where sentencing is higher. It is argued that African Caribbean origin males and females are over-represented in prisons, and treatment in prisons has been found to be discriminatory.

One third of black inmates reported racial attacks and felt unfairly treated in disciplinary procedures (Denney, 1997). A later report by NACRO (2000) assessed progress in the prison service. In 1995, the CRE and the Prison Service published joint research on 'race' relations in seven prisons. The study found that although 'race' relations management teams were in place, there were variations in how often they met and in their effectiveness. Ethnic monitoring systems were in place but were not always used effectively. Communicating policy to staff had a low profile, and there was a low rate of reporting of racist incidents compared to their incidence. Responses to these incidents were ineffective, despite the fact that monitoring began in 1981, almost 15 years earlier. Over half of the black prisoners, for example, reported racial victimisation by staff. A further snapshot survey of prisons and 'race' by NACRO (2000) concluded that racist incidents were just as common as they were 20 years ago. They were just as rarely reported or acted upon. However, there was a mismatch between what staff thought and what prisoners thought. For example, only 20% of prisoners thought that 'race' relations were good compared to 47% of staff.

Crown Prosecution Service

In the Crown Prosecution Service, evidence of racial bias was found in many stages of prosecution, including plea bargaining and choosing jury trial (Gus John Partnership, 2003). The qualitative analysis of written materials showed that the police found it almost impossible to acknowledge racial aggravation in criminal offences even when there was clear evidence. This was amplified by the Crown Prosecution Service. The police accepted a lesser charge on plea bargaining, and the Crown Prosecution Service downgraded these offences.

Recent research shows that professional interventions here have also mostly failed. Denney (1997) argues that this is because of a failure to be clear about goals and a tradition in interventions in concentrating on *changing the historically disadvantaged groups themselves.* The complexity of 'race', gender, class and age is not often examined. In fact, antiracism has not been used in making interventions in the criminal justice system. Lastly, racial bias exists, but complaints against the professional groups in criminal justice have traditionally been handled from within the professional group either inside the police, within probation or within the prison service. Independent handling of complaints might, in fact, reveal racial bias. The inquiry into the death of Zaheed Mubarak (a young Asian man killed by his racist cellmate) suggests that prison officers were culpable, purposely putting the two young men together to see the outcome.

Arts, leisure and sport

The arts, leisure and sport area is wide ranging and encompasses the following: equality of access of audiences to performances and events, participation in arts and leisure activities locally and nationally, as well as tackling inclusion through one-off or short-term specific arts or sports projects. Treating ethnicised groups differently is also part of the arts approach to tackling racism and equality. These arts interventions on difference are discussed in the next chapter on multicultural interventions.

Arts

Initiatives in the arts are overseen and encouraged by the Arts Council. Up until 1994, arts in Britain defined interventions in relation to the monitoring of numbers of ethnic minorities and their representations as audiences and performers in Britain. In 1998 the Arts Council reports admit that 'diversity' is not about focusing on problematic and marginalised groups, but structures and institutions that have a tendency to marginalise individuals and groups. At the same time they have also targeted the capacity building of community-based organisations and the resourcing of black arts. The Arts Council Diversity Plan argues that access to the arts is dogged by historic issues and attitudes that are entrenched in social practices (Khan, 2002). The Arts Council have began to unravel the misconceptions around the concept of cultural diversity and decided to demonstrate nationally and internationally the *strengths* of a diverse society.

The Arts Council has thus set up a New Audiences Programme and has targeted funding for black and minority ethnic capital projects. These projects have been evaluated, and audiences' access to mainstream theatre has increased (Khan, 2002). They have made appointments of black and minority ethnic people at a senior level, and these ambassadors represent a new face of Britain with connections overseas. They are used in forums in reinterpreting/re-representing British heritage. The initiatives involve the allocation of resources and a determination to work in real partnership with groups (Khan, 2002). 'Diversify' is one example of a project which aims to build capacity in the sector. Postgraduate training for young black and minority ethnic people is funded, the rationale being the need to break the cycle of closed networks in the arts world. Vocational areas include curators, or senior managers in museums, libraries or archives (see Appendix A (3) 'Arts Council').

The interventions described here are interesting because they focus on changing the image of Britain, encouraging new audiences into the mainstream, as well as resourcing the access of black and minority ethnic performers and artists into the arts. They have engaged with the multiplicity of factors which perpetuate racism, as well as deal with effects.

Black artists are also slowly being included in prestigious prizes (for example, Booker or Turner Prizes). We cannot do justice here to the wealth of art and achievement contributed to British society by black theatre, musicians, painters and novelists, and of course there is no way of empirically assessing if these interventions have made a difference to tackling racism. Undoubtedly being exposed to black artists of all descriptions has encouraged an understanding of the wide range of talent and potential in Britain, and has helped social cohesion.

Sport and leisure

Sport England has written up a series of case studies across the country that encourages participation in sport. These have been creative in including the racialised groups who have been excluded in football and cricket (Sport England, 2002). Sport access for girls and older people is also particularly emphasised. This is effective in helping access, but we do not know if it tackles the causes of racism.

One project on football racism is perhaps exceptional here (Bradbury, 2001). It has attempted to tackle racism in a local area, by both supporting black people, but also trying to create better interaction between groups. Project organisers discovered that local minority residents were fearful because they regularly experienced racial abuse, harassment and victimisation by white football supporters. Professional clubs, they found, had been unable to connect with minority ethnic communities because of their concerns over community safety and spectating. These communities were also not being employed by the clubs. Thus many members of these groups had become marginalised.

They had clear aims and objectives, and they encouraged the participation of minority youth through specialised coaching, which eventually led to the creation of a team. They used articles and announcements in the football press and magazines to convey important messages about racism. They liaised successfully with the police with regard to community safety, and they set up a team club of mixed racial origins, including white participants.

The evaluation of the project attributes the reduction of racial chanting to their interventions. Anecdotally, it is argued, black and minority fans feel safer and feel less excluded. Project coordinators have also set up a black footballers exhibition, developed various initiatives for local schools, and used plays and theatre as well as 'chant it' poetry to get messages across. This project in Sheffield was seen as good practice by the national initiative of 'Kick it Out' (see Appendix A (10), 'Football – Sheffield'). They also organised a Community Day. A by-product of this was that white fans who were not connected to the different ethnic minority groups attending, turned up, and enjoyed themselves.

Social capital, 'race' and ethnicity

Social capital has been seen as a recent intervention in tackling exclusion and encouraging equality of access to employment and services. The concept has been championed by the Prime Minister's Strategy Unit (Strategy Unit, 2003; Halpern, 2004) and has been influenced by Putnam's seminal book, *Bowling alone* (Putnam, 2000). The book argues that there is an increasing lack of trust and social engagement in American society. Social capital is a wide-ranging multi-level concept, which includes social relationships at the local level (for example, neighbourliness and involvement in local voluntary organisations and civic engagement) as well as engagement, access and participation in wider societal institutions. It is measured by surveys that ask people to discuss the levels of trust they have in other people at local, regional and national level (Runnymede Trust, 2004).

Linking social capital to 'ethnicity'

Research suggests that while social capital, as measured on these criteria, is in decline for the working classes, it is *not* declining for the middle classes (Duffy, 2004). So what is the relationship between the use of the concept of social capital for 'race' and ethnicity?

It has been argued that 'ethnic' minorities may lack contacts or networks with the wider community for access to networks about jobs and opportunities. It has been found, for example, that African Caribbean groups are much less likely to know their neighbours than white people. Organisations that have involved more diverse memberships including contact with different ethnicities and origins are seen to stimulate higher levels of trust than those that consist of homogeneous groups (Performance and Innovation Unit, 2002). The findings on differences between groups on trust in British institutions (see above) are also relevant for those wishing to use the term. Asian and African Caribbean origin groups have reportedly much lower levels of trust in institutions than their white counterparts (Runnymede Conference, 2004).

Research findings also include the fact that the more 'ethnic' diversity there is in a local area, the more there is dissatisfaction with services. Exploring ethnic groups' access to services such as health, housing, education, justice and welfare, it becomes clear that it is not so much their lack of civic engagement that explains their disadvantage but the way in which they are treated and perceived. Access to services such as health and welfare are hindered by perceptions, for example, that assume that 'ethnic' minorities may lack contacts or networks with the wider community or have lower levels of 'trust' and are less integrated into the social fabric of society. Thus interventions are nearly always aimed at training to 'understand difference', or develop cultural and familial competency, or monitor access and enhance communication.

It has been argued that the 'underclass theory' of urban decay and ghetto cultures of poverty are covertly reworked in our contemporary discourses of social exclusion and social capital (Byrne, 2000). Contemporary preoccupations with black masculinity, gun and gang violence, single-parent families, black underachievement, deficient mothering and poor parenting, and 'backward' cultural practices such as wearing of the hijab or forced marriages are seen as 'everyday' characteristics that lock certain black and minority communities into their own patterns of social exclusion (Wilson, 1987, 2003). Thus, lack of social capital becomes an explanation for the continued poverty and inequality of some communities.

Using social capital to define social policy

The breadth of the concept makes it impossible to define tightly. Some argue that the concept is worthless because it ranges over everything in society and thus should be rejected (Fine, 2002). By using the concept so widely, Fine argues, it functions to obliterate difference and is a panacea for poor people. Social policies (aimed at working-class communities) can thus use the concept of social capital to intervene on any pretext. The concept, Fine argues, is silent on power and inequality, and concentrates on 'social' questions, ignoring economic ones.

It may be that the concept is too problematic and should be discarded. But its use is growing in government, and its meanings have to be revealed. In discussing the role of the state in social capital at the local level, many policy initiatives appear to be aimed at *preventing* the exclusion of poor people and the working classes. They represent a way of re-discussing concepts of 'disadvantage' and *access* to resources and services, so that new social policy can once more 'manufacture consensus'. The use of the concept, then, may currently be particularly pertinent. Recent years have witnessed a growing mix of providers of services at a local level, fuelled by global change and the decline of the welfare state. These shifts are leading to a more differentiated form of social policy and a restructuring of how welfare is organised and delivered. Across Europe, a mixed economy of welfare is apparent now with a shifting emphasis away from the state to private, voluntary and informal provision (Johnson, 1998). This has implications for those deemed to have less social capital to access services and resources.

The black voluntary sector and capacity building

Social capital is central to the government's vision for 'civil renewal' (Blunkett, 2003). The Active Communities Directorate in the Home Office sees capacity building through neighbourliness, involvement in local voluntary organisations and civic engagement and citizenship as crucial in tackling social exclusion.

The concept of social capital is also being utilised to address exclusion by local non-government providers of services. For example, the Welsh Assembly has encouraged minority ethnic engagement with decision-making by using the concept of social capital to mean exclusion from political participation (Fevre, 2004). The black voluntary sector has grown substantially in recent years, with upwards of 700 'black' non-governmental organisations in Leicester and 3,000 in London, but it is viewed primarily as a service deliverer, rather than one that contributes to civic engagement (Chouhan and Lusane, 2004). Research has been funded into the contribution of the voluntary sector to inclusion strategies in a London borough (Lees et al, 2003). Key policy think-tanks as well as the Home Office have been concerned with strengthening the black voluntary sector (Home Office, 1999; McLeod et al, 2001).

However, the levels of civic engagement among the black and minority ethnic communities are high (Foster, 1997; Pharoah and Smerdon, 1998). While members of these communities are very ready to volunteer, they are rarely found in more prestigious visible public service, but in the informal grassroots organisations connected to church, community and caring networks. Black women's organisations are vibrant and underpin community cohesion at the local level (Sudbury, 1998; Mirza and Reay, 2000b; Davis and Cooke, 2002). This commandeering of feminised cultural and social capital is rarely acknowledged in the social exclusion debates.

The voluntary sector in local authority areas has also become important and vocal due to the recognition that this sector is increasingly providing services, which previously would have been delivered by the council. Funding to the voluntary sector is now increasingly service-led (Bhavnani and Foot, 2000). Luncheon clubs, preventative healthcare, counselling, enhancing safety, monitoring racial harassment, providing English classes as well as a variety of community events are just some of the activities in which they are involved (Lees et al, 2003). These activities have proved effective in enhancing equality of access to a variety of services and events that have reduced exclusion (Lees et al, 2003). For example, there have been initiatives to help ethnic minority children at risk of abuse (Roshni, 2004), and a variety of domestic violence projects for girls and women (Gupta, 2003). The use of the concept of social capital, then, may be used to encourage racialised matching of services to residents. It may also be used to encourage political participation.

There is also some indication, however, that councils may not be acting in a reciprocal way towards the black voluntary sector. Councils themselves may be partly responsible for these declining levels of trust. A recent audit for a London borough revealed that voluntary organisations did not feel equity in partnership; they felt that they were regarded with mistrust, as potentially corrupt and incompetent. The council's intervention to check if the voluntary organisation was monitoring ethnicity was perceived as harsh, nit picking, controlling and insensitive (Bhavnani and Foot, 2000). These latter views were not seen to apply to white-dominated organisations, and therefore were construed as racist. The council, on the other hand, perceived that they had made great efforts to involve and fund this sector.

Unlike mainstream voluntary organisations, however, this sector also has another role, by acting as advocates and representatives of the black community. For example, Operation Black Vote (www.obv.org.uk) aims to raise awareness of wider political issues among the black community. Interventions that ensure under-implementation of racial justice come from within the minority ethnic communities. For example, the Joseph Rowntree West Yorkshire Racial Justice Programme works with local community groups, enabling them to seek funding and to develop their own needs as they see fit (see Crosskill, 1997; Williams and Ali, 1999).

The black voluntary sector has become increasingly important in consultation exercises to encourage participation in decision making in, for example, health, and education, and will become even more so given the requirement to consult in the 2000 Race Relations (Amendment) Act. A recent review of 'race' equality by the Office of the Deputy Prime Minister shows that in consultation exercises local authorities did provide information in various formats, but no constructive engagement took place (ODPM, 2003). An ESRC-funded project which is concerned with the involvement of under-represented groups in the Welsh Assembly found that the composition of the black and minority ethnic sector involved primarily those who were well-educated and middle class (Fevre, 2004).

The Audit Commission report on 'race' equality also highlighted that black and minority residents felt there was poor feedback and communication from the council, which was often accompanied by slow responses to their requests for change (2003). By co-opting organisations to be formally consulted in town halls, or to deliver services, the function of their campaigning or advocacy roles may diminish. This situation needs constant monitoring.

Interventions regarding funding and resources are important if racism is to be tackled through engaging the black community. For the black voluntary sector to build capacity it needs resources, but the regional devolvement of funding means less access and more competition for limited pots of money (Grant, 2004). Umbrella organisations such as the Council for Ethnic Minority Voluntary Organisations (CEMVO) campaign for a more cohesive funding strategy for the black voluntary sector.

Conclusion

- Social policy has encouraged 'equal' access to services, and interventions have been introduced in order that barriers to access are removed. In examining the review of studies across a wide range of sites in the public sector, it can be concluded that most 'access' interventions do not address the causes and perpetuation of racism.
- There have been exceptions to this. In education, there have been several initiatives on teaching about racism to teachers and pupils, and in the arts, several initiatives have attempted to challenge traditional images of who *represents* the arts in Britain. There are also the beginnings of antiracist work with perpetrators of racial harassment, and there have been interesting evaluated projects on racism in football. Furthermore, social movements in the black communities on education and the provision of voluntary sector-led services to challenge racism in mainstream institutions are also in evidence.
- However, research on the effectiveness of these interventions in most service provision is sadly lacking, with the few exceptions discussed above. Many other services examined, via public inquiries and academic studies, in the areas of education, housing, arts and leisure, health and the criminal justice system continue to show varying degrees of racism. Some interventions ignore racism completely in a 'colour-blind' approach; others focus on the racialised

groups themselves as needing to change, while the rest automatically assume a singular focus on 'cultural' or 'racial' explanations for complex social problems of disadvantage and poverty.

- It may be that the separation of the causes of racism from the dominant discourse on interventions in social policy is part of the problem. Dominant discourses such as 'social capital' stress equality of access and stemming social exclusion. In the absence of data on the effectiveness of these 'access' interventions, coupled with the continued evidence of racism in various services, it is hypothesised that these interventions deal, in a highly variable manner, with the *effects* of racism, rather than the *causes*.

EIGHT

Multicultural interventions

This chapter explores multicultural or difference interventions and their usefulness in tackling racism. National policy has also implemented interventions based on ethnic or 'racialised' difference side by side with notions of equality of opportunity. We will term these 'multicultural' interventions.

There is a deep ambivalence to, as well as a variety of interpretations of, 'multicultural' interventions (Hall, 2001). Some interventions, for example, could be construed as entrenching segregation and artificially separating 'racialised' groups. Others could be interpreted as providing different services for differing groups, since 'one size does not fit all'. The latter interpretation could legitimately apply to the setting up of interventions in translation or interpreting services, or understanding and respecting that differing groups observe their religions on different days and in different ways. These differences, then, need to be taken into consideration within schools, workplaces or other centres providing services.

On the other hand, by only examining 'difference' between and among communities against a narrow definition of culture, 'culture' can become 'fixed' and interpreted as unable to change. Relationships between differing ethnic cultures in Britain are always subject to change and influence, whether within the broad category of black (for example, Somali, Ghanaian, Barbadian) or Asian (for example, Gujarati, Turkish) or within the broad category white (for example, Geordie, Irish, Cornish, Lancastrian, Welsh, orthodox Jews, reformed Jews). Differing alliances may be made across groups, based not only on colour, but cross-cutting identities, such as motherhood, job seeker, privately or publicly educated and so on. Multiple identities exist for people all at the same time, and it is difficult to separate one from the other in all contexts (see Chapter Four). At the same time, some ethnicised groups have also stepped up their demands for 'separate' treatment and 'separate' provision.

These differing interpretations and ensuing ambivalences characterise interventions based on 'cultural' difference. Interventions and their rationales remain subject to contestation.

The rise and fall of multiculturalism

Multiculturalism in its many forms has had a long and troubled history in Britain (Hall, 2000). In the 1960s and 1970s there was a policy emphasis on the *assimilation* of racialised groups into existing society, but 'culture' was always present, seen to be 'disruptive' of a stable national identity (Lewis, 2000). These initiatives were closely followed by discourses on *integration*. It was argued that one way to foster good 'race' relations was to learn about 'other' cultures and to ensure all children learned about them too. This type of multiculturalism has been categorised as *strong multiculturalism*, ways in which 'other cultures' can be accorded recognition and respect (Harris, 2001).

However, the kinds of interventions in this 'strong' multiculturalism were hotly debated at the time. The 'left' argued that understanding the 'other' or black cultures did not tackle the power relations of racism. This 'saris, steel bands and samosas' approach led to an 'exoticisation' of black cultures, which left the 'white' cultures unexplored and untouched. The 'right' argued that it was important to keep 'cultures' distinct and campaigned for this (Ratcliffe, 2004). Many different arguments were used to argue for keeping 'cultures' or religions distinct and 'authentic' (Sahgal and Yuval-Davis, 1992).

Multiculturalism suffered a demise and was replaced by municipal antiracism in the 1980s and 1990s (Gilroy, 1992). After the backlash on racism awareness training and antiracism units in the 1990s, several discursive shifts took place that brought cultural diversity back into the limelight.

First, disappointment about EO policies, together with demographic forces, shifted the discourse towards 'diversity' policies. Business reasons were now argued as being critical to embrace difference, and hence multiculturalism. This has been termed *demographic multiculturalism* (Harris, 2001). Its equivalent is 'diversity' in employment policies.

Second, the publication of the Runnymede Trust report on the future of multiethnic Britain (Runnymede Trust, 2000) brought cultural differences and the role of the state centre stage. It put forward the idea of cultural pluralism. Lord Parekh's views on creating both a 'community of communities', while also aiming for *social* cohesion led to a major debate in the press about Britishness and national identity (McLaughlin and Neal, 2004).

In 2000 the moral panic about asylum seekers added to the confusion and debates about the nation state, both within Europe and around the globe. The disturbances in the northern towns in 2001, and the White Paper *Safe havens, secure borders* continued to conflate immigration with 'race' and cultural difference (see Chapter Five). Recommendations on cultural pluralism and integration (often seen as the same), came to be viewed side by side with notions of equality of opportunity.

Research discourse also highlighted the increasing diversity among Britain's racialised populations of colour. While it was accepted that racialised minorities shared experiences of racialised exclusion, evidence showed a wide complexity of experiences and a growing internal diversity within and between groups (Modood et al, 1997; Runnymede Trust, 2000). Historical experience of racialised exclusion and labour market segregation encouraged racialised groups to identify with the idea of a 'secure' ethnicity. The lack of political will to tackle racism encouraged racialised groups to look inwards into themselves, and to search for certainty in their 'culture'.

These 'ethnicised' differences have been legitimised in the interpretation of the 2000 Race Relations (Amendment) Act with its focus on racial data collection as a means of monitoring racism. The aftermath of September 11th, together with the incorporation of religion into human rights discourse, has also led to the targeting of interventions aimed at 'Muslims' (Commissions and Forums on Islamophobia, 2004) .

As we have discussed in the previous chapter, the multiculturalist formula of 'celebrating difference' (in a marginalised kind of a way) is now replaced by the concept of 'community cohesion'. Instead of celebrating difference, and discussing the 'vibrancy' of other cultures, we are confronted with the fact that certain groups are now 'too different' and prone to 'self-segregation'. Dominant policy emphasis is now on their need to be 'assimilated' through citizenship and engagement (Back et al, 2002).

These divisions have increased the prevalence of professional interventions on intercultural understanding. In this chapter we explore the impact these interventions have had in combating racism.

Multicultural interventions

Recent multicultural interventions based on difference have included a variety of 'institutionalised' initiatives within government, such as separate faith schools, heritage projects, the setting up of translation and interpreting services for those who do not speak English, as well as the marketing of products to specific groups.

Policies in Northern Ireland, as well as those originating from policy on community cohesion, have led to what we term interventions based on *intercultural* understanding. Some projects with young people have used conflict resolution to encourage deeper understanding. We consider these in turn. All these interventions are imbued with the differing and contested interpretations of multiculturalism.

Faith schools

The case for faith schools could be legitimately argued for as an intervention in valuing other cultures, in 'strong multiculturalism' or even under the concept of cultural pluralism (a 'community of communities'; see Runnymede Trust, 2000). On the other hand, recent research has indicated that segregated schools can breed intolerance (Burgess and Wilson, 2004). Clearly there has to be a distinction between faith schools where parents 'choose' a certain faith-based education and one where parents have no choice, if, for example, the local school is in an area which is racialised, segregated and with poor housing. The only alternative for a decent education may be to attend a faith-based school. However, it can be argued that racialised faith schools are also a response by some community leaders to the marginalisation or absence of the understanding of all 'cultural traditions' in state schools, police inaction on racial harassment, or living in poorly resourced areas. The complicated reasons for parents choosing, or not choosing, 'faith' schools have, unfortunately, been simplified by government.

For example, Tony Blair is argued to be a great enthusiast for faith schools (Woodward, 2001). The fact that there were state-sponsored Catholic, Church of England (in total for both almost 7,000) and Jewish schools (5), whereas Muslims were refused them initially, added to lobbying pressure in the light of the rise of 'ethnicisation' described above. The Secretary of State for Education and Employment accepted applications for Muslim schools in Birmingham, Brent and London for grant-maintained status with public funding (Carvel, 1998; Mac an Ghaill, 1999). In the state-sponsored sector there are now four Muslim, two Sikh and one Hindu school as well as one for Seventh Day Adventists. Faith schools could be interpreted as 'gift giving' to racialised communities. The policy may be an easy way out of lobby pressure, and may suit the needs of government. On the other hand, they could also be interpreted as the government's espousing of multiculturalism.

Why, then, have faith schools been legitimated? Some commentators (see, for example, Woodward, 2001), have argued that the increased granting of state sponsorship to faith schools is related to the Prime Minister's own beliefs in faith-based education, coupled with a pragmatic desire to encourage them as a result of their assumed higher achievement levels. Attainment levels are supposed to be better than in non-faith schools, making the idea more attractive to a government interested in providing 'choice' as well as setting targets for attainment improvements. On the other hand, higher achievement levels could be explained by admitting fewer children with special needs and from poorer backgrounds. Figures show 17.6% of primary age children overall are entitled to free school meals, but this figure is lower in Catholic schools (16%), Church of England schools (11%), Sikh schools (5.6%), and Jewish schools (4%) (Woodward, 2001).

Some feminists, for example, might also argue that faith-based schools could legitimate women's subordination (Sahgal and Yuval-Davis, 1992). The London-based organisation, Women Against Fundamentalisms (www.waf.gn.apc.org), argues for the development of an antiracist approach rather than a multicultural educational policy to address the inequalities of power that exist between groups. The struggles by Muslim girls (Haw, 1998) to decide where, and for how long they attend school can be interpreted as struggles against religious and cultural control. On the other hand, the assertion by the girls that they want to wear the hijab in schools as an independent religious choice could also be interpreted as a response to racism and the inferiorisation of their cultures (Dwyer, 1999; Timmerman, 2000).

Whatever the ultimate conclusion, research on the effects of faith-based schools is much needed. These religious schools may entrench intolerance, or they may reduce it. So far, in terms of an antiracist initiative aimed at reducing racism in schools, there have been no conclusive findings as to their positive or negative benefits.

Heritage resources and multicultural arts

Various resources on history and heritage have constituted important interventions in 'strong' multiculturalism. These resources can provide alternative ways of viewing history. They can affect attitudes towards 'differing' groups and peoples. The following are examples of these types of interventions.

The reports *Holding up the mirror* (London Museums Agency, 2003) and *Delivering shared heritage* (GLA, 2005) document the range and diversity of projects in Britain. A total of 30 museums, archives and libraries provided digital versions of items from their original collections. The National Archives 'Moving Here' project documents everyday stories and memorabilia. It ranges over how and why immigrants arrived in Britain over the last 200 years. It lays particular emphasis on Caribbean, Jewish, Irish and South Asian communities. This archive is funded by the Heritage Lotteries Fund. There is also a Black Cultural Archive, the Runnymede Collection, the Future Histories project and the Bernie Grant Collection, affiliated to Middlesex University. The latter holds collections of multicultural postwar history and artefacts related to theatre, dance, political activism and social history. Black History Month targeted particularly at schools across the UK, but also at the general population, has become an annual October event (www.realhistories.org.uk). Unlike the US where Black History Month has been supported by state funding, the British event has been poorly resourced and haphazardly organised (Morris, 2004).

British heritage is being reinterpreted and contested. We have seen the development of a Museum of Empire and Commonwealth in Bristol and the small-scale Museum of Immigration and Diversity in the East End (not always open). Arts Councils have also formed partnerships with refugee organisations and encouraged refugee arts work across the country. There is also a Commission on African and Asian heritage funded by the Greater London Authority. The Commission lobbies for an equitable and visible representation of black and minority ethnic contributions to London's development as a multicultural city (GLA, 2005). High profile projects such as 'Africa 2005', which celebrate the contribution of African art and culture, are important statements on the African presence now and historically in relation to Britain. However, how do we measure its impact on challenging ethnocentric perspectives within the large national museums and galleries where many African artefacts are kept?

The Heritage Lotteries Fund in conjunction with the Victoria and Albert Museum supported a series of events celebrating Sikh Arts across four cities with high proportions of Asian origin residents. Again we do not know the impact of these initiatives in terms of challenging racism experienced by Asian communities in Britain. However, many of these initiatives are few and far between. A search of the Heritage Lottery site for multicultural projects revealed six out of the hundreds that have been funded under the category 'multicultural'. The search for projects on racism revealed none. A national scheme to celebrate and encourage young people to celebrate their heritage, 'Young Roots' was launched in 2002. Out of the total 240 projects funded in the first year, the numbers allocated to multicultural initiatives are not available.

One-off events in the arts include, for example, organising

multicultural festivals and football tournaments in response to concerns about the stigmatisation of refugees. For example, arts organisations have worked with Refugee Action. Others work to counter stigma, using drama with children and young people. Eastside Arts and the Refugee Council organised poetry and performance sessions for 7- to 14-year-olds in Tower Hamlets, London, to encourage thinking about what it means to be a refugee. A similar project in Derby simulated refugee experiences with children in a local school. These one-off events are important interventions in tackling hostility exacerbated by the media and politicians. Their aim is to encourage children to empathise with an experience with which they may have no direct knowledge. These initiatives may or may not have long-term positive benefits, since data is not available. Research on stereotyping suggests that these experiences need to be sustained and reinforced in a variety of educational situations (Richardson, 2004).

Other annual festivals such as the Mela in Bradford, the Notting Hill Carnival and Respect in London and the St Paul's Carnival in Bristol are examples of ongoing interventions in the arts. Most are organised by 'racialised' groups, with funding provided nationally or locally. These festivals may make a difference in bringing groups together and encouraging understanding. There is, however, no research evidence of their effects in combating racism, either way.

Translation and interpreting

Various organisations in the public sector have set up translation and interpreting services. A Home Office research paper maps the provision of interpreting and translation services across five local authorities (Turton et al, 2003). Of course it is as well to remember that 307 languages, for example, are spoken in London and there are many regional dialects, so comprehensive provision in certain areas is clearly difficult. But the problem of interpreting appears to be one of a non-recognition of needs in translation and interpreting; the needs of users are not only unmet but undetected (EITI, 2002: eiti.com/latest news). When exploring access to English provision, it may be important to remember that women may be unwilling to learn it because they either perceive no need to learn English and/or because male members of their families take over to retain control (Audit Commission, 2003). The Audit Commission report reminds us of the lack of resources devoted to these services. In the area of health and ethnicity it has also been argued that provision for translation, advocacy and interpreting services are poorly developed (Johnson, 1998).

A review of translation, interpreting and communication services in the public sector in Scotland found little change in the provision of such services since the 1990s, despite numerous critical reviews. Implementation of policy and guidelines is poor. Failure to recognise the skills developed by a variety of translators and interpreters has led to low pay rates, limited training opportunities and difficulties in recruitment and retention. Ad hoc practices involving bilingual children and friends are commonplace, reflecting widespread attitudes that 'even a child can do it' (McPake et al, 2001).

Communication in a language other than English needs to take account of other factors. Users express the need for better personal understanding, patience and respect, rather than a 'pure' emphasis on the provision of technical expertise in the language.

Private sector products and services

Patterns of consumption have changed due to globalisation. The flexibility offered by new technology and the ability to develop new products rapidly has opened up new markets. Consumers are arguably better informed about products and services, and are able to demand them. This meshing of supply and demand has encouraged 'boutique' multiculturalism, the marketing of products to specific groups, as well as the wider society (Harris, 2001).

Specific minority groups have been targeted because they have increased spending power, such as the Jaguar sponsorship of the Asian Mela in Bradford. HSBC is the first bank to offer Islamic financial products. These products are offered since they do not conflict with aspects of the Muslim faith, such as the repaying of mortgages. The presence of two million Muslims helped drive this change. Similarly the Legal Action Group has developed a course to help practitioners identify Islamic matrimonial rights and ways of securing these under English law.

These examples of private sector interventions represent important initiatives in the provision of services, given the debates above about our diverse society. 'One size does not fit all.' As with other multicultural interventions, it is difficult to conclude either way that these initiatives have or have not made a dent in the causes of racism. Certainly, the sponsorship or development of certain products by large corporations ensures that the debate on racism, cultures and differences remains on the wider corporate agenda.

Community cohesion

On 11 December 2001, the government published a policy report of the Ministerial Group on Public Order and Community Cohesion entitled *Building cohesive communities*. This Ministerial Group was set up in response to a summer of 'disturbances' or 'riots' in the northern towns of England. The report identified the key factors or causes responsible for the summer disturbances:

> A lack of a strong civic identity; fragmentation and polarisation of communities based on economic, geographical racial and cultural lines; disengagement of young people from the local decision making process; intergenerational tensions; an increasingly territorial mentality in asserting different identities; weak community political leadership; inadequate provision of youth facilities; high levels of unemployment; activities of extremist groups; weaknesses in the police response to community issues particularly racial incidents and irresponsible coverage of 'race' stories by sections of the local media. (Home Office, 2001a, p 11)

Reports pertaining to the localities of Bradford, Burnley and Oldham, with associations independent of government followed (see Ouseley, 2001). The Cantle Report (Home Office, 2001b), a report of the independent review team appointed by ministers, identified the national themes emerging from localities. Following a variety of conferences to discuss the emerging policy agenda on cohesion the Home Office published a consultation document on community cohesion and 'race' equality called *Strength in diversity* in 2004. The outcome is the government's new strategy that focuses not just on community cohesion but also links the concept to 'race and faith' (Home Office, 2005).

The concept of community cohesion

The current government use of the phrase *community cohesion* in the British context originates partly with the urban disturbances in the North of England in 2001. The term 'community' has been highly theorised in political discourse, but under New Labour it has been used as a bridge between notions of citizenship and notions of criminality to 'cohere' nationhood at a local level, and exclude those who cannot be conceived of as 'active' citizens (Burnett, 2004). What is more, the importance of the government's approach to community cohesion was to reduce 'community' tensions, implying the causes lay with young working-class men, of white and of Asian origin.

The term 'cohesion' itself was used together with concepts of equality and difference in the Runnymede-inspired Parekh report on the future of multiethnic Britain, published in 2000. Here the term 'cohesion' was designated to refer to 'social' cohesion or how Britain could become a more cohesive political community, given its diverse regional, ethnic, national, religious and other communities. The authors came down firmly on the side of common values and equal citizenship rights as a necessary basis for social cohesion, but went further to argue for a need to re-conceptualise 'common belonging' and what that means in terms of identity for a multiethnic Britain.

It is now being argued that religion and faith are becoming the new axis for the articulation of the new racism, superseding culture and ethnicity which was dominant in the 1980s and 1990s (Modood, 2005). Community cohesion, with its emphasis on 'one nation' (Ratcliffe, 2004), demonstrates a move away from multiculturalism toward monoculturalism and cultural homogenisation. In the climate of increased global insecurity and the heightened media fear of Islamic extremism there has been a resurgence of 1960s' assimilationism, as witnessed in anti-immigration and security laws, citizenship tests, compulsory English language tests, and codes of conduct for trustees of mosques (Back et al, 2002; Fekete, 2004b).

Debates on community cohesion

Community cohesion has gained increasing importance and is being much debated. It is argued that the concept is particularly important for legitimating the link between citizenship and nationhood (Burnett, 2004). Others focus on the fact that issues of industrial decline and deprivation across both white and Asian communities have been sidelined when using the concept (McGhee, 2003; Burnett, 2004; Ray and Smith, 2004). Yet other authors have highlighted the fact that Asian youth, rather than white young men, bore the brunt of demonisation and stigmatisation by a hysterical media in the aftermath of the 'disturbances' in the northern towns in 2001 (Kalra, 2003). It is the 'Asian community' that are seen as insular and inward looking, encouraging a construction of criminalisation (Burnett, 2004; Ray and Smith, 2004). This community was beset by intergenerational conflict, with the 'elders' disapproving of the violence, yet similar interpretations which could be made of the white community were ignored (Burnett, 2004). Others have argued that the concept of community cohesion defined agendas for policing in particular areas, while inverting the usual relationship between victim and perpetrator of racial violence (Ray and Smith, 2004).

In the aftermath of the disturbances in the northern towns, problems of community cohesion were also defined by large sections of the media and others as *self-segregation* of ethnicised communities, not ones forced on people because of racial harassment and fear (Webster, 2003; Burnett, 2004).

> There is clear evidence however, that concentrations of people from one ethnic background in certain areas of housing and their separation from other groups living in adjacent areas has contributed significantly to inter-community tensions and conflicts. (Local Government Association, 2002, p 36)

In fact, research shows that communities did not '*self*-segregate' (Ouseley, 2001). Ouseley discusses the fact that local authority leaders and community leaders maintained the status quo of control and segregation through fear, ignorance and threats. People in local areas were rarely told what was going on. Some sections of the white community, he reported, resented the Asian community, and perceived the community leaders as advocates of segregation. He argued that the problems were also about resources. Regeneration processes forced communities and neighbourhoods to compete with each other for scarce resources, thus creating resentment. For example, both minority ethnic and majority ethnic women and young people were aggrieved that they were excluded from decision making and having a voice in community-based projects.

Another view is that this assumption of segregation itself has to be questioned. First, these Pakistani and Bangladeshi origin young people showed wide varieties of 'cultural' identities, with many often crossing cultural repertoires and racial divides (Webster, 2003). Second, both white and Asian people also shared leisure spaces mixing together.

Power's work (1999) demonstrates a further perspective on 'segregation'. She showed that it was local authorities who had entrenched segregation. In her work on the social consequences of mass housing on estates in Northern Europe (1999), she argues that the causes of segregation and decline on housing estates did not lie with the 'problems' brought by 'immigrants'. It was pressure that had been created *for* local authorities. Authorities had to rapidly house previously excluded groups at a time when the estates themselves were in decline and difficult to let. These estates had multifactorial problems. The combination of 'place', that is, located on the edges of cities, poor architectural design, factory-like tower blocks and a lack of services, contributed to their unpopularity. Minorities were not the *cause* of the decline or segregation; they were at the receiving end of the consequences of the design of mass housing estates. Since minorities were associated with deteriorating conditions, they were *blamed* for them:

> The public perception of the estates deteriorated significantly, partly through racial stereotyping – but also through discrimination. The standard of services dropped because of the image of 'black' and ethnic minority areas as a bad area. (Power, 1999, p 279)

Community cohesion projects and their effects

It is too early to conclude the effectiveness of the approach of community cohesion to tackling situated racisms as explored in Chapter Four. Policy responses in community cohesion projects have, however, been about creating, together with community relations councils, Pathfinder projects on interfaith understanding, with community facilitators.

After the northern disturbances, the government set up a funding initiative on cohesion at the local level, asking local agencies, particularly local authorities, with the voluntary sector to bid for Pathfinder programmes. There are some examples of good practice on these initiatives on the Home Office website, including arranging groups to come together (www.crimereduction.gov.uk activecommunities53.pdf). The vast majority of projects are just beginning. Key staff are involved in writing a strategy and trying to involve local people in it. There have been some initiatives regarding the role of the press, where a 'pullout' within a local paper has been produced, to show the ways that 'communities' are working together. There is also advice on setting up area-based initiatives for neighbourhood renewal, to ensure funding allocations do not become a source of tensions and that these are clearly explained.

Community cohesion was also extended to educate the receiving community about refugees and Travellers. It was further extended to wider social exclusion strategies. Community cohesion became further re-defined as a problem of *cultural* understanding, when local government guidance in this area was produced. There was an emphasis on strengthening community leadership, arguably to discipline black resistance and thus form the perfect colonial arrangement (CARF, 2002).

Cross-community contact: Northern Ireland

Although the situation in Northern Ireland is not directly comparable to the northern towns, examining some lessons on cross-community contact may be helpful. Lessons from Northern Ireland show that creating contact between groups who have been segregated as a result of deep-seated social structural and attitudinal factors will have limited effect (Hughes and Donnelly, 2003). Since the 1980s, community relations in Northern Ireland became a priority for British governments. This approach was primarily about promoting cross-community contact, and religion was taken as the key divide to encourage this contact.

In addition, a range of equality measures were introduced to tackle what were defined as problems of discrimination and disadvantage experienced by the Catholic community. Criticisms of this approach were revealed by various authors who argued that these initiatives had had little effect in reducing *social and economic* differentials (Hughes and Donnelly, 2003). Contact initiatives were viewed with suspicion by the Catholic Church and nationalist politicians as being about *assimilating* into the Northern Ireland State. It was argued that the British government had entrenched divisions by protecting Unionist interests and had failed to tackle the power held by Protestants in the upper echelons of the public service. The contact policies were viewed as deflecting attention away from the relationship of Catholics with the British government. Since the Belfast Agreement in 1998, policy has shifted from addressing symptoms of the conflict, that is, segregation and division to trying to tackle its roots, that is, causes of inequality and discrimination. These initiatives have also been about recognising that the religious divide is not the only divide that needs to be confronted. In other words, the unity of class or gender has to be addressed, not just the axis of religion equated with advantage or disadvantage (Hughes and Donnelly, 2003).

Intercultural understanding

Amin (2002) argues that interculturalism is about removing the fear and intolerance of the 'other'. It is about coming to terms with the fact that groups are *all* made up of individuals, many of whom will have things in common with those who appear to be defined as removed from them, for example, socially and ethnically. If we adopt this approach, people will then hopefully live with a cultural pluralism in all its vibrancy and evolution.

The question here is how can we challenge racism through multicultural coexistence? One way is to use public spaces for festivals, for example. Although this is important as an intervention, these events are short term and have limited impact. The really prejudiced stay away and even those who are present carry the imprint of deeper negative attitudes.

Ideas of intercultural understanding are not new. JCORE (Jewish Council for Racial Equality) has had a cross-cultural programme of black–Asian–Jewish dialogue for some time (www.jcore.org.uk). More recently, a manifesto of British Muslims and Jews, who have joined together to create Alif Aleph UK, was launched in June 2004. The co-ordinators of this project have already mapped positive contacts between communities. They aim to further this work through aiding informal contacts, and they give examples of joint initiatives in universities to defend each other's rights to rooms for prayer, religious holy days and examinations and the availability of Halal and Kosher food. They are also planning joint visits to religious sites, developing artist links through calligraphy, for example, and holding small discussion groups about Israel and Palestine (Alif Aleph, 2004).

We believe that these contacts between previously 'segregated' groups can be important, but the idea that intercultural understanding under the concept of community cohesion is the *sole* answer to related problems of stereotyping, poverty and racism and the decline of the infrastructure of housing and schools, is very much open to question.

Conclusion

• Multicultural interventions and their underlying interpretation have been much debated since the 1970s. Interpretations have ranged from rejecting multiculturalism (assimilation tendencies), to integrative concerns (living with some difference, but also wanting an adaptation to dominant norms) as well as cultural pluralism (a mutual tolerance in a community of communities). These interpretations have been used at a national level, and at a local level, by official agencies as well as racialised grassroots groups.

- Many interventions based on recognising 'difference', whether faith schools, translation services, heritage projects, or projects on intercultural understanding, have not been evaluated for their effectiveness in reducing racism and lowering intolerance. The hotly contested nature of multiculturalism in all its guises leaves many with deep ambivalences about the nature of these interventions. On the one hand, it is important to recognise and cater for difference in service provision; on the other hand, to use a narrow definition of 'culture' as a sole axis for interventions between groups and people can entrench essentialised, 'fixed' notions of how the 'other' lives. It can deflect us from looking at the 'norm'.

- Community cohesion is hailed as the new 'multiculturalism'. It identifies segregation and difference between communities as the problem and stresses assimilation through common values and citizenship. The interventions emphasise intercultural understanding, especially faith-based interventions. It is too early to know the effectiveness of these interventions, but lessons for Northern Ireland suggest cross-community contact has a limited effect in reducing racism if deep-seated attitudes and structural, social and economic issues are not addressed.

NINE

Lessons for success

Not only should successful interventions address the causes of racisms and their everyday reproduction, they should also address the *why*, *what* and the *how*. We have argued that most professional policy interventions concentrate primarily on the 'what' (to do) and frequently ignore the 'why' (the causes of racism). The 'how' (it affects racism) is very rarely quantified or measured. In this chapter we describe examples of success, with all these three questions in mind.

Previously we made a distinction between the reproduction of everyday racisms by elites, *and* those made by ordinary members of the public, which we termed situated local racisms. It was suggested that although both these kinds of racisms were linked, 'elite' racisms had more power and often legitimated the expression of local situated racisms. Both of these racisms are important to understand if we are to get to the root causes of racism, and so they both need to be addressed. We group our interventions below under these two broad headings of situated local and elite everyday racisms.

Situated local racisms

Any intervention needs to work through a situated social dynamic. Interdependence and habitual engagement are critical for change to take place (Amin, 2002). In one housing estate, some sanctions against racist language will be critical, while in another, youth workers could use their imagination to bring people together. Similarly discussions with children on the curriculum may work in one context; in others it may be important for the children to work on common ventures together. Youth or child care projects, for example, could have common sites with common goals. Various groups across classes, could be given a civic duty for a given period, for example, cleaning up a housing estate, working with HIV/AIDS patients and so on.

Another way is to encourage people to step *outside* of everyday routines. For example, engaging with strangers is commonplace and disrupts easy labelling. Changes in attitudes and behaviour can result from lived experimentation. Amin points out that many of these experiences can be short lived and need an intensity of memory to survive. We begin our illustrations with tackling racisms among young people.

Young people and conflict resolution: the 'why', the 'what' and the 'how'

Most reports on intercultural conflict and the experience of day-to-day racism discuss the alienation of young people and the pressing need for good youth provision, which ensures that young people are occupied and mix across housing estates. While the police have been slow and 'incompetent' in their responses to racist attacks (Kalra, 2003), youth activities are encouraged as a positive way to reduce race hate crime.

The Bede Anti Racist Youth Work Project intervened with the leaders and members of gangs of young white working-class men (Dadzie, 1997), in response to a rising number of racist attacks in the local area of Bermondsey. Interventions also took place with young white women and young black Somali origin men. The project established that in South East London, racist attacks in the 1990s increased by 36% (Connections, 1999). It was recognised that the intervention would need a long-term commitment, so resources were devoted and workers were recruited to the idea of challenging racism (see Appendix A (1) 'Bede Anti Racist Youth Work Project').

This intervention would take place in relation to the young people's lived and everyday experience. Team meetings of youth workers developed strategies for open discussion of racist feelings. They discussed, for example, how to ensure that young people viewed the black female youth worker as a positive role model, without explicitly pointing this out. The youth worker was placed in a decision-making role in many discussions with the young people, and other workers deferred to her, openly admiring her style.

Racism was explicitly discussed, but not *artificially* placed on the agenda. On many occasions it was not discussed at all; it was discussed at planned strategic moments. The evaluation of the project showed interesting results. Young white people who had been aggressively racist in their views and behaviour started to opt out when their friends made racist comments. One year later, many of the 200 young people said the project had changed their lives. Racist incidents on the housing estate where the project operated reduced by 46% over three years, whereas they increased as a whole in Bermondsey.

The Bede project also found that some girls were more self-aware and less aggressive than the boys. They were less influenced by peer group pressure and were more receptive to antiracist ideas. The girls could be useful in challenging the racism of the boys, but only when they felt secure and confident in their ability to make decisions in their lives that related to their position *as girls*.

A key lesson from this intervention, apart from its longer-term focus, is the understanding of 'why'. In this context, it was clearly important to address the young people's own self-image and identity at the same time as discussing racism. Gender and class influenced this self-identity. Furthermore, not all teaching interventions were made by 'banning' racist comments; rather a more subtle approach was created, using both an understanding of 'unconscious' and emotional reactions to where these young people lived and their relationships with each other.

Outside of England, in Paris, for example, an intervention with youths (assuming that they were young *men*) bent on writing graffiti, was based on creating *auto écoles*. Youth workers used a loose curriculum to re-engage young people in the school system, invited young boys from all over the world to play in a world tournament and animated public debates on relevant themes. In Marseille, theatre was used with professionals and residents to work on common problems in their local areas (see Appendix A (22) 'Paris – Youth').

Greenwich Council has funded a project run by a probation officer working with the *perpetrators* of racial violence. They underwent a course that analysed the reasons for their behaviour, and began to understand that they shared a common history, with common antisocial behaviour problems, alcohol and housing problems. They worked on aspects of their own family trees, kept a diary and reflected on their national identities. Videos, anger management and relaxation tapes were also used. The modules included understanding unconscious beliefs and attitudes. The perpetrators were encouraged to understand how prejudiced attitudes had contributed to their behaviour. Although the report makes clear that there has been no formal evaluation, since the work is in its early stages, there are some indications that those who have completed the programme have re-examined their racist attitudes, accepted greater responsibility for their actions, and have failed to re-offend (see Appendix A (2) 'Greenwich Council').

Enabling discussion: involving all

In working with diverse people living together, interventions that *enable* discussion to take place across differing axes are pertinent. Talking about racism openly and without fear of either 'political correctness' and a genuine aim of articulating confusion and ambivalence appears to be an important prerequisite. In the US, a nationwide project on Study Circles that were funded by a charity aimed to involve local people in discussions about racism. Several groups were set up across the country and everyone was included (Roberts and Kay, 2000). Some evaluations using qualitative techniques such as interviews, focus groups and observation, showed that people involved in the groups (which were facilitated) became more aware, and some wanted to take action in their workplaces.

Evaluations also showed that Study Circles provided an arena where anyone interested in community improvement could form new relationships and connections with people they would otherwise be unlikely to meet. These relationships sometimes bridged racial and other divides. Participants reported that being part of the Study Circle gave them a deeper sense of community and commitment. They could see several hundred fellow citizens working for hours on an interest for collective good. Participants reported becoming more active in challenging racist statements and more willing to interrupt racist jokes and behaviour. They further felt that the experience of dialogue about 'race' and racism itself constituted a change for the better. They welcomed discussing 'race' issues with those from diverse racial and ethnic backgrounds. These open discussions also transferred into participants' workplaces. Aside from the process of becoming more aware, other more tangible outcomes are also in evidence. Study Circles have led to a greater number of multicultural festivals, arts events and task forces being launched within organisations. Study Circles on 'race' have also been replicated within work organisations, for example, MBNA Corporation and Andersen Consulting (see Appendix A (17) 'Study Circles').

A project in Copenhagen on a declining housing estate drew on community development and tenants' involvement (Amin, 2002). Issues of 'difference' were at the centre of that involvement, and not separated out. Many different groups were involved in the design of the housing estate, from gardening to regeneration, as well as using communal areas. Although some tensions between groups remained, a viable estate was created, with multiculturalism at its heart (see Appendix A (18) 'Environmental Project', Taastrupgaard).

Teaching antiracism: unlearning racism

In an all-white teacher training course students from white residential areas were taught about racism. These students had previously not had much contact with racialised groups. A follow-up three years after they had left showed that they continued to use antiracism approaches in their work as teachers. The author, Gaine (2001), argues that challenging behaviour and attitudes without personalising the issues had made a clear difference. Although hostility and tension were generated through the teaching, this was not necessarily destructive.

In the US, Bigler (1999) looked at the multicultural curricula in schools to determine whether different types of teaching interventions were effective. She examined 'additive' interventions, using counter-stereotypic information and teaching about stereotyping. Empirical data show that most of these interventions do not in fact change children's attitudes and have very limited positive effects. Most programmes are what she categorises as *additive* approaches. These approaches prescribe inclusion. Symbols of minority group role models are included in books and projects to dispel ignorance about people's cultures. There are also interventions that aim to present deliberate *counter*-stereotypic information. These may involve extensive changes to content of curricula. They involve the deliberate inclusion of famous black heroes and heroines in unexpected fields. Explicit teaching about stereotyping and discrimination, using role playing and understanding differences in economic power and status between groups have also been introduced.

In the exploration of why these interventions had little or no effect, she hypothesises various factors. She found, for example, that counter-stereotypic information sometimes increased racial bias (Bigler, 1999). Those with racially biased attitudes were more resistant to challenging the meanings they had already held. She argues that the limited success of these programmes is due to a poorly theorised understanding of how children learn/unlearn. Children are constructed as passive learners, rather than active constructors of reality. These interventions are, therefore, not without meaning for children.

The age of the child was also a factor. Young pre-school children, for example, did not remember much about other people's cultures. Age also mattered in relation to the type of thinking that teachers introduced, whether it was concrete or abstract. Young children may also concentrate on salient criteria, such as colour in the first instance, and ignore individuating aspects. Skills of multiple classification may help to counter these perceptions, whereas singular classifications may entrench this focus on colour.

Affective or motivational aspects of children's learning also made a difference. If children have no experience of African-Americans as scientists, they will not incorporate counter-stereotypic information about them. Some children may be resistant to knowledge being imparted by authority figures. Finally, narrowly focused interventions have less effect than those that are broad-based. The latter include addressing attitudes, beliefs, and behaviour in a variety of situations. She also concludes that drawing attention to a group and its characteristics facilitates inter-group bias. However, tasks that encouraged children to attend to individuating characteristics between individuals within differing 'racialised' groups, and to look for similarities across groups, helped to reduce racist stereotypes.

Unpacking racist talk

Understanding the conversational and language context is also important in tackling attitudes and behaviours. Guerin (2003) suggests that actions fulfil social purposes and are socially motivated. There may be no such thing as individual agency. For example, anthropologists point to the increasing use of rituals to bind social groups and to maintain social relationships. When the discussion occurs in the course of a conversation, an intervention may need to be quite specific. If you exclude certain topics or ban them, they may be rarer in appearance, but they may appear in starker form, if the aim of the speaker is to draw attention to themselves.

Much racist talk is made in the context of having fun, making jokes, getting attention or status in a relationship, or telling wildly racist stories (Guerin, 2003). Guerin gives an example of someone using 'racist' talk to boost status and standing with humour. By distancing yourself from the actual comments, for example, "I'm not a racist..." or using hedging strategies, "perhaps it was an Asian", or quoting someone else, or even a more insidious approach such as "I'm only joking", and so on, perform a social function for the talker.

Interventions in racism have tried to reduce racial discrimination, based on a rational imparting of information to counter attitudes. Guerin argues that these interventions consist purely of telling people the facts. Practitioners assume that imparting knowledge will have the desired effect and participants will reflect and change their behaviour. Guerin argues, however, that the interventions in question may not be about countering statements with lecturing, or giving lists of facts. He suggests approaching the intervention in its context, and addresses how to respond in informal conversations. He advocates an understanding of 'why'. Conversational language, such as stories and jokes, are used to regulate social relationships. These conversations are not about persuading listeners to act in racist ways. These conversational 'throwaways' are part of understanding the function of such language. They should therefore be responded to in that particular context. Instead of trying to change someone's mind by giving them a list of facts, or telling them off, a different approach is needed.

Countering such expressions in everyday conversational encounters by responding with another joke or a story will be more effective. He gives an example of Refugee Week in New Zealand, where members of the public were given sheets of typical comments made about refugees, followed by some conversational appropriate replies.

For example:

"Refugees come here without adequate English which means they can never fit in properly."

Was followed by:

"Refugees only find out which country they are going to a week before they leave their refugee camp. Unlike other migrants they do not have time to learn English."

"More needs to be done to help them learn English, but most do a good job of picking up the language quickly if they do not already have some."

"Many refugees speak a number of languages and are helpful in translating for others."

He believes that conversational encounters can be taught, and gives further examples of responding with counter jokes, or preventing laughter by interruption with a repartee.

Sport and the arts

Images and ideals of racial prowess between the 'races' in sport are long-standing. Black sportsmen and women are imbued with ideas that they have 'natural' talent. This taken-for-granted assumption that "White men can't jump, but black men can run fast" is part of everyday common-sense talk (Kohn, 1996). 'Race' and sport are at the very heart of nationalistic concerns. Sport is frequently saturated with symbols of the national flag and collective anthems are sung in order to support representative heroes and heroines. These actions exist side by side with racist chants. Sport can therefore be a prime site for the reproduction of racism (Carrington and McDonald, 2001). There is much rhetoric at the national level about zero tolerance of racism in sport and we have seen several national initiatives in football such as 'Kick it Out' and 'Show Racism the Red Card'.

However, while sport can reproduce racism, it can also bring people together.

One project on football racism is worth noting (Bradbury, 2001). It is worth stressing that the project coordinators had clear aims and objectives. They encouraged the participation of minority youth through specialised coaching, and they eventually created a team. But the project was not solely about tackling exclusion. Organisers also used the written word and the football media to get across messages about racism. They liaised successfully with the police with regard to community safety. They managed to set up a team club of mixed racial origins, including white participants. They held a sports tournament, developed positive images through a black footballers' exhibition and worked with local schools, using drama. Evaluations indicated a decline in racial chanting and minority young people felt safer. Their interventions, as Bigler (1999) argues, used several initiatives in several sites and worked long term to achieve their results.

Arts are also important since they convey important messages about the cultural image of a country. Chapter Six discussed how the Arts Council had attempted to change their interventions through a greater reflection of what diversity meant, and how racism could actually keep audiences away or present an image of Britain as white male and middle class. They made appointments of black and minority people at a senior level. These 'ambassadors' were then seen to represent a new face of Britain with connections made overseas. They have been used in forums in reinterpreting/re-representing British heritage.

Self-help and struggle: the challenge to 'closed' ethnic communities

Racialised groups have been involved for a long time in 'self-help'; designing ways to intervene in their own and group's lives. Examples range from top-down interventions such as specific museums and heritage sites that expose past treatment. Examples of this are the Jewish Museum and the Museum of Slavery. Organisations that liaise with local and regional communities and lobby for change such as Southall Black Sisters are also part of this campaigning and self-help approach.

Most interventions, however, take place at a local level, with Saturday schools, projects which work with excluded pupils, and projects designed to convert buildings for community use and supporting those who are most vulnerable (Mirza and Reay, 2000). They have also been about struggles for belonging to specific central urban spaces. These projects have been aided by both white and racialised individuals working to address change in creative and innovative ways.

For example, lessons from a recent campaign by Muslims to build a mosque in Toronto, Canada (Isin and Siemiatycki, 2002) deserve our attention. The authors of this article argue that Muslims are marginalised and racialised in urban spaces in England, the US and Canada. The most critical struggles, they argue, have taken place over the right to 'own' urban space. Examples given by these authors include conflicts over mosques, Jamaican community centres, Chinese retail malls and funeral parlours.

The reports of these struggles contain important insights in the legitimating and forging of people's identities. They help to consolidate feelings of inclusion and integration. These clashes often raise the question, *who belongs and on what terms*? Opposition to the fight for urban space is often expressed as a technical concern over car parking or the size of the building, or the location. It can, however, also be interpreted as racialised and open to racialised discourse from neighbours. For example, campaigners for the mosque argued that a different discourse had been used about arguments made for churches and synagogues. The struggles for urban spaces have particular resonances for those who may be feeling particularly vulnerable in the light of September 11th anti-terrorist measures. The clashes have deeper meanings, since they are about forging the idea of the 'active' citizen, without locating the notion of citizenship solely in a Western framework. Activists wanted to move beyond 'multicultural' notions of citizenship, to deeply question the 'Western' idea of citizenship, which is orientalist and racialised.

These interventions have related the intervention to the situational context. Community mobilisations and capacity building of groups have been strategically and timely implemented, despite short-term funding. These interventions have made a difference in tackling both internalised racism and in exposing the ways in which racism operates. Lessons from these interventions need to be shared and debated.

The historical experience of racialised exclusion and labour market segregation has also encouraged racialised groups to identify with the idea of a 'secure' ethnicity. But this 'secure' ethnicity may be interpreted by members of the group in a singular way. Thus combating sexism and homophobia *within* ethnic communities has now become as important as combating racism from outside. It is important to prevent the fixing of identities of those who are construed as being 'outside' their 'cultures'.

The Safra Project (2003: www.safraproject.org) aimed to provide support for Muslim lesbians and transsexuals and to identify difficulties in accessing legal and social services. The project argued that the media and 'community' leaders reinforced a denial that Muslim women could be lesbian, or bisexual. Women did not know how to deal with their feelings because of this denial. The idea that homosexuality is 'unnatural' was continually reinforced. Information was not available relating to Islam. If it was, the focus was on *male* homosexuality. Muslim women were placed in a position where they had to choose between their cultural or their sexual identity. This led to mental health problems. However, these women did not trust mental health counsellors either. They felt that counsellors did not understand Islam and nor did they make distinctions between patriarchal values and religious values. They needed to seek help in a 'gendered', or 'race' centre, because it was not enough to attend a Muslim women's group. The women also needed information on how to relate to identities that were positive. Services for Muslim women that were safe and confidential were planned and set up (see Appendix A (4) 'Safra Project').

These examples of 'self-help' are a response to situational contexts where racism has impacted. The interventions may take place in different sites, such as education, or welfare, or they can target particular groups, such as lesbians, or older women, or disabled children (see discussion in Chapter Four on 'multiple racisms' and 'disability and age'.)

Everyday elite racisms

We argued in Chapter Five that legislation on 'race' relations and discrimination has been passed in the same policy and discourse context as repressive immigration and nationality policies. These latter discourses have implicitly legitimated the idea of a 'white' Britain, while also reinforcing notions of racialised groups as 'outsiders'. These attitudes have been legitimised by the popular press and some sections of the media. The PressWise project on exposing the racism of the press towards asylum seekers is a good example of a successful intervention in exposing 'media' racism and leading to change (see Chapter Three, and Appendix A (16) 'Presswise'). They monitor on a regular basis the ways in which racisms are expressed by politicians and commentators in the media.

While discourses in the press, media and politicians need to be exposed and illuminated for their misinformation and reproduction of racism, the media also need to be congratulated for their imaginative and antiracist portrayal. Below we give examples, primarily from other countries, how everyday elite racism can also be contested by sympathetic members in governments. These interventions by politicians and others challenge the 'norm' of everyday racism.

International lessons: just saying 'sorry'

Even though different countries have differing contexts in which racism is expressed (Bonnett, 2000a), it is interesting to see how national antiracist debates can be legitimated by politicians. Sometimes the wording of a debate matters. For example, the diversity statement on the official Australian government website uses the word 'we' to tell us the country speaks over 200 languages. They list languages including English, Italian, Greek, Cantonese, Arabic, Vietnamese and Mandarin. They use the word 'our' to indicate the main religions of Christianity, Buddhism and Islam (www.img.gov.au/multicultural).

In this declaration of its diversity, Australia, as a nation of immigrants, may be stating the obvious. But the hierarchy of languages and religions, beginning with English and Christianity is deep. Furthermore, the impact of Australia's 'white only' immigration policy has compounded the legacy of racism, a policy only recently rescinded (Greer, 2004).

The absence of indigenous Aboriginal language and culture in this statement underscores the amnesia of Australia's racist origins in its 'national story'. It is debatable as to whether the 'Sorry' campaign will have long-term effects on improving relations between Aboriginal groups and the dominant white majority. But the government has at least officially acknowledged the atrocities done to the Aboriginal people. It has, for example, recognised the cruel and enforced separation of children. Even though this recognition has not immediately led to better relations, it appears to be an important first step. The inclusive use of 'we' or 'our' also suggests Australia is struggling with the construction of itself as a diverse and multicultural nation. These constructions are contested. Australia continues to infringe the human rights of asylum seekers and refugees, through its policy of internment. At the same time Australia has also established the celebration of 'Harmony Day'.

National statements can have healing effects and open up the possibilities of multicultural intent in white postcolonial nations. In 2002, the Prime Minister of New Zealand made a speech to Parliament on the Chinese New Year celebrations. She apologised for immigration restrictions, as well as the ways in which regulations had separated families. She apologised for the imposition of taxes that had impoverished Chinese people in the later 19th and 20th centuries, and stressed the need for reconciliation. Words were also followed up by action. She was keen to fund aspects of Chinese heritage, culture and language, including a national essay writing competition for school children on the 'history of the contribution of the Chinese' in New

Zealand (see Appendix A (24) 'Interventions on the Chinese in New Zealand').

More dramatic and forthright approaches to 'Sorry' have been embodied in the movements toward Truth and Reconciliation (*Race and Class*, 2002). These movements have made an important intervention in setting out antiracist aims for a just society. There have been commissions and hearings in Guatemala, Rwanda, Chile and Northern Ireland. In post-apartheid South Africa, open trials of perpetrators have come face to face with their victims. These trials have opened up a powerful mechanism in dealing with racist crimes through attempts to reconcile, face the past and move forward (Hamber, 2002; McLaughlin, 2002).

It is currently difficult to ascertain the effectiveness of such approaches. On the one hand, it can be argued that such 'forgiveness' is futile, given the human rights atrocities. How far can problems of personal accounting be an answer to politically sanctioned and collective institutionalised racism? On the other hand, laying bare the psychology of racist acts and a desire to break down barriers may make an impact in healing rifts. The ultimate success of these Truth and Reconciliation Commissions will be measured by how much future political education is generated (Adam and Moodley, 2003).

Similarly, the reparations movements have attempted to heal the rifts of racism by revisiting the silences in European and American historical memory. The injustice of post-abolition slavery promises of 'one acre and a mule' to each freed slave was not honoured in the US. Reparations for the slave trade have led to demands for aggregating financial totals of the cost to human beings and their countries of origin (Hutton, 2001; Mack, 2001).

These may be highly controversial movements, as witnessed by the uproar they caused at the World Conference against Racism in Durban (Ajadi, 2002). They appear to confuse the focus on current and present-day problems of racism. However, they demonstrate a deep need for acknowledgement *in the present* to people wronged in the past. They reveal the power of both dialogue and acts of forgiveness and contrition for the past. Racist injustice, perhaps, can only be countered once the past is acknowledged and dealt with.

In Britain English National Heritage has projects that acknowledge the wealth and capital accumulation during British slavery. Some efforts, though limited, have been made in stately homes to recognise in their exhibitions how the wealth of the aristocracy was gleaned from forced black slave labour in the plantations. However, no national statement has yet been made with regard to Britain's role in the slave trade. No antislavery monument has been erected in Britain. As Bernie Grant, a champion of the reparations movement pointed out, the lived memory and pain of human subjugation is still carried by generations of African and Indo-Caribbean displaced people (Bernie Grant Trust: www.berniegrantarchive.com).

Making antiracism and multiculturalism part of national policy or the constitution

New Zealand recognises its indigenous people in its constitution. The 1975 Treaty of Waitangi Act is a permanent Commission of Inquiry on Maori claims relating to the land. It enables the negotiation between the Crown and the Maori people, on any aspect which concerns grievances against policies, practices or legislation (see Appendix A (23) 'Waitangi Tribunal'). There is, however, still a long journey to go in terms of cultural differences between 'pakeha' (white) and Maori understandings (Bishop and Glynn, 1999). Instead New Zealand has focused on its international image abroad. Every 21 March, it celebrates Race Relations Day in memory of the Sharpeville massacre in South Africa in 1960. It also remembers the subsequent introduction of the UN Convention on the Elimination of all Forms of Discrimination.

It has been argued that self-confidence in one's own ethnic identity leads to a more 'mature' multiculturalism. The official multicultural policy adopted by the Canadian Federal government in 1971 was largely inspired by the conception of addressing 'immigrant ethnicity'. It treated ethnocultural affiliation as voluntary, and therefore to be encouraged. The differing ethnic groups were facilitated to interact, share their cultural heritage, and to participate in common educational political, economic and legal institutions (see Appendix A (21) 'Multiculturalism policy'). Evidence suggests that this policy has had some impact on national identity. Twenty years on, in 1991, 95% of minorities agreed that they were proud of being Canadian *and* their own ethnic identity at the same time. Almost 80% felt they shared values in common with other Canadians (Kymlicka, 1998). However, the problematic positioning of black and Asian people as marginal in the process of Canadian nation building (Dua, 2000; Lenk, 2000), and the 'vanishing' of First Nation indigenous people in the 'popular' national story, is ever present (Castagna and Sefa Dei, 2000).

In Sweden, multiculturalism has meant taking an holistic look at notions of citizenship. This is a citizenship not bequeathed to people by a sovereign state. It is rather one that engages people to address difference and participate in community development at a local level.

Antiracism was centrally adopted in the Swedish national constitution to promote and protect democracy. Policies encouraged the open discussion and combating of racism. By linking antiracism with democracy, participation and involvement by a variety of groups became integral to their engagement with institutions. Multiculturalism did not mean 'separated'-out consultation mechanisms for racialised groups, while the real work gets done elsewhere (Osler and Starkey, 2002). Once more, it is not all so simple. The lack of integration and continued discrimination of indigenous Sami people, a growing fascist far right, and persistent racial attacks on asylum seekers still needs to be explained against the image of Sweden as a country of tolerance and democratic participation (see Appendix A (25) 'Approaches to Antiracism').

Conclusion

- Examples of these successful interventions illustrate that challenging racism can take very different and wide-ranging forms. The ways in which racism changes depends on the macro and micro contexts in question. The micro day-to-day situated local racisms include interventions based on conflict resolution, communication and education. Tackling the macro level of elite racism includes interventions based on monitoring the media, and committed national political leadership.
- Racism is legitimated by the media and government, who have been involved in reproducing panics about 'race'. Racisms have (re)-appeared when issues of national identity are in question. These macro contexts have helped to explicitly reproduce the causes of racism, already embedded through history and everyday acts of marginalisation in ordinary people's lives. The marginalisation of 'race' equality and racism helps us think of how we can incorporate antiracist aims into our national and local core values and objectives
- We have argued that there is not one racism, but multiple racisms. There are racisms expressed by politicians and the press. There are the racisms expressed as part of the normal everyday situations in which people find themselves. They are embedded in our 'normal' ways of seeing the world. These understandings of racisms help us to plan interventions. The invisibility of government and media racism enables us to think about how this racism can be made more visible. It can help us acknowledge a different interpretation of history.

- The problematisation of the 'other' helps us design interventions that include all those involved, without focusing solely on 'minority ethnic communities'. Interventions which only consider the 'ethnic' axis in examining evidence of discrimination can 'fix' 'cultural' and 'racial' identities. Understanding the complexity of human relations enables us to recognise people's multiple identities across gender, age, disability and class.
- Exploring further what kinds of interventions may work best involves bringing together multidisciplinary and cross-cultural research. Understanding the 'why', the 'what' and the 'how', makes it possible to facilitate a more open discussion about connecting the causes of racism with appropriate interventions.

TEN

Tackling the roots of racism

"Society itself has got to change. It's got to be able to accept black people as black people, because you won't accept us as English people. So now we've been forced apart, we've been categorised and we've got to do it ourselves, and then ask you to accept us the way we are because you don't want us the same as you." (young black resident from Broadwater Farm Estate, Tottenham, London, quoted from Zipfel, 1986, in Power, 1999, p 214).

In the aftermath of the 'racial' uprisings on the Broadwater Farm Estate in 1985, this young black person articulates the dynamics of everyday racism. Here the experience of racism is shaped by societal exclusion, racial categorisation and fixed, entrenched identities. Racism is experienced as a general attitude and as a way of thinking that pervades society.

In the current climate of western liberal democracy where racism is officially and culturally condemned, racism is now viewed as something that is bad or deviant behaviour, practised by a few 'bad apples'. Racists are constructed as those who commit individual intentional acts of discriminatory behaviour, such as that prohibited in the 'race' relations legislation. Racism is not understood as patterns of behaviour, which are collectivised and ingrained in both British structures and British cultural representations. This does not mean that everyone therefore *acts* in individualised racialist ways, but that these attitudes and ideologies based on ideas of inferiority and subordination of certain groups, like those of class and gender, are embedded in the very ways in which British society has developed.

What is racism?

This book concludes that the ways in which racism changes depends on the macro and micro contexts in question. For example, racism has become less overt and more covert since the 1980s. It has 'appeared' in our societies at times of moral panics around immigration, at times of a decline of the provision of social housing, at moments where white working-class young people's identities are in crisis or when the demands of the labour market are rapidly changing. It is legitimated by the media and government, who have been involved in reproducing panics about 'race'. It has re-appeared when national identity is in question. These macro contexts reproduce racism.

We have argued that there is not one racism, but multiple racisms. There are racisms expressed by politicians and the press with the aid of immigration legislation, which are a counterweight to legislation aiming to combat discrimination. Some of these racisms have greater power than others. The struggles over meanings and contexts of these powerful racisms must be illuminated. There are also the racisms of professionals and managers in denying racism, or considering it unimportant, and locating it in areas where there are greater numbers of black and minority ethnic residents. There are the racisms expressed through working-class young men's crisis of masculinity in the context of declining state resources. There are the racisms perpetuated through legislation, on, for example, the right to jury trial, which disproportionately affects black people in the criminal justice system. There are the racisms of 'cultural' assumptions, for example, that everyone who has the label Muslim must be someone of whom we must be suspicious. There are the racisms of young African Caribbean origin men as 'lawless and threatening'. There are the racisms which suggest that all young South Asian origin women are subject to repression in their homes. There is the internalised racism of minorities which is expressed against other racialised groups, as well as through 'identity' crises. There are the racisms of British or English, Scottish, Irish or Welsh national identities.

Racisms are expressed at an interpersonal level, for example, in the form of throwaway remarks, jokes and debates. They are also expressed silently through white middle-class flight from racialised localities, through non-verbal behaviour, and through informal networks. They are expressed through images in our media. They are expressed through ignoring and denying racism. They are expressed through racist attacks and murders.

Everyday racist practices are created and situated within current ideologies and structures. These everyday practices include hating and harassing black neighbours, discriminatory local authority housing allocation policies and overt racist immigration policies of dispersal and internment. They are reflective of, and informed by, the deeper causes of racism. These roots of racism have evolved through centuries of social and psychological power.

Both macro and micro racisms need carefully designed interventions.

However, professional policy interventions in racism have been limited in their effects in tackling the *causes* of racism. By causes of racism, we mean both the origins, or roots, of racism, and the ways in which it is reproduced on an everyday basis. Professional interventions on the whole primarily deal with the *effects* of racism.

In this final chapter we consider interventions in racism in terms of their effectiveness in tackling the root causes of racism as it manifests itself in the current British discourse of 'race' and racism. The analysis of the effectiveness of policy-based professional interventions has evolved in the context of changing British social policy on 'race'. These policy interventions are categorised on the basis of 'equality of opportunity' and 'multicultural difference'.

Roots of racism: from legislative to political interventions

In order for causes of racism to be addressed, there is a need to expose the operation of macro racism within wider societal structures. These types of racism are more influential because they are perpetuated by those who have more power in our society. They interact with everyday situated racisms.

For example, we cannot understand the *causes* of 'racial' differentiation and discrimination against certain groups in Britain if we do not understand the dynamics of the history of the Empire and slavery. But this is not the whole story. We also need to understand how this history links to postcolonial migration, and the fact that the arrival of ex-Commonwealth immigrants was driven by postwar reconstruction and the changing labour market in Britain. We need to understand the political struggles these migrants met on their arrival and the racist legislation that shaped their experience. Finally we need to understand the complexity of 'race' as well as class, gender, age and disability, which act together to produce a complex system of inequality.

Racism cannot be understood on its own. The ways in which it is reproduced is related to the nature of political and economic change in society. Racist exclusion and exploitation has been differently expressed in different times and places. Racism is not about objective measurable physical and social characteristics. It is about the ideological legitimation of relationships of domination and subordination in different social and historical contexts.

For example, the official government discourse on 'social cohesion and social exclusion' has superseded the previous discourse of 'assimilation and integration' to explain racialised discontent and unrest among white, black Caribbean/African origin and South Asian youths in Britain. In a shift of language and rhetoric, religious and 'racial' segregation coupled with cultural 'rigidity' is seen as the problem. Thus capacity building, a reliance on (male) community leaders to act as bridges, citizenship oaths and inter-faith communication frame the debate for civic participation and renewal. The camera lens remains on the ethnicised communities, who are pathologised as problems.

Structural causes, such as a lack of educational resources, or racialised poverty, are sidelined. Intergenerational unemployment, and a non-inclusive, middle-class construction of Britishness are not included in these explanations.

There needs to be a recognition that racism is not a 'thing' outside of society and brought in by black people. It cannot be isolated out, and easily defined in policy interventions. Measuring and quantifying 'black' achievement, for example, does not make sense when compared solely along the axis of 'racial' categories, while ignoring socioeconomic status, parental background, gender, age and disability. We need a complex understanding that conceptions of racism and their manifestations are constantly changing in relation to specific historical and political conditions.

What kinds of interventions can address the causes?

In short, we need interventions aimed at revealing the interrelationship of the past to the present. In particular, we need educational initiatives that seek to understand the complexity of historical links. Museums, archives, libraries, schools and universities all have a role to play in opening up new ways of seeing the world beyond the entrenched notions of multiculturalism and Britishness that we see debated ad nauseam in the media. Mainstreaming diversity in our national galleries and museums showing the interrelationships that knit together our diverse heritage will slowly and cumulatively tell us an 'other' story which will be more balanced.

Citizenship education with teachers confident in diversity issues can offer one such opportunity to explore diversity and challenge racism. Similarly we need projects that understand how children learn about 'race' and racism. We need to appreciate that different cultural contexts of learning can influence change.

The changing nature of racism and interventions

'Race' is a social construction. Since the 1950s the 'new racism' has moved from a scientific biological kind, towards a cultural racism and more recently it is shifting to a religious expression. These shifts in the conceptions of racism are linked to the macro process of globalisation. The interdependence of nations and the mass movements of people have increased with global change. Culture, nation and identity continue to be caught up with changing conceptions of racism. These processes are not understood and analysed in everyday debate. Instead we see overtly racist 'political discourse' that unashamedly plays on people's insecurities and fears. It fuels the lack of certainty the population feels by displacing this on to the 'racialised aliens'.

Interventions that disrupt politically inspired racist immigration legislation and the racist media are essential. Media monitoring groups such as PressWise are important mechanisms of contestation. Newsletters such as the Institute of Race Relations' *Race Bulletin* provide up-to-date information on the rise of racism in Europe. It keeps us vigilant about elite racism.

Activists counter official propaganda on 'illegal' immigrants with facts, highlighting the fictions that pervade 'commonsense' fears of swamping and invasion by the alien 'other'. As 200 years of slave resistances in the West Indies demonstrates, the role of committed activists is critical. The campaigns by many families and their friends (such as Doreen and Neville Lawrence), who have suffered deaths in custody or whose loved ones have been killed in racist murders, have placed the issues of 'racial' injustice into the public consciousness. The publication of *The Stephen Lawrence Inquiry* is really a culmination of their dogged campaigning. Institutional racism and externally driven reform of an unmodernised and unaccountable police force would not be on our agendas but for these campaigners.

Civil society's influence in shaping progressive antidiscrimination and human rights legislation must also not be overlooked. The patterns of the antislavery movement, who campaigned for a formal end to slavery in 1833, can be currently discerned. In the European Union, it was non-governmental organisations, such as ECRE (European Council on Refugees and Asylum) and MPG (Migration Policy Group), who campaigned for the rights of third country nationals. It was they who struggled for the freedom of movement and the inclusion of antidiscriminatory legislation at EU summits in Maastricht and Tampare.

In the UK, the black voluntary sector, including the 1990 Trust, the

National Assembly Against Racism, and Southall Black Sisters, are examples of these campaigners. Established independent 'think-tanks' such as the Runnymede Trust, Liberty and Justice among others, have all impacted on the British legislation that protects the rights of racialised people, such as the 1998 Human Rights Act and the 2000 Race Relations (Amendment) Act. Government-independent funding of many of these radical groups provided through charitable trusts (for example, Joseph Rowntree Charitable Trust and Cadburys) has been a powerful yet silent intervention in changing the direction of racial justice in Britain. These independent groups have helped to counter the effects of illiberal, racist and politically fuelled asylum and immigration acts since the 1950s.

Everyday racisms: from interpersonal to situational interventions

The everyday inequities experienced by black and minority ethnic groups are perpetuated through everyday practices. The micro level everyday behaviours and attitudes which maintain the social structures of racism become critical to the causes of racism. One sustains the other. While there are interventions concerned with interpersonal and face-to-face racism, the macro contexts of ideologies and discourses are rarely addressed in policy interventions. Micro processes of everyday 'lived out' racisms are perhaps 'easier' to focus on than the macro, more discursive manifestations. Most interventions in everyday racism involve the young, the powerless and the working classes, or the employee rather than the powerful and the influential. The former are important interventions, but they must not become the sole understanding of interventions in racism.

At a local level, successful interventions in racism have understood the situational context of, for example, white young men's racist expressions, and attempted to address these in an inclusive way by involving young men and women, black and white. Youth projects have enabled dialogue and understanding to develop among previously hostile and violent black and white young people in an open, yet challenging environment. These projects show that racism is not monolithic. It can be understood in terms of a locally shared experience of deprivation and scarce resources. Business opportunities, jobs and housing policies can (unwittingly?) place racialised minorities into declining white areas. These minorities become associated with the decline of the service or the area. They come to take the blame for the 'crisis' of white working-class identities, people abandoned by the middle-class political elite of 'New Labour'.

The interfaith and intercultural social cohesion projects set up in the aftermath of the northern 'race' riots of 2001 are predicated on the importance of dialogue. But intercultural understanding as an intervention also depends on the situation and the context. While sanctions against racist language may work in one place, joining together to clean up the local environment may work in another. While this may lead to conflict resolution in the short term, in the long term, as in Northern Ireland, causes may not be addressed. The root causes of political and religious rifts or economic and social inequalities are rarely used as a basis for designing interventions. Such projects may or may not impact on a short-term personal level, but deep-rooted structural problems will not go away.

International interventions, such as the Truth and Reconciliation hearings in Chile, South Africa and Rwanda, which bring the victim face to face with the perpetrator, may have some mileage in addressing causes. The pain produced by racist regimes can be healed. These reconciliation interventions constitute important interventions in putting 'on trial' the heart of 'normalised' everyday racism. Political recognition and reparations statements by senior politicians on behalf of a nation's shameful past can have a considerable impact on a culture to move forward. Examples of these are the Aboriginal 'Sorry' movement and the Maori Treaty of Waitangi.

Everyday racism has also to be addressed in the workplace. The level of unreported sexual and racial harassment is particularly of concern. The limitations of accessing the race relations legislation to deal with the everyday manifestations of sexual and racial taunts must be recognised. Actions by colleagues and managers, including both subtle and overt blocking of promotions or appointments, are in urgent need of carefully designed interventions. Leaders of organisations need to address organisational cultures which allow these behaviours and attitudes to flourish.

Safety for black and minority ethnic people (particularly young people and asylum seekers) in public spaces is also critical. Whether it is the office, the school playground, the bus or the street, 'race' hate can often be exacerbated and legitimated by some parts of the press. The racist murder of Stephen Lawrence who was chased and stabbed by a group of white young men is one such case. The murder of Damilola Taylor by other boys in the neighbourhood points to the issue of black on black crime. Masculinised territorial conflicts between rival Muslim and Sikh gangs, African Caribbean and Somali youth, and high-profile Jamaican yardie drug gun crime, needs to be confronted. Forced marriages and honour killings perpetrated against women in the ethnic communities need to be constantly exposed.

These issues are partly rooted in the current political context. At times where cultural and religious identities are increasingly constructed as 'fixed', the notion of 'black' as 'uncivilised', 'backward' and 'prone to crime' can be legitimised. Health, social welfare, crime and educational systems can reproduce these pathological discourses of innate violence and aggressiveness (for men) or passivity and oppression (for women) in their policies, laws and procedures.

Professional policy interventions: equality versus difference

There have been two key types of professionalised interventions in relation to racism. There are those initiatives which are concerned with promoting *equality*, particularly in employment and in access to services. There are those which are about the promotion of *difference*, which are aimed at differing ethnicised groups. These latter approaches include multicultural policies on social cohesion. They have been introduced to both legitimate differences as well as bring groups together. These two different approaches have characterised British social policy since the 1960s. Fundamental tensions inhere between these two types of interventions. The tensions are based on both philosophy and outcome, and both have underpinned the confusing range of initiatives we now have in the 'race relations industry'.

Equality interventions are the most commonly understood form of intervention of 'race' equality initiatives. These interventions are derived from the equality struggles of feminist and civil rights movements. They are underpinned by arguments for positive and protective measures, such as EO policies and antidiscrimination legislation. These measures are commonly agreed as ones to ensure fair and equal treatment of groups, who have been hitherto marginalised.

For black and minority ethnic groups, equality interventions based on the notion of equal access have largely resulted in a focus on recruitment and promotion and more recently in access to services. Increases in the recruitment of racialised groups have been hailed as a success. It is not possible to decisively conclude that this is due to the effectiveness of the interventions themselves, rather than labour market and demographic changes. It may be a combination of these factors.

But the recruitment changes have also brought to light the employment of black workers serving the black community in areas where greater proportions of the black populations live or have been channelled. Many black professionals are to be found serving their 'own' communities, or in positions such as 'race' advisers or as 'token' teachers and professors. Their visibility can be proudly acclaimed. There may be instances where numerical targets can thus be 'easily' met, but racism will not have changed. Ethnic monitoring, without an equal emphasis on gender, age and class, results in the 'fixing' of ethnic categories, as if these categories are 'real, concrete divisions'. In the new racism, this cultural expression of difference reproduces racism rather than challenges it.

Equality interventions that seek to facilitate access to health, welfare, education and other services are also problematic with regard to addressing the causes of racism. Discourses on social cohesion and civil renewal stress the importance of including the alienated and the disengaged. Social capital addresses the building of 'trust' rather than challenging the structural and political reproduction of racism. It would be fair to say that inclusion interventions which recognise racialised exclusion such as the Sure Start programmes for mothers and pre-school children, and translation and interpretation services are important as a first step. On the other hand, they do not often address the experience of racism and exclusion. They do not tackle why these groups have been excluded and how they are treated once they are 'included'.

The under-funded black voluntary sector can provide creative interventions to combat racism. Projects such as the Community Empowerment Network provide an important advocacy and support service for excluded children (see Appendix A (15) 'Community Empowerment Network').

Difference interventions include multicultural initiatives such as national policy interventions based on ethnic or racialised difference. These interventions have been implemented side by side with notions of equality of opportunity. They have arisen for a variety of reasons explored in Chapter Eight. The separating out of different racialised groups in social policy (for example, in the Census, or in monitoring categories) has encouraged a stronger self-definition by the groups themselves. Ethnic and religious groups, originating as Hindus, Muslims, African Caribbeans, or Africans, may not want to be seen as the 'same' as each other. These settled communities want to assert their separate and unique identities, particularly since overlapping or changing identities is not something recognised by official discourse.

However, multiculturalism is not just about an innocent cultural recognition in a plural society with shared values. Political concern about conflicts between 'cultures' has been part of the motivation. Recent policies on social and community cohesion and civil renewal have been introduced under the banner of 'multiculturalism'. These policies aim to deal with the issues of community leadership, inter-faith and intercultural understanding rather than tackling the social effects of 'racialised disadvantage'.

The business case for diversity is the new manifestation of the difference and multicultural discourse. There are pleas for 'excluded' groups to be included in an expanding public service sector and in global private corporations. While demographic changes and 'business' arguments have informed this approach, many opportunities for skilled and talented black and minority graduates have been opened up. Such initiatives should not be seen as special case scenarios to 'unqualified' black employees. We need to strengthen these interventions by addressing the culture of work. This culture needs to be underpinned by a culture of rights in order for such interventions to be sustainable.

Probably the most important intervention to emerge from the 'difference' interventions is the recognition of multiple identities. Interventions that appreciate the complexity of sex, 'race', religion, sexual orientation, disability and age within racialised groups have the capacity to challenge the structural causes of racism by revealing the common roots of prejudice and discrimination which reproduce inequality and exclusion. We need an analysis that can show common threads which link a project on lesbian Muslim women's sexuality with a project on the sign language needs of Asian deaf children. By understanding the commonalties, we can make improved interventions that tackle the root causes of racist exclusion in service provision for all those with marginalised identities.

While this book has set down the *strong causes* of racism, professional policy interventions are arguably *weak solutions*. They have skimmed the surface of the *effects* of racism, dealing with symptoms rather than *causes*.

Professional interventions on equality or difference have also not had neutral impacts. By not examining the causes of racism and designing appropriate interventions, difficulties in addressing racism have been compounded. By not implementing real change, the rhetoric of 'race' equality assumes a tangible reality. It conveys an impression that action on 'race' equality and multiculturalism has been going on for years. It suggests an idea that plenty of resources have been 'given' to 'ethnic minorities'. The lack of implementation coupled with a widespread rhetoric acts together to fuel a backlash.

Conclusion

The conclusions of this book on interventions in racism are not easy to summarise. Part of the problem lies with a lack of literature which evaluates success in interventions related to racism. As we have discussed, this problem is related to a lack of clarity about what racism means. Combating racism has come to be seen as primarily about changing policies and procedures in order to provide 'equality of opportunity' to address the effects rather than the causes of racism. Understanding racism with reference to ideology, nation, identity construction, the role of whiteness and the nature of ethnicity, essential to tackling racism, are ignored.

Defining success is problematic when the problem of racism has not only been around for several hundred years, but keeps changing form and appears in different ways, in different situations, contexts and societies. We live currently in a culture that valorises success by calculating quantifiable outcomes such as 'evidence-based policy'. But this does not help us to measure success in combating racism in any meaningful way. We can only make *assumptions* that racism has declined if, for example, more black and minority ethnic people have been recruited into an organisation, such as the police force. However, numbers as a means of measuring success is highly misleading, since we know the internal culture of the police remains suffused with racism, despite the recruitment of 'minority ethnic' police officers. It is this intangible aspect of tackling the root causes of racism that makes evaluating successful interventions a difficult task.

Rather than search for the key to success, what has emerged in this book are underlying themes which direct us to areas where interventions may have an impact on the root causes of racism.

Addressing the causes of racism

The three areas of *education, communication* and *vigilance* are strong themes that course through our findings. These themes could shape a more systematic strategy for thinking about future interventions in an integrated way.

First, if the definition of an 'intervention' is 'stepping in to affect the outcome of a situation' then *education* has the means to do just that by bringing about change through knowledge and understanding. We have seen the impact of youth projects where young people who have been perpetrators of racism unlearn their racism. A diverse multicultural curriculum can inspire children to learn about their past to build a future. Our schools and institutions of higher learning have a leadership role to play in building a more confident sense of Britishness. Antiracist education at work, among other educational initiatives, can drive change from the bottom to the top. Black and 'minority ethnic' groups understand the power of education to transform their lives. They invest in alternative schools in which they are protected from the racism which devalues their children. Black self-help and empowerment through education is a key intervention in combating racist expectations.

Communication is crucial in developing global cross-racial, cross-cultural relationships. Communication means enabling dialogue between ethnic groups, torn apart by histories of violence and political opportunism. Women have been critical in the peace and opening dialogue relationships in Northern Ireland, Bosnia and Israel–Palestine (see Cockburn, 1998). The Truth and Reconciliation movements and soundly designed and implemented everyday forums for exchanging intercultural understandings, such as international youth projects, can help us understand the dynamics of racism. Communication and dialogue through sports, arts and cultural projects enable face-to-face contact which relies on the power of human relations to transcend historical and political divides that thrive on racist constructions. Good communication and understanding means we can understand the needs of racialised and multiple identity groups to access services, and so challenge the reproduction of inequality that underpins the dynamics of racism. One of the most important means of countering racist infiltration of the far right in our mainstream organisations is also through the use of the Internet (Fernandez Esteban, 2001). This use of technology will become an increasingly important intervention in the struggle against the growing right-wing racism, such as the BNP.

Finally, and probably most importantly, is the issue of *vigilance*. By this we mean the monitoring of the invisible racist elite who occupy the silent 'normative space of whiteness'. These are the powerful in our society such as politicians, social commentators, heads of corporations and the media who are rarely considered when racist pronouncements are discussed; yet they are central to the reproduction of everyday racist ideology. Independent activists, lawyers and non-governmental organisations who monitor press attacks on asylum seekers or campaign against racist legislation make substantial contributions to tackling the causes of racism.

Closing remarks

We began this book with a discussion of the World Conference Against Racism in Durban in 2001. The Conference was beset with conflicts and controversies over Arab charges of Israeli racism against Palestinians, African demands for slavery reparations, and disputes over India's caste system, China's rule in Tibet and Europe's treatment of Romany Gypsy communities. The roots of racism in slavery and the caste system, as well as current manifestations through wars and conflicts over disputed territories, all entered the debate about racism and its causes.

What the Conference illustrated and indeed as do the contents of this book, is that there is no one definition of racism, no one history of racism, and no one cause of racism. The multiple, situated and changing nature of racism in different times and places means it is impossible to find one ideal successful intervention which addresses the roots and reproduction of racism.

Bibliography

Adam, H. and Moodley, K. (2003) 'Reconciliation without justice', in J. Stone and R. Dennis (eds) *Race and ethnicity: Comparative and theoretical approaches*, Oxford: Blackwell.

Adorno, T.W., Frenkel-Brunswik, E., Levinson, D.J. and Sanford, R.N. (1950) *The authoritarian personality*, New York, NY: Harper.

Ahmad, W.I.U. (1996) 'Making black people sick: "race", ideology and health research', in W.I.U. Ahmad *'Race' and health in contemporary Britain*, Buckingham: Open University Press.

Ahmad, W.I.U. and Jones, L. (1998) 'Ethnicity, health and health care in the UK', in A. Peterson (ed) *Health matters*, London: Allen and Unwin.

Ahmed, S. (2004) *The cultural politics of emotions*, Edinburgh: Edinburgh University Press.

Ajadi, A. (2002) 'Reparations now!', *Inclusion*, Summer, pp 8-12, Bristol: Equality Foundation and Inclusive Management Solutions.

Alderson, P., Williams, C. and Farsides, B. (2004) 'Practitioners' views about equity within prenatal services', *Sociology*, vol 38, no 1, February, pp 61-80.

Alexander, C.S. (1996) *The art of being black: The creation of black youth identities*, Oxford: Clarendon Press.

Alexander, C.S. (2000) '(Dis)entangling the Asian gang: ethnicity, identity and masculinity', in B. Hesse *Un/settled multiculturalisms*, London: Zed Books.

Alexander, Z. (1999) *Study of black, Asian and ethnic minority issues*, London: DH.

Alibhai Brown, Y. (1999) *True colours: Public attitudes to multiculturalism and the role of the government*, London: Institute of Public Policy Research.

Alibhai Brown, Y. (2000) *Who do we think we are? Imagining the new Britain*, London: Allen Lane.

Alif Aleph (2004) *Manifesto*, June, London: Uniting Britain Trust.

Allen, S. (1973) 'The institutionalisation of racism', *Race*, vol 15, July, pp 99-105.

Amin, A. (2002) *Ethnicity and multicultural city: Living with diversity*, Liverpool: Economic and Social Research Council.

Amin, A. (2004) 'Multi-ethnicity and the idea of Europe', *Theory, Culture and Society*, vol 21, no 2, pp 1-24.

Anderson, B. (1983) *Imagined communities*, London: Verso.

Andrew, F. (1996) *An exploration of opportunities and barriers to the development of black managers in public services*, July, London: Office for Public Management.

Anthias, F. (1999) 'Institutional racism, power and accountability', *Sociological Research Online*, vol 4, no 1, March.

Appiah, L. (2001) *Mentoring: Business and schools working together*, London: Runnymede Trust.

Audit Commission (2000a) *Another country: Implementing dispersal under the Immigration and Asylum Act 1999*, London: Audit Commission.

Audit Commission (2000b) *A new city: Supporting asylum seekers and refugees in London*, London: Audit Commission.

Audit Commission (2002) *Widening participation in Higher Education in England*, HC 485 session 2001-2002, London: National Audit Office.

Audit Commission (2003) *Journey to race equality*, London: Audit Commission.

Back, L. (1996) *New ethnicities and urban culture*, London: Routledge.

Back, L. (2001) 'Reading the signs on the street', Mimeo, Department of Sociology Goldsmith's College, London: University of London.

Back, L. and Nayak, A. (1999) 'Signs of the times? Violence, graffiti and racism in the English suburbs', in T. Allen and J. Eade (eds) *Divided Europeans: Understanding ethnicities in conflict*, London: Kluwer Law International.

Back, L. and Solomos, J. (2000) *Theories of race and racism: A reader*, London: Routledge.

Back, L., Keith, M., Khan, A., Shukra, K. and Solomos, J. (2002) 'The return of assimilationism: race, multiculturalism and new labour', *Sociological Research Online*, vol 7, no 2.

Banks, M. (1996) *Ethnicity: Anthropological constructions*, London: Routledge.

Banton, M. (1997) *Ethnic and racial consciousness* (2nd edn), London: Longman.

Barber, L. (2004) 'Interview: my TV job wasn't my life, it gave me my life', *The Observer*, 6 June.

Barker, M. (1981) *The new racism: Conservatives and the ideology of the tribe*, London: Junction.

Barn, R. (2001) *Black youth on the margins: A research review*, York: Joseph Rowntree Foundation, with York Publishing Services.

Baxter, P. and Sansom, B. (1972) *Race and social difference: Selected readings*, Harmondsworth: Penguin.

Bell, D. (1992) *Faces at the bottom of the well*, New York, NY: Basic Books.

Berthoud, R. (1999) *Young Caribbean men and the labour market: A comparison with other ethnic groups*, York: Joseph Rowntree Foundation.

Bhattacharya, G., Gabriel, J. and Small, S. (2002) *Race and power: Global racism in the 21st century*, London: Routledge.

Bhavnani, R. (1994) *Black women in the labour market: A research review*, Manchester: Equal Opportunities Commission.

Bhavnani, R. (2001) *Rethinking interventions in racism*, Stoke on Trent: Trentham Books.

Bhavnani, K. and Bhavnani, R. (1985) 'Racism and resistance in Britain', in D. Coates, G. Johnson and R. Bush *A socialist anatomy of Britain*, Cambridge: Polity Press.

Bhavnani, R. and Coyle, A. (2000) 'Black and minority ethnic women managers in the UK: continuity or change?', in M.J. Davidson and J. Burke (eds) *Women in management: Current research issues*, Volume II, London: Sage Publications.

Bhavnani, R. and Cheung-Judge, M. (1990) *Review of Lambeth Council equal opportunities policy (1978-1989)*, London: Lambeth Council.

Bhavnani, R. and Foot, J. (2000) *Value for all: A review of race equality – Race matters in Lambeth*, London: London Borough of Lambeth.

Bhavnani, R., Arya, A., Ashton, C. and Meetoo, V. (2003) *Project Domino: Promoting race equality through leadership: Promoting minority ethnic managers*, London: Centre for High Performance Development.

Bigler, R.S. (1999) 'The use of multicultural curricula and materials to counter racism in children', *Journal of Social Issues*, Winter (www.findarticles.com/cf_dls/m03414_55/62521563/print.jhtml).

Bignall, T. and Butt, J. (2000) *Between ambition and achievement: Young black disabled people's views and experiences of independence and independent living*, Bristol/York: The Policy Press/Joseph Rowntree Foundation.

Bishop, R. and Glynn, T. (1999) *Culture counts: Changing power relations in education*, London: Zed Books.

Blair, M. (2001) *Why pick on me? School exclusions and black youth*, Stoke on Trent: Trentham.

Blair, M. (2004) 'Aiming high project', Paper presented at 'Raising achievement: towards a whole school agenda', Nexus conference, Woburn Place, 20 May.

Blair, M. and Bourne, J., with Coffin, C., Creese, A. and Kenner, C. (1998) *Making the difference: Teaching and learning strategies in successful multi-ethnic schools*, London: Department for Education and Employment.

Blink: Black Information Link (2002) 'Many companies fail to provide equal opportunities for all' (IPPR survey of company directors: 'What's on the agenda?', 4 December: www.blink.org.uk/print.asp?key=1450).

Bloch, A. (2000) 'Refugee settlement in Britain: the impact of policy on participation', *Journal of Ethnic and Migration Studies*, January, vol 26, no 1, pp 75-88.

Bloch, A. (2004) *Making it work: Refugee employment in the UK*, London: IPPR.

Blunkett, D. (2003) *Civil renewal: A new agenda*, London: Home Office.

Bonnett, A. (2000a) *White identities: An historical and international perspective*, London: Prentice Hall.

Bonnett, A. (2000b) 'Whiteness in crisis: white race identity in early 20th century', *History Today*, December, vol 50, no 12, p 38.

Bourne, J. (2001) 'The life and times of institutional racism', *Race and Class*, vol 43, no 2, pp 7-22.

Bowser, B.P. (ed) (1995) *Racism and anti-racism in world perspective*, London: Sage Publications.

Bradbury, S. (2001) *Football unites, racism divides: An evaluation of the period 1998-2000*, Leicester: Sir Norman Chester Centre for Football Research, University of Leicester.

Brah, A. (1992) 'Difference, diversity and differentiation', in J. Donald and A. Rattansi (eds) *'Race', culture and difference*, London: Sage Publications.

Brah, A. (1996) *Cartographies of diaspora: Contesting identities*, London: Routledge.

Braham, P., Rattansi, A. and Skellington, R. (eds) (1992) *Racism and anti-racism: Inequalities, opportunities and policies*, London: Sage Publications.

Branigan, T. (2004) 'I'm not racist, says Princess, I even pretended to be half-caste', *The Guardian*, 24 July.

Brown, C. (1992) 'Same difference: the persistence of racial disadvantage in the British employment market', in P. Braham, A. Rattansi and R. Skellington (eds) *Racism and anti-racism: Inequalities, opportunities and policies*, London: Sage Publications.

Brown, G. (2004) 'The golden thread that runs through our history', *The Guardian*, 8 July.

Brownill, S. and Darke, J. (1998) *'Rich mix': Inclusive strategies for urban regeneration*, Bristol/York: The Policy Press/Joseph Rowntree Foundation.

Bulmer, M. and Solomos, J. (eds) (1999) *Racism*, Oxford: Oxford University Press.

Burgess, S. and Wilson, D. (2004) 'Ethnic mix: how segregated are English schools?', *Market and Public Organisation*, Issue no 10, Spring, University of Bristol.

Burnett, J. (2004) 'Community, cohesion and the state', *Race and Class*, vol 45, no 3, pp 1-18.

Burnley Task Force (2001) *Burnley speaks, who listens? A summary of the Burnley Task Force Report*, June.

Byrne, D. (2000) *Social exclusion*, Buckingham: Open University Press.

Cabinet Office (2001) *Towards equality and diversity: Implementing the employment and race directives*, London: Cabinet Office.

Carby, H. (1982) *White woman listen! Black feminism and the boundaries of sisterhood*, London: Hutchinson.

CARF (2002) 'Community cohesion ... Blunkett's new race', Doctrine no 66, February/March (www.carf.demon.ac.uk/feat56.html).

Carmichael, S. and Hamilton, C. (1967) *Black Power*, Harmondsworth: Penguin.

Carrington, B. and McDonald, I. (2001) *'Race', sport and British society*, London: Routledge.

Carter, J., Fenton, S. and Modood, T. (1999) *Ethnicity and employment in higher education*, London: Policy Studies Institute.

Carvel, J. (1998) 'Muslim schools get the grants', *The Guardian*, 10 January.

Cashmore, E. (2002) 'Behind the window dressing: ethnic minority police perspectives on cultural diversity', *Journal of Ethnic and Racial Studies*, vol 28, no 2, April, pp 327-41.

Cassell, C. (2000) 'The business case and the management of diversity', in M. Davidson and R. Burke (eds) *Women in management: Current research issues, vol 2*, London: Sage Publications.

Castagna, M. and Sefa Dei, G.J. (2000) 'An historical overview of the application of the race concept on social practice', in A. Calliste and G.J. Sefa Dei *Anti-racist feminism*, Nova Scotia: Fernwood.

Castells, M. (1996) *The information age: Economy, society and culture, vol 1: The rise of the network society, vol 2: The power of identity, vol 3: End of millennium*, Oxford: Blackwell.

Castles, S. (1996) 'The racisms of globalisation', in E. Vasta and S. Castles (eds) *The teeth are smiling: The persistence of racism in mulitcultural Australia*, St Leonards: Allen and Unwin.

CBSE (Commission for Black Staff in Further Education) (2003) *Challenging racism: Further Education leading the way: The full report of the Commission for Black Staff in Further Education*, London: CBSE.

Centre for Contemporary Cultural Studies (1982) *The Empire strikes back: Race and racism in 1970s Britain*, London: Hutchinson.

Centre for Educational Research (2003) *Minority ethnic exclusions and the Race Relations (Amendment) Act 2000, Interim summary*, November, Canterbury Christ Church University College (www.dfes.gov.uk/exclusions/uploads).

Centre for Ethnicity and Racism Studies (2002) *Institutional racism in Higher Education: Building the anti-racist university: A toolkit*, Leeds: University of Leeds.

Chahal, K. (1999) *We can't all be white: Racist victimisation in the UK*, York: York Publishing Services/Joseph Rowntree Foundation.

Chahal, K. (2003) *Racial Harassment Support Projects: Their role, impact and potential*, York: Joseph Rowntree Foundation.

Chahal, K. (2004) 'Experiencing ethnicity: discrimination and service provision', *Foundations*, York: Joseph Rowntree Foundation.

Chalmers, D. (2001) 'The mistakes of the good European', in S. Fredman (ed) *Discrimination and human rights: The case of racism*, Oxford: Oxford University Press.

Chouhan, K. and Lusane, C. (2004) *Black voluntary and community sector funding: Its impact on civic engagement and capacity building*, York: Joseph Rowntree Foundation, with York Press Services.

Church and Race (Bulletin for Churches Commission for Racial Justice) (www.ctbi.org.uk).

Clancy, A., Hough, M., Aust, R. and Kershaw, C. (2001) Ethnic Minorities Experiences of Crime and Policing: Findings 146 Home Office, www.homeoffice.gov.uk/rds/bcs1.html

Coard, B. (1971) *How the West Indian child is made: ESN in the British school system*, London: New Beacon Books.

Cockburn, C. (1991) *In the way of women*, Basingstoke: Macmillan.

Cockburn, C. (1998) *The space between us: Negotiating gender and national identities in conflict*, London and New York, NY: Zed Books.

Cohen, P. (1986) *Anti racist cultural studies*, Curriculum Development Project in Schools and Community Education, London: Institute of Education.

Cohen, P. (1997a) *Rethinking the youth question: Education, labour and cultural studies*, Basingstoke: Macmillan.

Cohen, P. (1997b) 'Getting through: new approaches to tackling youth racism', by CARF, *Bulletin* no 1, November.

Cohen, P. (ed) (1999) *New ethnicities, old racism*, London: Zed Books.

Coker, N. (2001) *Racism in medicine: An agenda for change*, London: Kings Fund.

Colley, L. (1999) 'Britain as Europe', Beall-Russell Lecture, Baylor University.

Collier, R. (1998) *Equality in managing service delivery*, Buckingham: Open University Press.

Commissions and Forums on Islamophobia (2004) (www.runnymedetrust.org/projects/commissionOnBritishMuslims.html and Forum Against Islamophobia and Racism: www.fairuk.org).

Connections (1999) *Young, white and wicked*, Leicester: National Youth Agency.

Connor, H., Tyers, C., Modood, T. and Hillage, J. (2004) *Why the difference? A closer look at higher education minority ethnic students and graduates*, Research Report 552, London: DfES.

Cook, R. (2001) 'Robin Cook's chicken tikka masala speech', *The Guardian*, 19 April.

Cornell, S. and Hartmann, D. (1998) *Ethnicities and race: Making identities in a changing world*, London: Sage Publications.

Cottle, S. (2000) *Ethnic minorities and the media: Changing cultural boundaries*, Buckingham: Open University Press.

Coyle, A. (1995) *Learning from experience: The equal opportunities challenge for the 1990s – The seven million pounds project working paper 5*, London: Demos.

Crawley, H. (2004) *Moving forward: The provision of accommodation for Travellers and Gypsies*, London: IPPR.

CRE (Commission for Racial Equality) (1993) *Housing associations and racial equality: England and Wales: A general investigation*, London: CRE.

CRE (1995) *Racial equality means business: A standard for racial equality for employers*, London: CRE.

CRE (1998) *Stereotyping and racism: Findings from two attitudes surveys*, London: CRE.

CRE (2000) *Equal opportunities and private sector employment in Scotland*, September, London: CRE.

CRE (2004a) 'CRE survey shows little integration among UK's white majority community with ethnic minorities', 19 July (www.cre.gov.uk/media/nr_arch/2004/nr010719.html).

CRE (2004b) 'Statistics: education – race equality impact assessment' (www.cre.gov.uk/duty/reia/statitics_education.html).

Creegan, C., Colgan, F., Charlesworth, R. and Robinson, G. (2001) *Walking the talk: Perspectives on the implementation of a local authority race equality action plan*, CERB Research Paper No 7, London: University of North London.

Creegan, C., Colgan, F., Charlesworth, R. and Robinson, G. (2003) 'Race equality policies at work: employee perceptions of the "implementation gap" in a UK local authority', *Work, Employment and Society*, vol 17, no 4, pp 617-40.

Crenshaw, K. (1993) 'Whose story is it anyway? Feminist and anti-racist appropriations of Anita Hill', in T. Morrison (ed) *Race-ing, justice en-gendering power*, London: Chatto and Windus.

Crenshaw, K. (1998) 'Race, reform and retrenchment: transformation and legitimation in anti-discrimination law', *Harvard Law Review*, vol 101, no 7, pp 1331-87.

Crosskill, D. (1997) *The scales of justice: West Yorkshire Racial Justice Programme – Independent programme review*, April, York: Joseph Rowntree Charitable Trust.

Cumberbatch, G., Gauntlet, S., Richards, M. and Littlejohns, V. (2001) *Top 10 TV: Ethnic minority group representation on popular television*, London: CRE.

Curtis, L.P. (1971) *Apes and angels: The Irishman in Victorian caricature*, Newton Abbot: David and Charles.

Dadzie, S. (1997) *Blood, sweat and tears: An account of the Bede anti-racist detached youth work project*, Leicester: Youth Work Press.

Dadzie, S. (2003) 'Trial and Error: learning about racism through citizenship education' (www.front-line-training.co.uk/trialand error; www.dfes.gov.uk/citizenship).

Daniel, W.W. (1968) *Racial disadvantage in Britain*, Harmondsworth: Penguin.

Davidson, M. (1997) *The black and ethnic minority woman manager: Cracking the concrete ceiling*, London: Paul Chapman.

Davidson, M. and Burke, R. (eds) (2000) *Women in management: Current research issues vol 2*, London: Sage Publications.

Davis, M. (2003) 'Community living and community safety', *Runnymede Bulletin* no 333, March.

Davis, S. and Cooke, V. (2002) *Why do black women organise? A comparative analysis of black women's voluntary sector organisations in Britain and their relationship to the state*, London: Policy Studies Institute/Henry Ling Ltd.

Delgado, R. (ed) (1995) *Critical race theory: The cutting edge*, Philadelphia: Temple University Press.

Delgado, R. and Stefancic, J. (eds) (1997) *Critical white studies: Looking beyond the mirror*, Philadelphia: Temple University Press.

Denney, D. (1997) 'Anti racism and the limits of equal opportunities policy in the criminal justice system', *Social Policy and Administration*, vol 31, no 5, December, pp 79-95.

Denney, C. and Elliot, L. (2004) 'Migration rhetoric belies the fact', *The Guardian*, 6 April.

DfES (Department for Education and Skills) (2001) *Permanent exclusions from school and exclusion appeals, England 2000-2001*, London: DfES.

DfES (2003) *Aiming high: Raising achievement of ethnic minority pupils*, Consultation, March, London: DfES.

DH (Department of Health)/Norfolk, Suffolk and Cambridgeshire Strategic Health Authority (2003) 'Independent Inquiry into the Death of David Bennett', December (www.image. guardian.co.uk/ sys-files/ Society/documents/2004/02/12/Bennett.pdf).

Dodd, V. (2001) 'Blunkett's blame game' (David Blunkett legislation conforming to British values), *The Guardian*, 11 December.

Donald, J. and Rattansi, A. (eds) (1992) *'Race', culture and difference*, London: Sage Publications.

Dorset Racial Equality Council (2003) *Racism and the rural idyll*, Devon: Devon Library and Information Services.

Dover Express, The (1998) 'Editorial: human sewage', 15 October (www.canterbury.u-net/Dover).

DTI (Department of Trade and Industry) (2002a) *Equality and diversity: The way ahead*, London: The Stationery Office.

DTI (2002b) *Equality and diversity: Making it happen*, London: The Stationery Office.

DTI (2004) *Fairness for all: A new Commission for Equality and Human Rights*, White Paper, May, London: The Stationery Office.

Dua, E. (2000) 'The Hindu woman's question: Canada, nation building and the social construction of gender for South Asian Canadian women', in A. Calliste and G.J. Sefa Dei *Anti-racist feminism*, Nova Scotia: Fernwood.

Duffy, B. (2004) *Understanding life, satisfaction and trust – Where you live matters*, London: MORI.

Dummett, A. (1973) *A portrait of English racism*, Harmondsworth, Penguin.

Dwyer, C. (1999) 'Veiled meanings: young British Muslim women and the negotiation of differences', *Gender, Place and Culture*, vol 6, no 1, pp 5-26.

EITI (2002) http://eiti.com/

Essed, P. (1991) *Understanding everyday racism: An interdisciplinary theory*, London: Sage Publications.

Ethnic and Racial Studies (2003) *Special Issue: Scholarship on Race and Urban Poverty*, vol 26, no 6, November.

European Monitoring Centre for Racism and Xenophobia (2001) 'Strategies for the local community', Stockholm Conference Report, 29-30 January.

Eysenck, H. (1971) *Race intelligence and education*, London: Temple Smith.

Faludi, S. (1992) *Backlash: The undeclared war against women*, New York, NY: Anchor Books/Doubleday.

Fanon, F. (1986) *Black skins, white masks*, London: Penguin.

Faulkner, D. (2004) *Civil renewal, diversity and social capital in a multi-ethnic Britain*, London: The Runnymede Trust.

Fekete, L. (2004a) Contribution to the Joseph Rowntree Racism Roundtable on 'Causes of racism and successful interventions', 6 May, London: National Council for Voluntary Organisations.

Fekete, L. (2004b) 'Anti-Muslim racism and the European security state', *Race and Class*, vol 46, no 1, pp 3-39.

Fenton, S. (1982) 'Multi something education', *New Community*, vol 10, no 1, 57-63.

Fenton, S. (2003) *Ethnicity*, Cambridge: Polity.

Fernandez Esteban, M.L. (2001) 'The internet: a new horizon for race hatred', in S. Fredman (ed) *Discrimination and human rights: The case of racism*, Oxford: Oxford University Press.

Fevre, R. (2004) 'Social capital and the participation of marginalised groups in government', forthcoming figures from an unpublished ESRC-awarded study.

Financial Times (2004) 'Guidance for employers from the CRE runs to over 93 pages', 5 May.

Fine, B. (2002) 'They f**k you up those social capitalists', *Antipode*, September, vol 34, no 4, pp 796-9.

Fine, M., Weis, L., Powell, L.C. and Mun Wong, L. (eds) (1997) *Off white: Readings on race, power, and society*, New York, NY: Routledge.

Fiske, S. (1998) 'Stereotyping, prejudice and discrimination', in D. Gilbert and S. Fiske *The handbook of social psychology: Volume II* (4th edn), Oxford: Oxford University Press.

'Forced marriages action plan forges ahead' (2002) 12 November (www.redhotcurry.com/news/forced_marriages.htm).

Foster, J. (1997) 'Volunteering by members of the black and minority ethnic communities in Britain', in J. Butt and K. Mirza, *Dimensions of the voluntary sector*, London: Charities Aid Foundation.

Fox, N.J. (2003) 'Practice-based evidence: towards collaborative and transgressive research', *Sociology*, vol 37, no 1, February, pp 81-102.

Frankenberg, R. (1997) 'Introduction: local whiteness, localizing whiteness', in R. Frankenberg (ed) *Displacing whiteness: Essays in social and cultural criticism*, Durham, NC: Duke University Press.

Fredman, S. (2001) 'Combating racism with human rights: the right to equality', in S. Fredman (ed) *Discrimination and human rights: The case of racism*, Oxford: Oxford University Press.

Fredman, S. (2002) *The future of equality in Britain*, Working Paper series no 5, Manchester: Equal Opportunities Commission.

Fryer, P. (1984) *Staying power: The history of black people in Britain*, London: Pluto Press.

Fryer, P. (1993) *Aspects of British black history*, London: Index Books.

Gaine, C. (2001) 'If it's not hurting it's not working: teaching teachers about "race"', *Research Papers in Education*, vol 16, no 1, pp 93-113.

Ghaffur, T. (2004) *Race and diversity in the police force*, London: Metropolitan Police Service (www.monitoring-group.co.uk/).

Gillborn, D. and Mirza, H. (2000) 'Educational inequality: mapping race, class and gender – a synthesis of research evidence', November, London: Ofsted (www.ofsted.gov.uk).

Gillborn, D. and Youdell, D. (2000) *Rationing education: Policy, practice, reform and equity*, Buckingham: Open University Press.

Gilman, S. (1991) *The Jew's body*, New York, NY: Routledge.

Gilroy, P. (1987) *Ain't no black in the Union Jack*, London: Hutchinson.

Gilroy, P. (1990) 'The end of anti-racism', in W. Ball and J. Solomos (eds) *Race and local politics*, Basingstoke: Macmillan.

Gilroy, P. (1992) 'The end of anti racism', in J. Donald and A. Rattansi (eds) *'Race' Culture and Difference*, London: Sage/Open University.

Gilroy, P. (1999) 'Joined-up politics and post-colonial melancholia', ICA Diversity Lecture, London: Institute of Contemporary Arts.

Gilroy, P. (2004) *After Empire: Melancholia or convivial culture*, Oxfordshire: Routledge.

Greater London Authority (2005) *Delivering Shared Heritage: The Mayor's Commission on African and Asian Heritage*, London, GLA.

Goldberg, D.T. (1993) *Racist culture: Philosophy and the politics of meaning*, Oxford: Blackwell.

Goldstein, B.P. (2002) 'Catch 22 – black workers' role in equal opportunities for black service users', *British Journal of Social Work*, vol 32, pp 765-78.

Goodheart, D. (2004) 'Discomfort of strangers', *The Guardian*, 24 February.

Grant, M. (2004) Contribution to the Joseph Rowntree Racism Roundtable on 'Causes of racism and successful interventions', 6 May, London: NCVO.

Greenwich Council (2003) *Righting the wrongs of racism: Final report of the Race Equality Review Panel*, London: Greenwich Council.

Greer, G. (2004) *Whitefella jump up: The shortest way to nationhood*, London: Profile Books.

Griffiths, D. (2003) 'English language training for refugees in London and the regions', Home Office online report 14/03 (www.homeoffice.gov.uk/rds/pdfs2/rdsolr1403.pdf).

Guardian, The (2001) 'Full text of David Blunkett's speech' (David Blunkett legislation conforming to British values), 11 December.

Guardian, The (2000) 'Labour tries to reclaim the flag', 28 March.

Guardian, The (2000) 'What is Britishness', 28 March.

Guerin, B. (2003) 'Combating prejudice and racism: new interventions from a functional analysis of racism', *Journal of Community and Applied Social Psychology*, vol 13, no 1, pp 29-45.

Gundara, J. (2001) 'Multiculturalism in Canada, Britain and Australia: the role of intercultural education', *London Journal of Canadian Studies*, vol 17, pp 40-59.

Gupta, R. (2003) *From homebreakers to jailbreakers: Southall Black Sisters*, London: Zed Books.

Gus John Partnership (2003) *Race for justice: A review of CPS decision making for possible racial bias at each stage of the prosecution process*, October. London: Crown Prosecution Service.

Hall, S. (1992) 'New ethnicities', in J. Donald and A. Rattansi (eds) *'Race', culture and difference*, London: Sage Publications.

Hall, S. (1994) 'Questions of cultural identity', in D. Held and T. McGrew (eds) *Modernity and its futures*, Cambridge: Polity Press.

Hall, S. (ed) (1997) *Representation: Cultural representations and signifying practices*, London: Sage Publications.

Hall, S. (2000) 'The multicultural question', in B. Hesse *Un/settled multiculturalisms*, London: Zed Books.

Hall, S. (2001) 'The multicultural question', Pavis Papers in Social and Cultural Research No 4, Milton Keynes: Open University/Faculty of Social Sciences.

Hall, S., Critcher, C., Jefferson, T. and Roberts, B. (1978) *Policing the crisis: Mugging, the state and law and order*, London: Macmillan.

Halpern, D. (2004) *Social capital*, Cambridge: Polity Press.

Hamber, B. (2002) 'Ere their story die: truth, justice and reconciliation in South Africa', *Race and Class*, Special issue: *Truth*, July-September, vol 44, no 1, pp 61–79.

Hannaford, I. (1996) *Race: The history of an idea in the West*, Baltimore and London: Johns Hopkins.

Harding, J. (2001) *The uninvited: Refugees at the rich man's gate*, London: Profile Books.

Hargraves, A.M. (2002) *Multicultural broadcasting: Concept and reality*, November, Broadcasting Standards Commission and Independent Television Commission.

Harris, C. (2001) 'Beyond multiculturalism? Difference recognition and social justice', *Patterns of Prejudice*, vol 35, no 1, pp 13-34.

Harris, N. (2000) 'Racists are so blind', *The Guardian*, 2 May.

Harris, R. (2004) Contribution to the Joseph Rowntree Roundtable on 'Causes of racism and successful interventions', 6 May, London: National Council of Voluntary Organisations.

Harrison, F.V. (1995) 'The persistent power of "race" in the cultural and political economy of racism', *Annual Review of Anthropology*, vol 24, pp 47-74.

Harvey, D. (1989) *The condition of postmodernity: An enquiry into the origins of cultural change*, Oxford: Blackwell.

Hattenstone, S. (2004) 'A new force', *The Guardian Weekend Magazine*, 20 March.

Haw, K. (1998) *Educating Muslim girls: Shifting discourses*, Buckingham: Open University Press.

Heath, A. and Yu, S. (2001) 'Explaining ethnic minority disadvantage', Unpublished paper commissioned by the Strategy Unit.

Held, D. and McGrew, T. (eds) (1994) *Modernity and its futures*, Cambridge: Polity Press.

Hepple, B., Coussey, M. and Choudhury, T. (2000) *Equality and new framework: Report of the Independent Review of Enforcement of UK Anti-discrimination Legislation*, Oxford: Hart Publishing.

Hewitt, R. (1996) *Routes of racism: The social basis of racist action*, Stoke on Trent: Trentham Books.

Hill, M. (1997) *Whiteness: A critical reader*, New York, NY: New York Press.

Hollands, R.G. (1990) *The long transition: Class culture and youth training*, London: Macmillan.

Home Office (1999) *Strengthening the black and minority ethnic voluntary sector*, London: Home Office.

Home Office (2000) 'Full and equal citizens: a strategy for the integration of refugees into the United Kingdom', November, London: National Asylum Support Service, Immigration and Nationality Directorate (www.homeoffice.gov.uk/ind/hpg.htm).

Home Office (2001a) *Building cohesive communities: A report of the ministerial group on public order and community cohesion*, London: Home Office.

Home Office (2001b) *Community cohesion: A report of the independent review team*, chaired by Ted Cantle, London: Home Office.

Home Office (2002) 'Secure borders, safe havens: integration with diversity in modern Britain', 7 February, London: The Stationery Office (www.official-documents.co.uk/document/cm53/5387/cm5387.pdf).

Home Office (2004) *Strength in diversity: Towards a community cohesion and race equality strategy: Consultation*, London: Home Office.

Home Office (2005) *Strength in diversity: Towards a community cohesion and race equality strategy: A summary of responses to the Consultation*, London: Home Office.

Honeyford, R. (1984) 'Education and race: an alternative view', *Salisbury Review*, vol 6, pp 30-2.

Honeyford, R. (1988) *Integration or disintegration: Towards a non racist society*, London: Claridge.

hooks, B. (1989) *Talking back*, London: Sheba.

Housing Corporation (2001) *Race and housing inquiry: Challenge report*, London: The Housing Corporation/SPARK.

Hughes, J. and Donnelly, C. (2003) 'Community relations in Northern Ireland: a shift in attitudes?', *Journal of Ethnic and Migration Studies*, vol 29, no 4, July, pp 643-61.

Humphry, D. and John, G. (1971) *Because they're Black*, Harmondsworth: Penguin.

Hunt, T. (2004) 'Written in 1215. Needed today', *The Guardian on Saturday*, 24 July.

Husband, C. (ed) (1982) *'Race' in Britain: Continuity and change* (2nd edn), London: Hutchinson.

Hussain, M. (2000) 'Islam media and minorities in Denmark', *Current Sociology*, October, vol 48, no 4, pp 95-116.

Hussain, Y., Atkin, K. and Ahmad, W. (2002) *South Asian disabled young people and their families*, Bristol/York: The Policy Press/Joseph Rowntree Foundation.

Hutton, W. (1995) *The state we're in*, London: Jonathan Cape Ltd.

Hutton, W. (2001) 'Slaves to the past', *The Observer*, 26 August.

Ifekwunigwe, J.O. (2004) *'Mixed race' studies: A reader*, London: Routledge.

Iganski, P., Mason, D., Humphreys, A. and Watkins, M. (2001) 'Equal opportunities and positive action in the British National Health Service: some lessons from the recruitment of minority ethnic groups to nursing and midwifery', *Ethnic and Racial Studies*, vol 24, no 2, March, pp 294-317.

Iles, P. and Auluck, R. (1991) 'The experience of black workers', in M. Davidson and J. Earnshaw (eds) *Vulnerable workers: Psychosocial and legal issues*, London: John Wiley and Sons.

Institute for Employment Studies (2002) 'A review of training in racism awareness and valuing cultural diversity', Home Office Research Development and Statistics Online report OLR 09/02.

International Council on Human Rights Policy (ICHRP) (2000) *The persistence and mutation of racism*, Versoix, Switzerland (www.ichrp.org).

Isin, E. and Siemiatycki, M. (2002) 'Making space for mosques: claiming urban citizenship', in S. Razack (ed) *Race, space and the law: The making of a white settler society*, Toronto: Between the Lines.

JCWI (Joint Commission for the Welfare of Immigrants) (2002) 'Secure borders, safe haven: integration with diversity in modern Britain', JCWI's initial response, February (www.jcwi.org.uk).

Jenkins, R. (1998) *Rethinking ethnicity: Arguments and explorations*, London: Sage Publications.

Jenkins, R. and Solomos, J. (1989) *Racism and equal opportunities policies in the 1980s* (2nd edn), Cambridge: Cambridge University Press.

Jensen, A. (1969) 'How much can we boost IQ and scholastic achievement?' *Harvard Educational Review*, vol 39, pp 1-123.

Jessop, B. (2000) 'Restructuring the welfare state, reorienting welfare strategies, revisioning the welfare society', in B. Greve (ed) *What constitutes a good society?*, Basingstoke: Macmillan.

Jewson, N. and Mason, D. (1994) 'Race, employment and equal opportunities: towards a political economy and an agenda for the 1990s', *Sociological Review*, vol 42, no 4, pp 591-617.

Johnson, N. (1998) *Mixed economies of welfare: A comparative perspective*, Hemel Hempstead: Prentice Hall Europe.

Jones, R. (1999) *Teaching racism or tackling it? Multicultural stories from white beginning teachers*, Stoke on Trent: Trentham.

Joseph Rowntree Foundation Racism Roundtable (2004) 'Causes of racism and successful interventions', Notes, 6 May, London: National Council of Voluntary Organisations.

Julienne, L. (2001) 'The root to my tree: examining the experience of positive action training in housing', *Findings*, March, York: Joseph Rowntree Foundation.

Kalra, V. (2003) 'Police lore and community disorder: diversity in the criminal justice system', in D. Mason (ed) *Explaining ethnic differences: Changing patterns of disadvantage in Britain*, Bristol: The Policy Press.

Kandola, B. and Fullerton, J. (1994) *Managing the mosaic: Diversity in action*, London: Institute of Personal Development.

Karim, K.H. (1997) 'The historical resilience of primary stereotypes: core images of the Muslim other', in S.H. Riggins *The language and politics of exclusion: Others in discourse*, London: Sage Publications.

Kempadoo, M. and Abdelrazak, M. (eds) (1999) *Directory of supplementary and mother-tongue classes 1999-2000*, London: Resource Unit for Supplementary and Mother Tongue Schools.

Kennedy, H. (2004) *Just law: The changing face of justice – and why it matters to us all*, Ebury: Vintage.

Kershaw, C., Budd, T., Kinshott, G., Mattinson, J., Mayhew, P. and Myhill, A. (2000) *The British Crime Survey*, October, London: Home Office.

Khan, N. (2002) *Towards a greater diversity: Results and legacy of the Arts Council of England's cultural diversity action plan*, London: Arts Council of England.

Khan, O. (2002) *Perpetrators of racist violence and harassment*, London: Runnymede Trust.

Kilroy Silk, R. (2004) 'We owe Arabs nothing', *Express on Sunday*, 4 January.

Klein, N. (2005) 'Racism is the terrorists' greatest recruitment tool', *The Guardian*, 13 August (www.guardian.co.uk/Columnists/ Column/0,5673,1548480,00.html).

Klug, F. (2000) *Values for a godless age: The history of the Human Rights Act and its political and legal consequences*, London: Penguin Books.

Klug, F. (2003) 'Protecting human rights', *LSE Magazine*, vol 15, no 2, Winter, p 23 (www.lse.ac.uk/depts/human-rights).

Kohn, M. (1996) *The race gallery: The return of racial science*, London: Vintage.

Kundnani, A. (1998) 'Where do you want to go today? The rise of information capital', *Race and Class*, 1 October.

Kundnani, A. (2003) 'It's official: media coverage of asylum is distorted and unfair', 19 November, IRR News (www.irr.org.uk/2003/ november/ak000013.html).

Kymlicka, W. (1998) *Finding our way: Rethinking ethno cultural relations in Canada*, Toronto: Oxford University Press.

Ladson Billings, G. (2004) 'Just what is critical race theory and what's it doing in a nice field like education?', in G. Ladson Billings and D. Gillborn *Multicultural education*, London: Routledge Falmer.

Lane, J. (1999) *Action for racial equality in the early years: Understanding the past: Thinking about the present, planning for the future – A practical handbook for early years workers*, London: The National Early Years Network.

Law, I. (2002) *Race in the news*, London: Palgrave.

Law, I., Phillips, D. and Turney, L. (eds) (2004) *Institutional racism in Higher Education*, Stoke on Trent: Trentham.

Leach, C.W. (2002) 'The social psychology of racism reconsidered', *Feminism and Psychology*, vol 12, no 4, pp 439-44.

Lee-Cunin, M. (1989) *Daughters of Seacole: A study of black nurses in West Yorkshire*, West Yorkshire: Low Pay Unit.

Lees, S., Papadopoulos, R. and Meetoo, V. (2003) 'The role of the black and minority ethnic voluntary sector in promoting social inclusion, regeneration and quality of life: a case study of the London Borough of Enfield', NCVO: Researching the Voluntary Sector Conference.

Lemos, G. (2000) *Racial harassment: Action on the ground*, November, Plymouth: Lemos & Crane.

Lenk, H.M. (2000) 'The case of Emilie Ouimet: news discourse on hijab and the construction of Quebecois national identity', in A. Calliste and G.J. Sefa Dei *Anti-racist feminism*, Nova Scotia: Fernwood.

Lev-Wiesel, R. (2003) 'Indicators constituting the construct of "perceived community cohesion"', *Community Development Journal*, vol 38, no 4, October, pp 332-43.

Lewis, G. (2000) 'Discursive histories, the pursuit of multiculturalism and social policy', in G. Lewis, S. Gewirtz and J. Clarke *Rethinking social policy*, London, Thousand Oaks and New Delhi: Open University and Sage Publications.

Lipsitz, G. (1998) *The possessive investment in whiteness: How white people profit from identity politics*, Philadelphia: Temple University Press.

Local Government Association (2002) *Guidance on community cohesion*, London: The Chameleon Press.

London Museums Agency (2003) *Holding up the mirror: Addressing cultural diversity in London's museums*, October, London: Helen Denniston Associates.

Lusane, C. (2003) *A vision of equality: Statement on proposed Single Equalities Act and Single Equalities Body*, Policy Paper no 1, February, London: 1990 Trust.

Mac an Ghaill, M. (1999) *Contemporary racisms and ethnicities: Social and cultural transformations*, Buckingham: Open University Press.

McClintock, A. (1995) *Imperial leather: Race, gender and sexuality in the colonial contest*, London: Routledge.

McCrudden, C. (2001) 'International and European norms regarding national legal remedies for racial inequalities', in S. Fredman (ed) *Discrimination and human rights: The case of racism*, Oxford: Oxford University Press.

Macdonald Inquiry (1989) *Murder in the playground: The report of the MacDonald Inquiry into Racial Violence in Manchester Schools*, London: Longsight Press.

Macey, M. (1995) 'Towards racial justice? A re-evaluation of anti-racism', *Critical Social Policy*, vol 44/45, pp 126-46.

McGhee, D. (2003) 'Moving to our common ground – a critical examination of community cohesion discourse in twenty-first century Britain', Editorial Board of the *Sociological Review*, Oxford: Blackwell.

McIntosh, N. and Smith, D.J. (1974) *The extent of racial discrimination*, London: Political and Economic Planning.

Mack, T. (2001) 'Payback time', *The Guardian Weekend*, 11 August.

McLaughlin, C. (2002) 'Reparations in South Africa: a visit to Khulumani', *Race and Class*: Special issue, *Truth*, July-September, vol 44, no 1, pp 81–86.

McLaughlin, E. and Neal, S. (2004) 'Misrepresenting the multicultural nation: the policy making process, news media management and the Parekh Report', *Policy Studies*, vol 25, no 3, pp 155-74.

McLeod, M., Owen, D. and Khamis, C. (2001) *The role and future development of black and minority ethnic organisations*, York: Joseph Rowntree Foundation.

McPake, J., Johnstone, R., Lo Bianco, J., McColl, H., Rodriguez, J. and Speake, E. (2001) 'Translating, interpreting and communication support services across the public sector in Scotland: a literature review', Social Inclusion Research Programme, Research Findings No 6, Scottish CILT University of Stirling (www.scotland.gov.uk/cru/resfinds/sic6a-00.asp).

Macpherson, W. (1999) *The Stephen Lawrence Inquiry: Report of an inquiry by Sir William Macpherson of Cluny*, London: The Stationery Office.

Majors, R. (ed) (2001) *Educating our black children: New directions and radical approaches*, London: Routledge Falmer.

Malik, K. (1996) *The meaning of race: Race history and culture in Western society*, London: Macmillan Press.

Manchester Online News (2004) 'Husband defends Winterton over joke', 28 February (www.manchesteronline.co.uk/news/s/82/82615).

Mason, D. (2000) *Race and ethnicity in modern Britain* (2nd edn), Oxford: Oxford University Press.

Mason, D. (2003) 'Changing patterns of ethnic disadvantage in employment', in D. Mason (ed) *Explaining ethnic differences: Changing patterns of disadvantage in Britain*, Bristol: The Policy Press.

Maynard, M. (1994) 'Race, gender and the concept of difference', in H. Afshar and M. Maynard (eds) *The dynamics of race and gender: Some feminist interventions*, London: Taylor and Francis.

Metcalf, H. and Forth, J. (2000) *Business benefits of race equality: Race research for the future*, 6 March, Research Report no 177, London: DFEE.

Miles, R. (1982) *Racism and migrant workers*, London: Routledge, Kegan and Paul.

Miles, R. (1989) *Racisms*, London: Routledge.

Miles, R. (1993) *Racism after 'race relations'*, London: Routledge.

Miles, R. and Phizacklea, A. (1984) *White man's county*, London: Pluto.

Miles, R. and Small, S. (1999) 'Race and ethnicity', in S. Taylor (ed) *Sociology issues and debates*, Basingstoke: Macmillan Press.

Mills, G. (2002) 'Combating institutional racism in the public sector', *Industrial Law Journal*, vol 31, issue 1, March, pp 96-8.

Mirza, H.S. (1992) *Young, female and black*, London: Routledge.

Mirza, H.S. (1995) 'Black women in higher education: defining a space/ finding a place', in L. Morley and V. Walsh *Feminist academics: Creative agents for change*, London: Taylor and Francis.

Mirza, H.S. (1997) *Black British feminism*, London: Routledge.

Mirza, H.S. (1998) 'Race, gender and IQ: the social consequence of pseudo-scientific discourse', *Race, Ethnicity and Education*, vol 1, no 1, pp 109-26.

Mirza, H.S. (2003) '"All the women are white, all the blacks are men – but some of us are brave": mapping the consequences of invisibility for black and minority ethnic women in Britain', in D. Mason (ed) *Explaining ethnic differences: Changing patterns of disadvantage in Britain*, Bristol: The Policy Press.

Mirza, H.S. and Reay, D. (2000a) 'Redefining citizenship: black women educators and "the third space"', in M. Arnot and J. Dillabough *Challenging democracy: International perspectives on gender*, London: Routledge Falmer.

Mirza, H.S. and Reay, D. (2000b) 'Spaces and places of black educational desire: rethinking black supplementary schools as a new social movement', *Sociology*, vol 345, no 3, pp 521-44.

Mirza, H.S. and Sheridan, A.M. (2003) *Multiple identity and access to health: The experience of black and minority ethnic women*, Working Paper Series no 10, Manchester: Equal Opportunities Commission.

Modood, T. (2003) 'Ethnic differentials in educational performance', in D. Mason (ed) *Explaining ethnic differences: Changing patterns of disadvantage in Britain*, Bristol: The Policy Press.

Modood, T. (2005) *Multicultural politics: Racism, ethnicity and Muslims in Britain*, Edinburgh: Edinburgh University Press.

Modood, T. and Acland, T. (1997) *Race and Higher Education: Experiences, challenges and policy implications*, London: Policy Studies Institute.

Modood, T. and Werbner, P. (1997) *Debating cultural hybridity: Multicultural identities and the politics of anti racism*, London: Zed Books.

Modood, T., Berthoud, R. and Nazroo, J. (2002) '"Race", racism and ethnicity: a response to Ken Smith', *Sociology*, vol 36, no 2, pp 419-29.

Modood, T., Berthoud, R., Lakey, J., Nazroo, J., Smith, P., Virdee, S. and Beishon, S. (eds) (1997) *Ethnic minorities in Britain: Diversity and disadvantage*, London: Policy Studies Institute.

Montagu, A. (1997) *Man's most dangerous myth: The fallacy of race* (6th edn), Walnut Creek: Altamira Press.

Morris, J. (1998) *Still missing? Who cares?*, York: Joseph Rowntree Foundation.

Morris, J. (2004) 'Remember the riots of 1919', *The Guardian*, 30 September.

MPA (Metropolitan Police Authority) (2003) *The Metropolitan Police Authority independent evaluation into the Metropolitan Police Service community and race relations training*, London: MPA.

Multiverse (2004) 'Exploring diversity and achievement', *Newsletter*, issue 1, February, London: London Metropolitan University Institute of Policy Studies in Education.

Muir, H. (2004) 'Secret Whitehall plan to win over Muslim youth', *The Guardian*, 31 May.

Murphy Paul, A. (1998) 'Where bias begins: the truth about stereotypes', *Psychology Today*, May-June (www.findarticles.com/cf_0/m1175/n3_v31/20526120/print.jhtml).

Murray, C. and Hernstein, R.J. (1996) *The bell curve: Intelligence and class structure in American life*, London: Simon and Schuster.

NACRO (2000) *Race and prisons: A snapshot survey*, London: NACRO.

NACRO (2003) *Race and prisons: Where are we now? A race and criminal justice update*, London: NACRO

Nakayama, T.K. and Krizek, R.L. (1999) 'Whiteness as a strategic rhetoric', in T.K. Nakayama and J.N. Martin (eds) *Whiteness: The communication of social identity*, London: Sage Publications.

Nazroo, J. (1998) 'Genetic cultural or socio-economic vulnerability? Explaining ethnic inequalities in health', in M. Bartley, D. Blane and G.D. Smith (eds) *The sociology of health inequalities*, Oxford: Blackwell.

Nazroo, J. (2003) 'Patterns of and explanations for ethnic inequalities in health', in D. Mason (ed) *Explaining ethnic differences: Changing patterns of disadvantage in Britain*, Bristol: The Policy Press.

Observer, The (2004) 'What I said was racist – but I'm not a racist. I am an idiot', 25 April.

Observer, The (2004) 'Equality chief branded as right wing', 4 April.

O'Cinneide, C. (2002) *A single equality body: Lessons from abroad*, Manchester: Equal Opportunities Commission.

ODPM (Office of the Deputy Prime Minister) (2000) *Quality and choice – A decent home for all*, Housing Green Paper, London: ODPM.

ODPM (2003) 'Equality and diversity in local government', July, London: ODPM (www.local.odpm.gov.uk/research/crosscut/crosscut.htm).

Ohmae, K. (1990) *The borderless world*, London: Collins.

Oldham Independent Review (2003) 'Panel report', 11 December (http://image.guardian.co.uk/sys-files/Guardian/documents/2001/12/11/Oldhamindependentreview.pdf).

Omi, M. and Winant, H. (1987) *Racial formation in the United States: From the 60s to the 80s*, London: Routledge.

Osler, A. (1999) 'Citizenship, democracy and political literacy', *Multicultural Teaching*, vol 18, no 1, pp 2-15.

Osler, A. and Morrison, M. (2000) *Inspecting schools for race equality, Ofsted's strengths and weaknesses: A Report for the Commission for Racial Equality*, Stoke-on-Trent: Trentham Books.

Osler, A. and Starkey, H. (2002) 'Education for citizenship: mainstreaming the fight against racism?', *European Journal of Education*, vol 37, no 2, pp 143-59.

Osler, A. and Vincent, K. (2003) *Girls and exclusion: Rethinking the agenda*, London: Routledge Falmer.

Ouseley, H. (2001) 'Community pride not prejudice: making diversity work in Bradford', July, Report presented to Bradford Vision (www.bradford2020.com/pride/).

Owen, D. (2003) 'The demographic characteristics of people from minority ethnic groups in Britain', in D. Mason (ed) *Explaining ethnic differences: Changing patterns of disadvantage in Britain*, Bristol: The Policy Press.

Owusu, K. (ed) (2000) *Black British culture and society*, London: Routledge.

Panorama (2003) 'The secret policeman programme', broadcast on BBC1 21 October.

Parekh, B. (2000) 'Integrating minorities', ICA Diversity Lecture, London: Institute of Contemporary Arts.

Paul, A.M. (1998) 'Where bias begins: the truth about stereotypes', *Psychology Today*, vol 82, May/June, pp 52-5.

Performance and Innovation Unit (2002) *Social capital: A discussion paper*, London: Performance and Innovation Unit.

Petrova, D. (2001) 'Racial discrimination and the rights of minority cultures', in S. Fredman (ed) *Discrimination and human rights: The case of racism*, Oxford: Oxford University Press.

Pharoah, C. and Smerdon, M. (1998) *Dimensions of the voluntary sector*, London: Charities Aid Foundation.

Phoenix, A. (1988) 'Narrow definitions of culture: the case of early motherhood', in S.Westwood and P. Bhachu (eds) *Enterprising women: Ethnicity, economy and gender relations*, London: Routledge.

Phoenix, A. (1997) 'I'm white! So what? The construction of whiteness for young Londoners', in M. Fine et al (eds) (1997) *Off white: Readings on race, power and society*, London: Routledge.

Phoenix, A. (1998) 'Dealing with difference: the recursive and the new', *Ethnic and Racial Studies*, vol 21, no 5, pp 859-80.

Policy Action Team (2000) *Home Office Report of Policy Action Team 6 neighbourhood wardens*, London: Policy Action Team.

Poole, E. (2000) 'Media representation and British muslims', *Dialogue Magazine*, issue 14, April.

Power, A. (1999) *Estates on the edge: Social consequences of mass housing in Northern Europe*, London: Palgrave Macmillan.

Powney, J., Wilson, V., Hall, S., Davidson, J., Kirk, S., Edward, S., SCRE Centre and Mirza, H.S. (2003) *Teachers' careers: The impact of age, disability, ethnicity, gender and sexual orientation*, Research Report 488, London: DfES.

Presentation Housing (2000) *Diversity, quality and choice: A response to the Housing Green Paper*, July, London: Presentation Housing.

Prewett-Livingston, A.J., Field, H.S., Veres, J.G. and Lewis, P.M. (1996) 'Effects of race on interview ratings in a situational panel interview', *Journal of Applied Psychology*, vol 81, no 2, pp 178-86.

Prior, I. (2004) 'TV pundit Ron Atkinson sacked for racist remark', *The Guardian*, 22 April.

Punch, A. and Pearce, A. (2001) *Europe's population and labour market beyond 2000*, Strasbourg: Council of Europe.

Putnam, R. (2000) *Bowling alone: The collapse and revival of American community*, New York, NY: Touchstone.

Puwar, N. (2000) 'The racialised somatic norm and the senior Civil Service', *Sociology*, vol 35, no 3, pp 351-70.

Race and Class (2002) Special issue: *Truth*, July-September, vol 44, no 1.

Race for Opportunity Update (2003) Winter Special Issue: *Focus on the Financial Sector* (www.bitc.org.uk/resources/ publications/ rfo_newsletter.html).

Rai-Atkins, A. (2002) *Best practice in mental health: Advocacy for African, Caribbean and South Asian communities*, Bristol/York: The Policy Press/ Joseph Rowntree Foundation.

RAM (Refugees, Asylum Seekers and the Mass Media Project) (2001) *Bulletin*, no 10, July.

Rampton Report (1981) *West Indian children in our schools: Interim Report of the Committee of Inquiry into the Education of Children from Ethnic Minority Groups*, DES, London: HMSO.

Ratcliffe, P. (2004) *'Race', ethnicity and difference: Imagining the inclusive society*, Maidenhead: Open University Press.

Rattansi, A. (1994) *Race, modernity and identity*, Cambridge: Polity Press.

Ray, L. and Smith, D. (2004) 'Racist offending, policing and community conflict', *Sociology*, vol 38, no 4, pp 681-99.

Refugee Council (2002) 'News press myths', December (www.refugeecouncil.org.uk/news/myths/myth001.htm).

Rex, J. and Tomlinson, S. (1979) *Colonial immigrants in a British city*, London: Routledge and Kegan Paul.

Richardson, R. (2004) *Here, there and everywhere: Belonging, identity and equality in schools*, Stoke on Trent: Trentham Books.

Roberts and Kay (2000) 'Toward competent communities: best practices for producing community wide study circles' (www.studycircles.org/pages/bestpractices_ok.php).

Rose, E.J.B. (1969) *Colour and citizenship: A report on British race relations*, London: Oxford University Press.

Roshni (2004) 'Roshni – a ray of light for abuse victims', 3 May (www.rehotcurry.com/news/roshni.htm).

Rothon, C. and Heath, A. (2003) *20th British social attitudes report*, London: Sage Publications/National Centre for Social Research.

Runnymede Bulletin (2002) Building Community Cohesion Conference, March.

Runnymede Conference (2004) 'Social capital civil renewal and ethnic diversity', 24 June.

Runnymede Trust (1997) *Islamophobia: A challenge for us all*, London: Runnymede Trust and Commission on British Muslims and Islamophobia.

Runnymede Trust (1999) *This is where I live: Stories and pressures in Brixton*, London: Runnymede Trust.

Runnymede Trust (2000) *The Parekh Report: Commission on the future of multi-ethnic Britain*, London: Profile.

Runnymede Trust (2003) *Complementing teachers: A practical guide to promoting race equality in schools*, London: Runnymede Trust.

Safra Project (2003) 'Identifying the difficulties experienced by muslim lesbian, bisexual and transgender women in accessing social and legal services', January (www.safraproject.org).

Sahgal, G. and Yuval-Davis, N. (eds) (1992) *Refusing Holy Orders: Women and fundamentalism in Britain*, London: Virago.

Said, E. (1978) *Orientalism*, London: Penguin.

Sainsbury Centre for Mental Health (2002) *Breaking the circles of fear: A review of the relationship between mental health services and African and Caribbean communities*, London: Sainsbury Centre for Mental Health.

Sampson, A. (2004) *Who runs this place? The anatomy of Britain in the 21st century*, London: John Murray.

Scarman Report (1981) *The Brixton disorders 10-12 April 1981: Report of an inquiry*, London: HMSO.

Schneider Ross (2001) 'Equality in the university: setting the new agenda – a report on the equality audit for Cambridge University', January, Andiver: Schnieder Ross (www.schnieder-ross.com).

Schneider Ross (2002) *Towards racial equality: An evaluation of the public duty to promote race equality and good race relations in England and Wales*, London: CRE.

Schuster, L. and Solomos, J. (2003) 'Race, immigration and asylum: new Labour's agenda and its consequences', *Ethnicities*, June 2004, vol 4, no 2, pp 267-300.

Schutte, G. (1995) *What racists believe: Race relations in South Africa and the United States*, London: Sage Publications.

Sewell, T. (1997) *Black masculinities and schooling*, Stoke on Trent: Trentham.

Shakespeare, T. (1998) *The disability reader: Social science perspectives*, London and New York, NY: Continuum Books.

Shields, M.A. and Wheatley, S. (2000) *Racial harassment, job satisfaction and intentions to quit: Evidence from the British nursing profession*, Discussion Papers in Public Sector Economics, Leicester: University of Leicester.

Sibbit, R. (1997) *The perpetrators of racial harassment and racial violence*, Home Office Research Study 176, London: Home Office.

Sihera, E. (2002) *Managing the diversity maze*, Buckinghamshire: Answer Publishing.

Sivanandan, A. (2001) 'Poverty is the new black', *Race and Class*, vol 43, no 2, October–December, pp 1-6.

Sniderman, P.M. and Carmines, E.G. (1997) *Reaching beyond race*, London: Harvard University Press.

Social Exclusion Unit (1998) *Bringing Britain together: A national strategy for neighbourhood renewal*, CD 4045, London: The Stationery Office.

Social Exclusion Unit (2002) 'Tackling racist crime: minority ethnic issues in neighbourhood renewal', Policy Action Team, National Strategy for Neighbourhood Renewal (www.socialexclusionunit. gov.uk/publications/reports/html/bmezip/06.htm).

Social Exclusion and Policy Unit (2000) *Action Team no 12: Young People*, March, London: Stationery Office.

Solomos, J. (1999) 'Social research and the Stephen Lawrence Inquiry', *Sociological Research Online*, vol 4, no 1.

Solomos, J. (2003) *Race and racism in Britain* (3rd edn), Basingstoke: Palgrave Macmillan.

Solomos, J. and Back, L. (1995) *Race, politics and social change*, London: Routledge.

Solomos, J. and Back, L. (1996) *Racism and society*, Basingstoke: Macmillan.

Spencer, S. (ed) (1994) *Immigration as an economic asset: The German experience*, Stoke on Trent: Trentham.

Spencer, S. (2000) 'Building a human rights culture', in *Commission on the Future of Multiethnic Britain*, London: Runnymede Trust.

Sport England (2002) *Active communities: A review of impact and good practice – Individual project reports*, February, produced by Leisure Futures.

Stepan, N.L. (1990) 'Race and gender: the role of analogy in science', in T. Goldberg (ed) *Anatomy of racism*, Minneapolis: University of Minnesota Press.

Stoler, L.A. (1996) *Race and the education of desire*, Durham, NC: Duke University Press.

Strategy Unit (2003) *Ethnic minorities and the labour market: Final report*, March, London: Cabinet Office/Strategy Unit.

Sudbury, J. (1998) *Other kinds of dreams: Black women's organisations and the politics of transformation*, London: Routledge.

Swann Report (1985) *Education for All: Final Report of the Committee of Inquiry into the Education of Children from Ethnic Minority Groups*, DES, London: HMSO.

Tackey, N.D., Tamkin, P. and Sheppard, E. (2001) *The problem of minority performance in organisations*, IES Report 375, London: Institute for Employment Studies.

Tamkin, P., Pollard, E., Tackey, N.D., Strebler, M. and Hooker, H. (2003) *A review of community race relations (CRR) Training in the Metropolitan Police Service*, London: Metropolitan Policy Authority, December.

The FA.com (2003) 'Sporting equals', 14 May (www.thefa.com/TheFA/Ethicsandsportequity/racialequality/postings/2003/05/483).

The United Kingdom European Monitoring Centre for Xenophobia and Racism (2002) *Anti discrimination legislation in EU member states*, Vienna.

Tikly, L., Blair, M., Hill, J. and Vincent, K. (2002) *Ethnic Minority Achievement Grant: Analysis of LEA action plans*, Research Report no 371, London: The Stationery Office.

Timmerman, C. (2000) 'Muslim women and nationalism: the power of the image', *Current Sociology*, vol 48, no 4, pp 15-27.

Troyna, B. and Williams, J. (1986) *Racism, education and the state*, London: Routledge.

TUC (Trades Union Congress) (2004) *Moving on: How Britain's unions are tackling racism*, Black Workers Conference, London: TUC.

Turton, J., De Maio, F. and Lane, P. (2003) 'Interpretation and translation services in the public sector', (unpublished) Report to the Home Office by University of East London Harp, Social Inclusion Research Programme.

UN (2000) *Gender and racial discrimination*, Report of the Expert Group Meeting UN Division for the Advancement of Women, 21-24 November, Zagreb, Croatia (submission by K. Crenshaw).

van Dijk, T. (1999) 'Discourse and racism', *Discourse and Society*, vol 10, no 2, April, pp 147-8.

van Dijk, T. (1993a) *Elite discourse and racism*, London: Sage Publications.

van Dijk, T. (1993b) 'Denying racism: elite discourse and racism', in J. Solomos and J. Wrench, *Racism and migration in Western Europe*, Oxford: Berg.

van Dijk, T. (2000) 'New(s) racism: a discourse analytical approach', in S. Cottle *Ethnic minorities and the media: Changing cultural boundaries*, Buckingham: Open University Press.

Vertovec, S. (1999) 'Conceiving and researching transnationalism', *Ethnic and Racial Studies*, vol 22, no 2, pp 447-61.

Virdee, S. (1995) *Racial violence and harassment*, London: Policy Studies Institute.

Wander, P., Martin, N. and Nakayama, T. (1999) 'Whiteness and beyond', in T. Nakayama and N. Martin (eds) *Whiteness: The communication of social identity*, London: Sage Publications.

Ware, V. (1997a) 'Defining forces: "race", gender and memories of Empire', in I. Chambers and L. Curtis *The post-colonial question: Common skies, divided horizons*, London: Routledge.

Ware, V. (1997b) 'Island racism: gender, place and white power', in R. Frankenberg *Displacing whiteness*, Durham, NC: Duke University Press.

Webster, C. (2003) 'Race, space and fear: imagined geographies of racism, crime, violence and disorder in Northern England', *Capital & Class*, vol 80, pp 95-122.

West, C. (1993) *Keeping faith*, New York, NY: Routledge.

Wieivorka, M. (1995) *The arena of racism*, London: Sage.

Williams, M. and Ali, B. (1999) *The minority ethnic voluntary sector in Wakefield*, West Yorkshire Racial Justice Programme, York: Joseph Rowntree Charitable Trust.

Williams, P.J. (1991) *The alchemy of race and rights: The diary of a law professor*, Cambridge, MA: Harvard University Press.

Williams, P.J. (1997) *Seeing a colour-blind future: The paradox of race*, New York, NY: Noonday Press.

Wilson, F.M. (1995) *Organisational behaviour and gender*, London: McGraw Hill.

Wilson, E.M. and Iles, P.A. (1999) 'Managing diversity: an employment and service delivery challenge', *International Journal of Public Sector Management*, vol 12, no 1, pp 27-48.

Wilson, R. (2001) *Dispersed: A study of services for asylum seekers in West Yorkshire December 1999-March 2001*, June, York: Joseph Rowntree Charitable Trust.

Wilson, W.J. (1987) *The truly disadvantaged: The inner city, the underclass and public policy*, London: Chicago Press.

Wilson, W.J. (2003) 'Race, class and urban poverty: a rejoiner', *Ethnic and Racial Studies*, vol 26, no 6, pp 1096-114.

Wimmer, A. (1997) 'Explaining xenophobia and racism', *Ethnic and Racial Studies*, vol 20, no 1, January.

Winder, R. (2004) *Bloody foreigners: The story of immigration to Britain*, London: Abacus.

Wodak, R. and Resigl, M. (1999) 'Discourse and racism: European perspectives', *Annual Review of Anthropology*, vol 28, pp 175-99.

Woodward, W. (2001) 'Faith in the system', *The Guardian*, 12 December.

Yuval Davis, N. (1997) *Gender and nation*, London and Thousand Oaks, CA: Sage Publications.

Appendix A:
Successful interventions

Local

(1) Intervention: Bede Anti Racist Youth Work Project (Stella Dadzie)
Description: Intervened with the leaders and members of gangs of white working-class men, in response to a rising number of racist attacks in the local area of Bermondsey. Interventions also took place with young white women and young black Somali origin men, in relation to the young people's lived and everyday experience. Team meetings of youth workers developed strategies for open discussion of racist feelings. Racism was explicitly discussed, but not *artificially* placed on the agenda.
Further details: Dadzie (1997).

(2) Intervention: Greenwich Council
Description: Run by probation officer, David Court, on working with perpetrators of racial violence. The course analyses the reasons for behaviour: these acts are influenced by the fact there is a common history with common antisocial behaviour problems and alcohol and housing problems. Work is done on aspects of perpetrators' own family trees, writing diaries and thinking about their national identities. Videos, anger management and relaxation tapes are also used. The modules include unconscious beliefs and attitudes about others. Perpetrators are encouraged to understand how prejudiced attitudes have contributed to their behaviour.
Further details: Greenwich Council (2003).

(3) Intervention: Arts Council, National Arts intervention (various projects)
Description: Set up a 'New Audiences' Programme, to try and encourage different people to enter theatres. These new audiences were defined not just by ethnicity, but also by class, income, age, and

so on. The Arts Council also targeted funding for black and minority ethnic *capital* projects. They responded to refugee marginalisation by encouraging refugee arts work across the country, and made appointments of black and minority ethnic people at a senior level. These ambassadors represented a new face of Britain with connections overseas. The initiatives involved allocation of resources and a determination to work in real partnership with groups. The importance of reinterpreting British heritage led to new funding schemes and we have seen the development of the British Empire and Commonwealth Museum in Bristol and the Museum of Immigration and Diversity in Princelet Street in the East End in London. They have also formed partner-ships with refugee organisations and encouraged refugee arts work across the country.
Further details: Khan (2002).

(4) Intervention: Safra Project
Description: Aimed to provide support for Muslim lesbians or transsexuals and to identify difficulties in accessing legal and social services. The project argued that the media and 'community' leaders reinforced a denial that Muslim women could be lesbian, or bisexual, thus they needed to seek help in a 'gendered', or 'race' centre. The women also needed information on how to relate to identities that were positive. This intervention also set up services for Muslim women that were safe and confidential.
Further details: www.safraproject.org

(5) Intervention: Trial and Error
Description: Resource for teachers produced by Stella Dadzie for the Department for Education and Skills in July 2003 for citizenship suggests ways in which racism is incorporated into their teaching.
Further details: Dadzie (2003) (www.front-line-training.co.uk/ trialanderror; www.dfes.gov.uk/citizenship).

(6) Intervention: Black Police Officers Association
Description: Regularly exposes and comments on racialised policing matters, and has provided visible support for police officers who have complained about police discrimination.
Further details: www.nationalbpa.com/

(7) Intervention: Race for Opportunity
Description: A campaign involving large employers in the private and public sector in taking action on 'race' equality. This campaign

continues to persuade employers to demonstrate progress, primarily in recruitment and promotion. It has encouraged the setting up of networks of minority staff, encouraged applications from minority groups and also supported inclusion efforts in the wider community, particularly schools.
Further details: www.raceforopportunity.org.uk

(8) Intervention: Integrating racism into a curriculum
Description: An intervention that incorporated racism into teacher training modules in an all-white course followed up the students three years after they had left and analysed what made students' attitudes change. Challenging behaviour and attitudes without personalising the issue made a difference. Although hostility and tension were generated, this was not necessarily destructive. Many students from white residential areas, who had previously not had much contact with racialised groups continued to use antiracism approaches in their work as teachers three years after they left their training.
Further details: Gaine (2001).

(9) Intervention: Aik Saath
Description: An independent charity working on conflict resolution skills in Slough, London and surrounding areas. Aims to raise self-esteem, to empower and train young people to become peer trainers to work with other young people.
Further details: www.aiksaath.com/

(10) Intervention: Football – Sheffield
Description: Encouraged the participation of minority ethnic youth through specialised coaching, which eventually led to the creation of a team. Articles and announcements were used in the football press and magazines to convey important messages about racism. The team liaised successfully with police with regard to community safety and set up a team club of mixed racial origins, including white.

The evaluation of the project attributes the reduction of racial chanting to their interventions. Anecdotally, it is argued, black and minority ethnic fans feel safer and feel less excluded. A black footballers exhibition has also been set up, various initiatives for local schools have been developed, and plays and theatre have been used as well as 'chant it' poetry to get messages across. This project in Sheffield was seen as good practice by the national initiative, Kick it Out.
Further details: Kick it Out: www.kickitout.org

(11) Intervention: One-off events – Asylum seekers and refugees
Description: Organising multicultural festivals and football tournaments in response to the immediate concerns of the stigmatisation of refugees. Arts organisations work with Refugee Action. Others, for example, use drama with children and young people. Eastside Arts and the Refugee Council, for example, organised poetry and performance sessions for 7 to 14-year-olds in Tower Hamlets, London, to encourage thinking about what it means to be a refugee. A similar project in Derby tried to simulate refugee experience with children in a local school. They attempt to tackle the hostility created by the media and politicians to wards asylum seekers and refugees, and encourage seeing and learning about the experience from the other's point of view.
Further details: www.refugee-action.org.uk;
www.refugeecouncil.org.uk

(12) Intervention: Mentoring
Description: Began as a community-sourced initiative. Lessons from the US indicated that mentoring was successful within organisations in building confidence, encouraging a more proactive desire for improvement and job development, and was important under the right conditions for tackling internalised racism. Mentoring as an intervention has rarely been evaluated for its long-term effects, but the literature on short-term effects shows that black people who have been mentored increase their promotion rates and become more optimistic about their jobs and careers.
Further details: Bhavnani et al (2003).

(13) Intervention: The Commission for Black Staff in Further Education
Description: Sets out to establish the nature and extent of institutional racism in the sector using consultation, commissioned research and evidence from individuals, expert witnesses and key agencies. Produced guides for retention, recruitment and staff development. Found evidence of racialised stereotyping, and low expectations of managers, lecturers and students still exists.
Further details: CBSE (2003); (www.fento.org/staff_dev/race_equality/full_report.pdf).

(14) Intervention: Crossing the Line project, South Yorkshire
Description: Theatre funded by the Garnett Foundation to stage plays about 'race' and leadership. It was developed using the views and

opinions of 1,500 people who took part in forum theatre consultative workshops as part of the Race to Train project in South Yorkshire. The action is based on real incidents and real people. The aim of the plays is about identifying issues that concern all of us, as we work towards a more diverse and non-discriminatory society. Crossing the Line is being used by organisations striving to embrace the richness and value of the diverse community in which they live and work.
Further details: www.thegarnettfoundation.com/race.html

(15) Intervention: Community Empowerment Network
Description: Provides advice, counselling, support, representation and training for people experiencing mistreatment and disadvantage in education, especially exclusion from school. Provides current information through a newsletter, pamphlets, reports, manuals, e-mail and Internet contacts. Also provides representation and advocacy at adjudication hearings, advice on cases for judicial review and referral to the Parliamentary Ombudsman. Specialists are available to contribute to privately organised meetings, exhibitions, seminars and conferences as speakers and workshop facilitators. The Community Empowerment Network responds to media enquiries and is available to discuss ideas for programmes and articles, and provides short and long-term placement and work experience for volunteers and students.
Further details: www.compowernet.org/

(16) Intervention: PressWise Trust
Description: The PressWise Trust is an independent media ethics charity, supported by concerned journalists, media lawyers and politicians in the UK. It is based on the belief that press freedom is a responsibility exercised by journalists on behalf of the public. Its primary purpose is to provide advice, information, research and training on all aspects of media policy, practice and law. PressWise has taken a keen interest in promoting diversity within the media, not least because minorities are the most vulnerable to misrepresentation and abuse. In 1997 PressWise began looking for partners and funding to examine the consequences of inaccurate and sensational coverage of asylum seekers, refugees, Roma and other 'non-settled' groups. In 1999 they launched the Refugees, Asylum seekers and the Media (RAM) Project to promote best practice in media coverage of refugee and asylum issues.
Further details: www.presswise.org.uk

International

(17) Intervention: Study Circles
Country: USA
Description: Funded by a charity aiming to involve local people in discussions about a variety of topics, including racism. A Study Circle is a group of 8–12 people from different backgrounds and viewpoints who meet several times to talk about an issue. In a Study Circle, everyone has an equal voice, and people try to understand each other's views. The idea is to share concerns and look for ways to make things better. A facilitator helps the group focus on different views and makes sure the discussion goes well.
Further details: Roberts and Kay (2000) (www.studycircles.org/pages/bestpractices_ok.php).

(18) Intervention: Environmental Project, Taastrupgaard
Country: Denmark, Copenhagen
Description: By encouraging people to step out of their everyday routines, a declining housing estate drew on community development and tenants' involvement. Many different groups were involved in the design of the estate from gardening to regeneration, to using communal areas. Although some tensions remained, a viable estate was created with multiculturalism at its heart. In one estate sanctions against racist language will be critical, while in another youth workers could use their imaginations to bring people together.
Further details: Power (1999).

(19) Intervention: Good practice in migration, citizenship and integration
Country: Various
Description: A good practice guide bringing together various examples from Canada, the Netherlands and Australia in assisting with the integration of migrants. Specialised programmes include Canadian volunteers helping migrants to resettle, promotional material such as 'Welcome to Canada', and in the Netherlands, mutual contract responsibilities of the hosts and newcomers, internships offered to refugees in government departments, and mentoring on employment.
Further details: Foreign Policy Centre, 'Migration, integration and citizenship: lessons from around the world' (www.fpc.org.uk)

(20) Intervention: Truth and Reconciliation Commission (TRC)
Country: South Africa
Description: Set up by the Government of National Unity to help deal with crimes and injustices under apartheid. The conflict during this period resulted in violence and human rights abuses from all sides. It is based on the idea that truth telling is an important factor in promoting reconciliation. The Commission used personal narratives and dialogue to establish the building blocks of reconciliation.
Further details: www.doj.gov.za/trc/

(21) Intervention: Multiculturalism Policy
Country: Canada
Description: Official Multiculturalism Policy adopted by the Federal government is largely inspired by the conception of how immigrant ethnicity should be handled. Canada became the first country in the world to adopt an official Multiculturalism Policy. This policy provided for programmes and services to support ethnocultural associations and to help individuals overcome barriers to their full participation in Canadian society. It treats ethnocultural affiliation as voluntary, and encourages the differing ethnic groups to interact, to share their cultural heritage, and to participate in common educational, political, economic and legal institutions.
Further details: www.pch.gc.ca/progs/multi/respect_e.cfm

(22) Intervention: Youth Project
Country: France
Description: In Paris, youths bent on writing graffiti create *auto écoles* using a loose curriculum to re-engage young people in the school system, inviting young boys from around the world to play in a world tournament. Animated public debates on relevant themes have been held and using theatre with professionals and residents to work on common problems, for example, theatre in Marseille.
Further details: Amin (2002).

(23) Intervention: Waitangi Tribunal
Country: New Zealand
Description: The Tribunal was established in 1975 by the Treaty of Waitangi Act. The Tribunal is a permanent commission of inquiry charged with making recommendations on claims brought by Maori relating to actions or omissions of the Crown, which breach the promises made in the Treaty of Waitangi. It is supported by the Ministry of Justice. Areas covered include the use of various kinds of land and

the ability to investigate and negotiate between the Crown and the Maori people, on any other aspects concerning grievances against policies, practices or legislation.

Further details: www.waitangi-tribunal.govt.nz/

(24) Intervention: Interventions on the Chinese in New Zealand
Country: New Zealand
Description: Prime Minister's speech to Parliament on the Chinese New Year celebrations in 2002 included apologies for immigration restrictions, separations of families and taxes which impoverished Chinese people in later 19th and 20th century, declaring that there will be a reconciliation, and that the government will fund aspects of Chinese heritage culture and language. Also launched a national essay writing competition for New Zealand school children on the history of the Chinese in New Zealand.
Further details: www.ethnicaffairs.govt.nz/oeawebsite.nsf/wpg

(25) Intervention: Approach to antiracism
Country: Sweden
Description: Antiracism was centrally adopted in Sweden's national constitution to promote and protect democracy. Sweden encourages an open policy of discussing racism and combating it. By linking antiracism with democracy, participation and involvement, a variety of groups become integral to engagement with institutions. It means an holistic look at notions of citizenship, not one bequeathed to people by a sovereign state, but one which engages people to address differences and participate in community development at a local level.
Further details: Osler and Starkey (2002).

Appendix B:
Tables – legislation

Table 1: Legislation before 1900

Date	Legislation	What does it mean?
1807	Abolition of the Slave Trade Bill	Made it unlawful for any British subject to capture and transport slaves.
1813	Charter (1814 Regulations)	Required the East India Company to provide subsistence for Indian sailors in Britain until they returned to India, partly in order to prevent their settlement in Britain.
1823	Merchant Shipping Act	Meant that Indian seamen were not British subjects and not entitled to become so, known as the 'Lascar Act'.
1833	Slavery Abolition Act	Gave all slaves in the British Empire their freedom. The British government paid compensation to the slave owners.
1865	Abolition of Slavery (USA)	Although slavery was abolished at different times in different states across the US, the official end to slavery came in 1865 with the ratification of the 13th Amendment to the Constitution.
1894	Merchant Shipping Act	Agreement binding seamen to return to their country of origin, giving power to the Secretary of State to repatriate those who attempted to become residents in Britain.

Table 2: Immigration legislation before 1945

Date	Legislation	What does it mean?
1905	Aliens Order Act	'Alien' referred to all non-UK subjects, or those otherwise defined as aliens. It meant that aliens could be (1) refused permission to enter Britain if they did not have, or could not obtain the means to subsist in adequate sanitary conditions; (2) expelled from Britain without trial or appeal if they were found to be living in insanitary conditions or vagrancy, for example, overcrowding. Migrants who were refused entry could appeal to an immigration board. Immigrants could not be refused permission to enter Britain if they were the subject of religious or political persecution. This is set against the backdrop of high numbers of Jewish immigrants especially from Eastern Europe.
1914	Aliens Restriction Act	The government could decide on who to prohibit from entering Britain, who could be deported, and who could be restricted in terms of where they lived and travelled. The Restriction Act arose as a result of national security under the circumstances of the First World War.
1919	Aliens Restriction (Amendment) Act	Repealed the 1905 legislation and extended the 1914 Restriction Act for a further year, despite the fact that the First World War was over.
1920	Aliens Order	Immigration officers were able to refuse entry to those who were considered unable to support themselves. The Home Secretary was able to deport those who were not considered to be 'conducive to the public good'. If an immigrant wanted to work, he or she could only do so if a permit was issued by the Ministry of Labour, demonstrating that no British worker was able fill the job position.
1925	Special Restrictions (Coloured Alien Seamen) Act	Applied to colonial seamen who did not possess satisfactory evidence of being British subjects. They required the permission of an immigration officer to land and were subject to removal from Britain.

Table 3: Asylum and immigration legislation post-1945

Date	Legislation	What does it mean?
1948	British Nationality Act	Made a distinction between British subjects who were citizens of the UK and its colonies, and those who were Commonwealth citizens. Both had the legal right to enter and settle in Britain.
1962	Commonwealth Immigrants Act	The Act sought to control entry of Black Commonwealth citizens into Britain. It made the distinction between citizens of Britain and its colonies, and citizens of independent Commonwealth countries. Those who were exempt from immigration control (1) were born in Britain and (2) held British passports issued by the British government. Other Commonwealth citizens had to obtain an employment voucher issued by the Ministry of Labour to enter Britain provided that they (1) had a specific job to go to, (2) had a recognised skill or qualification that was in short supply or (3) had served in the British forces during the war.
1968	Commonwealth Immigrants Act (second)	To control the migration of Asians from East Africa, this Act imposed immigration restrictions on those who did not have one parent or grandparent born, adopted, or registered in Britain as a citizen, here or in its colonies.
1969	Immigration Appeals Act	Accepted the need for restriction on immigration but the new system of appeal would ensure that the restrictions were applied fairly. Applicants had to prove their relationship legally to the person residing in Britain.
1971	Immigration Act	Brought in to ensure that there would be no more large-scale immigration to Britain. It differentiated between citizens of Britain and its colonies who were patrial and non-patrial, the latter of which did not have the right to stay in Britain. Patrial included (1) citizens of Britain and its colonies entitled to citizenship by birth, or with parents or grandparents with citizenship and (2) citizens of Britain and its colonies who had settled and resided in Britain for five years or more.
1981	British Nationality Act	Divided the category of citizen in the UK and Commonwealth as follows: (1) British citizen, (2) British Dependent Territories Citizen and (3) British Overseas Citizen.
1988	Immigration Act	Amended the 1981 Act to incorporate free movement provision of European Community law. Made residents in Britain prove they could maintain their relatives here without recourse to public funds.

cont. . .

1993	Asylum and Immigration Appeals Act	Introduced the right of appeal for asylum seekers. They could not be forcibly removed from Britain between the time of making a claim for asylum and the state's decision.
1996	Asylum and Immigration Act	Produced a 'White List' of countries in which serious persecution was no risk and applicants from these countries were only entitled to the accelerated appeals procedure. The White List was later to be abolished by Labour in 1997.
1999	Asylum and Immigration Act	Introduced a voucher scheme instead of providing cash benefits, enforced dispersal, and stepped up the practice of detention on arrival.
2002	Nationality, Immigration and Asylum Act	Proposed an immigration hotline where the public could denounce irregular migrants, a further increase in detention facilities to enable more deportations, and stepping up boarder controls to prevent the arrival of asylum seekers. One of the announcements included the replacement of the voucher system by a cash voucher system.
2003	Section 55	On 8 January 2003, the government implemented section 55 of the 2002 Nationality, Immigration and Asylum Act. This allowed the Home Office to withdraw access to the National Asylum Support Service from those who do not apply for asylum 'as soon as reasonably practicable'. This policy effectively denies support to most in-country applicants.

Table 4: Antiracism legislation

Date	Legislation	What does it mean?
1965	Race Relations Act	A response to party political competitive responses to the Notting Hill and Nottingham riots/attacks in 1958 and based on the principal of ending discrimination towards black people on the grounds of race. Saw the establishment of special bodies to deal with problems faced by immigrants in terms of discrimination, integration and welfare, and educating the general population about race relations to minimise conflict. Set up the Race Relations Board as responsible for enforcing the Act and tackling discrimination.
1968	Race Relations Act	Set up Community Relations Commission as responsible for enforcing the Act and tackling discrimination.
1976	Race Relations Act	Extended the objectives of the law to cover, as before, intentional discrimination, but also racial disadvantage brought about by systematic racism. The Race Relations Board and the Community Relations Commission merged into the Commission for Racial Equality (CRE). Employment cases were to be handled through industrial tribunals rather than by the CRE. Introduced the concept of indirect discrimination into the legislation.
2000	Race Relations (Amendment) Act	Requires public sector bodies to actively 'promote' 'race' equality by preventing acts of racial discrimination before they occur, and ensuring that when public duties are performed, they have regard to the need to eliminate unlawful racial discrimination, and promote equality of opportunity and good relations between those of different racial groups.

Table 5: Northern Ireland

Date	Legislation	What does it mean?
1970	Prevention of Incitement to Hatred Act (Northern Ireland)	Made it a criminal offence internationally to stir up hatred against a section of the public in Northern Ireland on the grounds of religious belief, colour, race or ethnic or national origins.
1976	Fair Employment (Northern Ireland) Act	Made direct discrimination on the grounds of religious belief or political opinion unlawful in employment.
1987	Public Order (Northern Ireland)	Provisions rendering acts intended or likely to stir up fear unlawful are now contained in the Order, which makes it unlawful to use words or behaviour, or display any written material likely or intended to provoke hatred based on religious belief, colour, race, nationality (including citizenship) or ethnic or national origin.
1989	Fair Employment (Northern Ireland) Act	Amended and extended the 1976 fair employment legislation to outlaw indirect discrimination and provided for the use of affirmative action to secure fair participation in employment.
1997	Race Relations Order in Northern Ireland	Makes it unlawful to discriminate, either directly or indirectly on racial grounds in the areas of employment and training; education; the provision of goods, facilities or services; the disposal and management of premises and advertisements. It also places a statutory duty on district councils to make appropriate arrangements with a view to ensuring that their various functions are carried out with due regard to the need: (1) to eliminate unlawful racial discrimination; and (2) to promote equality of opportunity, and good relations, between persons of different racial groups.
1998	Fair Employment and Treatment (Northern Ireland) Order	Replaces and extends the 1976 and 1989 Fair Employment Acts (Northern Ireland). The concept of 'harassment' is now defined in the law for the first time as violating a person's dignity or creating an intimidating, hostile, degrading, humiliating or offensive environment. A new definition of 'indirect discrimination' focuses on whether an apparently neutral provision actually places persons of a particular religious belief 'at a particular disadvantage' rather than relying on the highly statistical approach of the previous definition.
1998	Northern Ireland Act	Equality legislation was further extended where designated public bodies are now under a statutory obligation to promote equality of opportunity in the areas of age, marital status, disability, political opinion, race, religious belief, sex, sexual orientation and whether or not people have dependants. These statutes also include measures that require the selected public bodies to promote good relations between people of different racial groups, religious beliefs or political opinions.

Table 6: International human rights mechanisms (UK ratified)

Date	Mechanism	What does it mean?
1949	Geneva Convention	Adopted to take account of the experiences of the Second World War, the Geneva Conventions still apply to modern armed conflicts. *Convention I*: Geneva Convention for the Amelioration of the Condition of the Wounded and Sick in Armed Forces in the Field. *Convention II*: Geneva Convention for the Amelioration of the Condition of Wounded, Sick and Shipwrecked Members of Armed Forces at Sea. *Convention III*: Geneva Convention relative to the Treatment of Prisoners of War. *Convention IV*: Geneva Convention relative to the Protection of Civilian Persons in Time of War.
1969	International Convention on the Elimination of All Forms of Racial Discrimination (CERD)	Adopted by the UN's General Assembly in 1965 and entered into force in 1969. Its provisions include the following: (1) State parties undertake to pursue "by all appropriate means [...] a policy of eliminating racial discrimination in all its forms" (Article 2); (2) State parties "shall declare an offence punishable by law all dissemination of ideas based on racial superiority or hatred" (Article 4); (3) a reaffirmation of the right to equal enjoyment of the civil, political, economic, social and cultural rights laid down in the two International Covenants (Article 5).
1998	Framework Convention for the Protection of National Minorities	Legal instruments developed within the Council of Europe in the field of protection of national minorities include the Framework Convention for the Protection of National Minorities and the European Charter for Regional and Minority Languages. Both provide for a monitoring mechanism of fulfilment of the obligations undertaken by their Contracting Parties.
	European Convention on Human Rights	The Convention protects a series of fundamental rights, including: The right to life; Freedom from torture, inhuman and degrading treatment; Freedom from forced labour or slavery; The right to liberty and to a fair trial; Freedom from facing retrospective crimes or penalties; A right to privacy; Freedom of conscience; Freedom of expression; Freedom of assembly; The right to marriage and family; Freedom from discrimination. In order to provide effective protection of these rights the ECHR has established the European Court of Human Rights with which States and individuals, regardless of their nationality, may lodge complaints about alleged violations by the Contracting States.
1998	Human Rights Act	Came into force in October 2000. For the first time individuals have the right to enforce their ECHR rights in UK courts.

Table 7: Equality legislation

Date	Legislation	What does it mean?
1970	Equal Pay Act (amended 1984)	Gives an individual the right to the same contractual pay and benefits as a person of the opposite sex in the same employment, where the man and the woman are doing: (1) like work; (2) work rated as equivalent under an analytical job evaluation study; or (3) work that is proved to be of equal value.
1975	Sex Discrimination Act (amended 1982)	Prohibits sex discrimination against individuals in the areas of employment, education, and the provision of goods, facilities and services and in the disposal or management of premises. It also prohibits discrimination in employment against married people.
1989	Employment Act (amended 2002)	Covers work and parents, dispute resolution in the workplace, improvements to employment tribunal procedures, including the introduction of an equal pay questionnaire, provisions to implement the Fixed Term Work Directive, a new right to time off work for union learning representatives, work-focused interviews for partners of people receiving working-age benefits and some data-sharing provisions.
1995	Disability Discrimination Act (amended October 2004)	The Disability Discrimination Act aims to end the discrimination which many disabled people face. This Act gives disabled people rights in the areas of (1) employment, (2) access to goods, (3) facilities and services, (4) buying or renting land or property.
1997	Protection from Harassment Act	Introduces three new criminal offences: (1) harassment; fear of violence; (2) breach of civil injunction; (3) breach of restraining order. Although it was passed primarily because of concern about 'stalking', the wording of the Act allows it to be used to cover other types of harassment as well as stalking.
1999	Sex Discrimination (Gender Reassignment) Regulations	The 1999 Sex Discrimination (Gender Reassignment) Regulations clarify British law relating to gender reassignment. It is a measure to prevent discrimination against transsexual people on the grounds of sex in pay and treatment in employment and vocational training. This reflects a ruling by the European Court of Justice that the dismissal of an employee undergoing gender reassignment is contrary to the European Equal Treatment Directive.
2000	Disability Rights Commission Act	The Disability Rights Commission was established by this Act to: (1) work towards ending discrimination against disabled people; (2) promote equal opportunities for disabled people; (3) encourage good practice in the treatment of disabled people; and (4) keep under review the working of the Disability Discrimination Act and the Disability Rights Commission Act.
2001	Special Educational	The Act removes the previous exemption of

	Needs and Disability Act	education from the 1995 Disability Discrimination Act, ensuring that discrimination against disabled students will be unlawful.
2003	Employment Equalities Regulation	States that it is unlawful to discriminate on the grounds of sexual orientation, religion or belief, before, during or after employment or in vocational training. The law covers direct and indirect discrimination, harassment and victimisation, whether such action is intentional or unintentional. It applies to applicants for jobs, employees, agency workers and some self-employed individuals.

Table 8: Criminal law that protects against racial harassment/ racist behaviour

Date	Legislation	What does it mean?
1986	Public Order Act	Makes incitement to racial hatred an offence. This covers the production and circulation of printed and other material.
1991	Football (Offences) Act	Makes racist chanting at football matches an offence.
1997	Protection from Harassment	Can be used in areas, such as social housing, to deal with racial harassment and abuse.
1998	Crime and Disorder Act	Covers new offences of racially aggravated violence, criminal damage and racial harassment.

Table 9: Nation: Scotland, Wales and the rest of Europe

Date Treaty/Act/ Agreement	What does it mean?
1959 The Treaty of Rome	Established the European Economic Community (EEC) and European Atomic Energy Community (Euratom). Both bodies were run by a Commission and all three bodies had one European Assembly (later becoming the European Parliament) and one Court of Justice in common.
1985 Schengen Agreement	The goal of the Agreement is to end border checkpoints and controls within the Schengen area and harmonise external border controls. All Schengen countries except Norway and Iceland are EU members. The UK and Ireland are in the EU but are not parties to the Schengen Agreement. Its purpose is to remove all controls at internal land, sea and airport frontiers. In order to maintain internal security, a variety of measures have been taken such as, for example, coordination of visa controls at the external borders of the member states through a common approach to visa policies and asylum procedures.
1987 Single European Act 1986	Introduced more specific single market objectives. It aimed to create an internal market by 31 December 1992, ensuring the free movement of goods, persons, services and capital between member states.
1992 Treaty on European Union (Maastricht Treaty)	Took effect in November 1993, formally establishing the EU. It also: (1) increased the power of the European Parliament; (2) reduced the scope of member state vetoes; (3) firmly established the route to EMU with the establishment of the European Central Bank. The Maastricht Treaty also contained a 'Social Chapter' relating to improved living and working conditions, significantly, introducing EU influence into many new areas. The UK opted out of this aspect of the agreement.
1997 Treaty of Amsterdam	Allowed for the possibility of 'closer cooperation' within the EU's single institutional framework, to enable certain member states to work together in the interests of the Union, at a time when not all member states wanted to or could do so. This agreement was based on the understanding that they would be free to join the group at a later date, aimed at building on the agreements reached in Maastricht in 1992. The Treaty of Amsterdam states that the EU is to respect the fundamental rights guaranteed by the European Convention on the Protection of Human Rights and Fundamental Freedoms (ECHR).
1999 Scotland Parliament (Devolution)	The main fiscal powers of government remain firmly embedded in London, and the Scottish Parliament can deal only with Scottish issues rather than trespassing into issues involving other regions. Important issues affecting Scotland, such as foreign affairs and major financial policies are still dealt with by London. Scotland remains part of the UK.

1999	National Assembly of Wales (Devolution)	As with Scotland, the Assembly develops and implements policies which reflect the particular needs of the people in Wales. Wales remains part of the UK.
2001	Treaty of Nice	Has been agreed, providing the possibility of enhanced cooperation in the field of common foreign and security policy (CFSP), except defence. The Treaty also ensures: (1) enhanced cooperation within the EU, with a minimum of eight member states required to establish enhanced cooperation; (2) respect for the role of the institutions; (3) future participation for states that that do not participate immediately, but later choose to. The Charter of Fundamental Rights of the European Union was proclaimed in Nice. It sets out the civil, political, economic and social rights of European citizens under six headings: (1) Dignity; (2) Freedom; (3) Equality; (4) Solidarity; (5) Citizens' rights; and (6) Justice. These rights are based on the ECHR and the constitutional traditions of the EU.

Appendix C:
Glossary of terms

The terms used in discussions in this book have been and are always open to contestation. Using a combination of key texts, definitions have been derived from the following publications: Essed (1991), van Dijk (1993a), Banton (1997), Mason (2000) and Solomos (2003).

Term	Definition
Affirmative action	A term commonly used in the US to refer to positive discrimination. Refers to activities aimed at specific racialised groups (see also **Positive discrimination**).
Anti-semitism	Prejudice or discrimination against Jews, based on negative perceptions of their religious beliefs and/or on negative group stereotypes. The term was originally used to refer to prejudice against Arab Muslims as well as Jews.
Assimilation	In the 1950s and 1960s this involved teaching immigrants to adapt to life in the UK, and to learn English.
Asylum seeker	While someone is waiting for their application to stay in the country to be considered by the government, they are known as an 'asylum seeker'.
Black	This is a collective term which can refer to anyone facing discrimination on the basis of skin colour. It refers to those of African and African-Caribbean origin. It can also include those of South Asian origin.
BME (black and minority ethnic)	The term BME has become current in official documents in recent years, not least

because it is conveniently short. However, this is not a term many 'ethnic minority' communities tend to use to describe themselves.

Culture The learned system of shared beliefs, systems of meaning, values, custom and behaviours which are transmitted from generation to generation. Because the relationship between what is taught and what is learned is not absolute (some of what is transmitted is lost, while new discoveries are constantly being made and cultural features from other groups are taken on), culture exists in a constant state of change. Defining and understanding 'culture' requires an understanding of how 'cultures' intersect with broad structures and processes in society.

Diaspora Refers to the movement of populations and groups, forced or voluntary. The term literally means to disperse or scatter.

Discrimination Actions and systems that disadvantage other people's lives and life chances. When some minority ethnic groups get second-rate treatment in access to work, education or the provision of services, that is 'racial' discrimination.

Diversity Has become a synonym for race. It is used primarily in the workforce to refer to the variety (diversity) of people that takes into account differences of culture, background, preferences and values, respecting individuals. Diversity recognises that everyone has a contribution to make and that services can be improved by harnessing the skills and contributions from all sectors of the workforce and community.

Elite racism	The perpetuation of racism takes place at all levels of society, but those who have more power, such as politicians, senior executives, academics and the media, need to be made more accountable, since the power of their actions have more widespread effects than those made by one neighbour to another (see van Dijk, 1993a, 1999). These social practices, named 'elite discourse', have been termed 'elite racism'.
Equal opportunities	Not discriminating on the grounds of race, sex, marital status, age, religion, disability and sexual orientation and providing equality of opportunity for all. An equal opportunities approach aims "to equalise the starting point by removing barriers at the point of selection for employment, education or other benefit" (Fredman, 2002, p 6). The equal opportunities approach still largely determines access to employment and training.
Ethnic cleansing	The systematic removal of a group of people identified by ethnicity from a certain area. This may be done through genocide (killing) or forced migration.
Ethnic minority / minority ethnic	The phrases 'minority ethnic' and 'ethnic minority' are in widespread official use to refer to all people who are visibly not white. Their use unhelpfully implies that white people all belong to a single group, 'the majority', and that there are no significant differences among them. There are many differences within the white population, including ethnic differences. The term 'ethnic' is frequently misused in the media and in everyday conversation as a synonym for 'not-white' or 'not-western', as in phrases such as 'ethnic clothes', 'ethnic restaurants', 'ethnic music'. Newspapers sometimes refer to 'ethnic writers', 'ethnic artists', 'ethnic communities'.

Recently ethnic minority people have
contested this collective term and prefer the
label 'minority ethnic'. The rationale is simple.
While those defined as 'ethnic' make up
majority populations globally, they find
themselves defined as 'minority' migrant
communities in the UK. Thus the term
'minority ethnic' rather than 'ethnic minority'
is now used.

Ethnicity   Essentially a process of group identification,
ethnicity is a sense of cultural and historical
identity based on belonging by birth to a
distinctive cultural group, for example,
English, Indian, Irish, African–Caribbean. We
may belong to at least one ethnic group and
may also identify with several groups at the
same time (for example, Yoruba, Nigerian,
African and Black Briton). Ethnicity has been
used frequently and interchangeably with
'race'. The use of the concept dates from the
1930s. It was first used in the US by
sociologists studying European immigrant
groups and their relationship to American
society.

Ethnocentricity   Viewing the world from the perspective of
one particular ethnic group, often with the
assumption that the values, beliefs and
achievements of that group are superior to
those of other ethnic groups.

Eurocentric   The assumption that the belief and values of
Western European or the 'West' are superior
to others.

Everyday racism   The integration of racism into everyday
practices that activate underlying power
relations. This process must be seen as a
continuum through which the integration of
racism into everyday practices becomes part
of the expected, of the unquestionable, and of

Appendix C: Glossary of terms

<table>
<tr><td></td><td>what is seen as normal by the dominant group (Essed, 1991).</td></tr>
<tr><td>Fascism</td><td>An ideology that advocates extreme nationalism, with a heightened sense of national belonging or ethnic identity. The term needs to be understood on a variety of levels: as a political ideology, as a style of rule, as a sub-division of totalitarian power politics, and as characteristic policies.</td></tr>
<tr><td>Genocide</td><td>The systematic and planned killing of an entire national, racial, political or ethnic group.</td></tr>
<tr><td>Immigrant</td><td>A person who leaves one country to settle in another.</td></tr>
<tr><td>Institutional racism</td><td>Procedures, practices and behaviour within an organisation or institution, which support and encourage direct or indirect racial discrimination, reinforcing individual prejudices and being reinforced by them in turn. Whereas individual racism is the expression of personal prejudice, institutional racism is the expression of a whole organisation's racist practice and culture. The Stephen Lawrence Inquiry report defined this as "The collective failure of an organization to provide an appropriate and professional service to people because of their colour, culture, or ethnic origin. It can be seen or detected in processes, attitudes and behaviour which amount to discrimination through unwitting prejudice, ignorance, thoughtlessness and racist stereotyping which disadvantage minority ethnic people" (Macpherson, 1999).</td></tr>
<tr><td>Integration</td><td>Integration was characterised in the 1960s by understanding the 'other' and other cultures where white culture was rendered invisible. It</td></tr>
</table>

was thought that this understanding of 'others' would lead to their integration.

Multiculturalism In the contemporary British sense this refers to the theory, policy and practice that are part of the struggle for racial justice, referring to an environment in which differences among people and groups are recognised, respected, celebrate and valued. Differences are seen as positive and desirable, rather than negative or threatening. Multiculturalism seeks to integrate minority cultures and communities without undermining their claims to be distinct.

Nationalism Distinctive sense of cultural and historical identity and or common destiny based on being a citizen of a particular nation state.

Patriotism Love of one's country and loyalty to one's country where virtuous citizens display a devotion to their country in words and deeds.

Positive action Offering special help to people who are disadvantaged because of prejudice, stereotyping and discrimination, in order that they may take full and equal advantage of opportunities in jobs, education, training, services etc.

Positive discrimination Treating people more favourably on the grounds of race, nationality, religion, gender etc. (Under the 2000 Race Relations [Amendment] Act this is illegal in the UK.)

Prejudice Pre-judging people in a negative way according to preconceived ideas about them. Prejudice is the affective manifestation of racism. Usually located by social psychologists in individuated processes rather than societal structures and institutions, categorisation and stereotyping comes to be seen as almost natural, and prejudice itself becomes almost 'natural' and inevitable.

Race 'Race' is a changeable term and we have to understand the ways in which ideologies and structures construct certain groups in ways that presume they are naturally distinct. In this sense, 'race' is not a real or measurable quality, hence the use of quotation marks to denote its social construction. 'Race' is a social relationship in which structural positions and social actions are ordered, justified and explained by reference to systems and symbols of beliefs which emphasise the social and cultural relevance of biologically rooted characteristics. Although the origin of these constructions for groups is in science and biology, since the early 1980s there is agreement that racism has increasingly been linked with 'culture' (see Mason, 2000).

Racial harassment Violence suffered by individuals or groups because of their nationality and ethnic or national origins. It may be verbal or physical and includes attacks on property as well as on the person.

Racism 'Race' is a social construct. Its changing manifestations reflect ideological attempts to legitimate domination in different social and historical contexts. Racism is therefore not about objective measurable physical and social characteristics, but about relationships of domination and subordination. Racism is rooted in the scientific discourse of Social Darwinism and the search for identifiable physical differences, based on a biological idea of 'race'. These physical differences were then linked to character traits and ideas of inferiority and superiority. Scientific racism has been partly replaced by the culturalisation of racism. Differences between groups are now 'judged' on the basis of 'cultural differences'. This culturalisation of racism has led to both hidden and covert racism, such as an unstinting 'gaze' on racialised peoples, legitimating in a subtle way their *difference* from the 'norm' and therefore problematising them. There are different types of racism which can manifest itself in many different ways depending on the site or group concerned. Hence the use of the plural term racisms. Racism in our current context, does not always refer to colour directly, but implies inferiority through the ways in which different groups live. Racism denotes attitudes and systems (for example, economic, political, cultural) that support and seek to maintain the superiority of one racial group. Racism may be personal, unconscious and unintentional as well as overt and deliberate. It has particular force when manifested in the major structures and institutions of society, which create and maintain the power and influence of one ethnic group at the expense of others (see **Institutional racism**). A way of conceptualising racism is to break it up into its causal component parts, the social and the cognitive (see van Dijk, 2000), both of which are reproduced every day. The social component consists of everyday discriminatory practices, and organisational, institutional and legal arrangements. The cognitive component concerns people's beliefs, namely knowledge, attitudes, values, ideologies and norms which are reproduced through discourse. Racism is expressed in different ways in particular historical, regional and national contexts. In other words, there are different racisms (Gilroy, 1987).

Refugee	A person who is forced to leave his or her home and seek safety outside of his or her own country. Under international law, the word 'refugee' has a very precise meaning; as set out in the 1951 United Nations Convention Relating to Refugees, a refugee is defined as someone who: "has a well-founded fear of persecution for reasons of race, religion, nationality, membership of a particular social group, or political opinion; is outside the country they belong to or normally reside in, and is unable or unwilling to return home for fear of persecution".
Stereotyping	This refers to cognitive aspects of the reproduction of racism. It involves making broad generalisations about particular groups of people and expecting all members of that group to think and behave identically. It has been argued that stereotypes emerge from what social psychologists call in-group/out-group dynamics. People like to feel that they are part of a group. We want to feel good about the way we are, so we denigrate those outside. In addition, stereotypes are seen as the 'other' in our minds. Stereotyping takes place in an 'automatic' way – people are so used to knowing and experiencing, for example, white men in key positions that those who have been racialised, as well as non-racialised women or disabled people are all seen as the 'other'. They become stereotyped as such because they are 'marked'.
Xenophobia	Fear and hatred of strangers or foreigners or of anything that is strange or foreign.

Index

L

Lane, J. 99
language 138-9
Law, I. 37, 98
Lawrence, Doreen 71, 153
Lawrence, Neville 71, 153
Lawrence, Stephen 33, 42, 155
  see also Stephen Lawrence Inquiry
Leach, C. W. 54
Lee-Cunin, M. 89
Lees, S. 112, 113
legislation 65, 76-7
  antiracism 65-6, 203
  before 1900 199
  criminal law 208
  equality 206-7
  human rights 72, 205
  immigration and nationality 67-9, 200-2
  limitations 74-6
  multiple identity and equality 72-4
  Northern Ireland 204
  race equality 71-2
  Scotland, Wales and Europe 209-10
  to promote equality 69-71
leisure 109
Lemos, G. 89, 98
Lenk, H.M. 145
Lewis, G. 47, 101, 118
Liberty 40, 154
Lipsitz, G. 49
Local Government Association 127
London Museums Agency 121
Lusane, C. 112

M

Mac an Ghaill, M. 34, 57, 120
McClintock, A. 8
McCrudden, C. 74
McDonald, I. 139-40
McGhee, D. 126
McIntosh, N. 66
Mack, T. 8, 144
McLaughlin, C. 144
McLaughlin, E. 44, 118
McLeod, M. 112
McPake, J. 124
Macpherson Inquiry *see* Stephen Lawrence Inquiry
mainstreaming 83-7
Major, John 44
Majors, R. 98

Malik, K. 36
Maori 145, 155, 197-8
Marseilles 135, 197
Mason, D. 33, 83, 85, 103, 211, 217
MBNA Corporation 136
media 48, 52, 142
  asylum seekers 39-40
  and everyday racism 37-9
  overt public racism 40-3
mentoring 91-2, 194
Metcalf, H. 70, 80
Metropolitan Police Authority 105-6
middle class racism 58-9
Miles, R. 8, 16, 66, 77
Mills, G. 76
Ministerial Group on Public Order and Community Cohesion 125
minority ethnic 13, 19, 37-9, 213-14
Mirza, H.S. 9, 15, 19, 24, 29, 46, 61, 72, 74, 86, 92, 99, 103, 104, 112, 140
Modernising Government 95
Modood, T. 18, 19, 119, 126
monitoring 69, 90-1
  criminal justice system 105, 106
  in employment 90-1
Montagu, A. 9
Moodley, K. 8
Morris, Bill 40
Morris, J. 61, 122
Morrison, M. 100
MPG (Migration Policy Group) 153
Mubarak, Zaheed 107
multicultural interventions 27, 31, 117, 119-20, 130-1, 158, 197
  community cohesion 125-9
  faith schools 120-1
  heritage resources and multicultural arts 121-3
  intercultural understanding 130
  private sector products and services 124
  translation and interpreting 123-4
multiculturalism 11, 118-19, 216
  Canada 145
  contestation 47-9
  elite discourse 43-7
  Sweden 145-6
multiple identities 72-4, 77, 117, 158
multiple racisms 60-1, 62
Multiverse 100
Murray, C. 9
Muslims 47-9, 130
  in media 38
  private sector interventions 124
  schools 120, 121
  self-help 140-2

Race Relations Act 1965 66
Race Relations Act 1968 66, 69
Race Relations Act 1976 66, 67, 69, 88, 105
Race Relations (Amendment) Act 2000 66, 73, 76-7, 154
  consultation 95, 113
  data collection 119
  positive action 99
  race equality policies 71, 75, 82, 90
  refugees and asylum seekers 68
Race Relations Order 1997 (Northern Ireland) 71
racial harassment 217
  employment 88-9, 93
  legislation 208
racialisation 18
racism 20-1, 149-51, 161, 217-18
  and class 56-9
  criminal justice system 105-7
  culturalisation 11-12, 13
  definitions 15-16
  denial 51-2
  disability and age 61-2
  equal opportunities impact 85-7
  and gender 59-60
  housing and neighbourhood renewal 95-8
  influence of psychoanalysis 55-6
  institutional 28-31
  multiple 60-1
  nation and race 12
  overt 40-3
  reproductions 17-18
  scientific 8-10
  tackling through education 99-101
  see also everyday racisms
Rai-Atkins, A. 104
Rampton report 98
Ratcliffe, P. 118, 126
Rattansi, A. 55
Ray, L. 126, 127
Reay, D. 24, 103, 112, 140
recruitment 80-2, 93
Refugee Council 39
refugees 33, 139, 219
  employment 81-2
  interventions 194
  multicultural interventions 123
Refugees, Asylum Seekers and the Media Project (SAM) 40
religion 71, 72, 120-1, 126, 129
reparations movement 144-5

Resigl, M. 12
Richardson, R. 99, 100, 123
Roberts and Kay 136, 196
Roshni 113
Rothon, C. 39
Runnymede Trust 15, 19, 24, 27, 31, 96, 100, 119, 154
  Britishness 43, 44
  Complementing teachers 101
  faith schools 120
  mainstreaming 83
  Parekh report 118, 126
  trust 110

S

Safe havens, secure borders 118-19
Safra Project 141-2, 192
Sahgal, G. 118, 121
Said, Edward 10
Sainsbury Centre for Mental Health 104
Sampson, A. 36, 37
Scarman Report 70, 105
Schneider Ross 82
school leadership 102
Schuster, L. 67, 68, 69
scientific racism 8-10, 20
Scotland 124, 209
Scotsman, The 39
Scruton, Roger 45
Seasonal Agricultural Workers' Scheme 81
Secure borders, safe havens (Home Office) 68-9
Sefa Dei, G.J. 145
segregation 127-8
self-help 140-2
services *see* accessing services
Sewell, T. 101
Sex Discrimination Act 1975 73
Sex Discrimination Act 2002 73
Shakespeare, T. 61
Sheffield 109, 193
Sheridan, A.M. 61, 72, 86, 104
Shields, M.A. 88, 89
Siemiatycki, M. 140
Sihera, E. 75
situated local racisms 56, 62-3
  class 56-9
  disability and age 61-2
  gender 59-60
  interventions 133-42
  multiple 60-1
slave trade 144-5

Wilson, E.M. 80, 85, 86
Wilson, F.M. 70
Wilson, W.J. 83, 92, 111
Wimmer, A. 11
Winant, H. 11
Winder, R. 45, 49
Windsor Fellowship 82
Wodak, R. 12
women 10-11, 12, 160
Women Against Fundamentalisms 121
Woodward, W. 120, 121
working class racism 56-8
Working Group Against Racism in
    Children's Resources (WGARCR) 99
World Conference Against Racism 7,
    144, 161

X

xenophobia 219

Y

Youdell, D. 100-1
young people 134-5, 197
Yu, S. 83
Yuval Davis, N. 11, 12, 118, 121

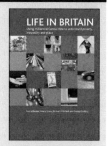

Migration and social mobility
The life chances of Britain's minority ethnic communities
Lucinda Platt, Department of Sociology, University of Essex

Drawing on data from the ONS Longitudinal Survey, this report traces patterns
of intergenerational social mobility for children from different ethnic groups
growing up in England and Wales. The study focuses on children born between
the late 1950s and the mid 1970s. Measures of their progress and class position
are compared, for the first time, with those of their parents. The report
therefore provides a unique insight into 'parent-to-child' class transitions across
'first' (immigrant) and 'second' generations.

Taking advantage of the new question on religion in the 2001 Census, the
report also asks whether patterns of intergenerational mobility vary by
religious affiliation and whether religion can add to our understanding of
ethnic group differences.

Migration and social mobility is essential reading for all those wishing to know
more about the extent and nature of ethnic minority achievement and
disadvantage.

Paperback £9.95 US$19.95 ISBN 1 86134 800 2
297 x 210mm 56 pages November 2005
Published in association with the Joseph Rowntree Foundation

To order further copies of this publication or any other Policy Press titles please
visit **www.policypress.org.uk** or contact:

In the UK and Europe:
Marston Book Services, PO Box 269,
Abingdon, Oxon, OX14 4YN, UK
Tel: +44 (0)1235 465500
Fax: +44 (0)1235 465556
Email: direct.orders@marston.co.uk

In the USA and Canada:
ISBS, 920 NE 58th Street, Suite 300,
Portland, OR 97213-3786, USA
Tel: +1 800 944 6190 (toll free)
Fax: +1 503 280 8832
Email: info@isbs.com

In Australia and New Zealand:
DA Information Services, 648 Whitehorse Road
Mitcham, Victoria 3132, Australia
Tel: +61 (3) 9210 7777
Fax: +61 (3) 9210 7788
E-mail: service@dadirect.com.au

Further information about all of our titles can
be found on our website.